Building Generative AI for Enterprise

A practical guide to developing GenAI systems to solve business problems

Devesh Rajadhyax

www.bpbonline.com

First Edition 2026

ISBN: 978-93-78541-353

Distributors:

BPB PUBLICATIONS
20, Ansari Road, Darya Ganj
New Delhi-110002
Ph: 23254990/23254991

DECCAN AGENCIES
4-3-329, Bank Street,
Hyderabad-500195
Ph: 24756967/24756400

MICRO MEDIA
Shop No. 5, Mahendra Chambers,
150 DN Rd. Next to Capital Cinema,
V.T. (C.S.T.) Station, MUMBAI-400 001
Ph: 22078296/22078297

To View Complete BPB Publications Catalogue Scan the QR Code:

Published by Manish Jain for BPB Publications, 20 Ansari Road, Darya Ganj, New Delhi-110002 and Printed by him at Repro India Ltd., Rewari.

www.bpbonline.com

Dedicated to

The colleagues, clients and supporters,
who helped me to build Cere Labs

About the Author

Devesh Rajadhyax is a successful entrepreneur and thought leader in software technology. He has co-founded three technology companies in his career spanning more than 25 years. Currently, he is the co-founder and CEO of Cere Labs, a company focused on developing enterprise AI solutions. Devesh has developed AI solutions for domains ranging from healthcare, manufacturing, pharmaceuticals and engineering. He has multiple patents to his name. This is his second book about generative AI. His first book on decoding GPT was enthusiastically received by both students and professionals.

Devesh is a post-graduate in control system engineering. He has written extensively on topics in ML and AI and has spoken on numerous platforms. He also serves as an industry expert on the board of many engineering and management institutions.

About the Reviewer

Neelesh is an applied scientist specializing in **natural language processing** (**NLP**), generative AI, and **large language models** (**LLMs**). He leads applied research in generative AI, driving innovation from foundational advances to large-scale enterprise adoption. He has held leadership roles in AI innovation, building cutting-edge, AI-driven solutions across domains. His work focuses on bridging advanced research with real-world applications, with key contributions in areas such as NL2SQL, agentic AI, and enterprise-scale AI systems. An alumnus of IIT Guwahati, Neelesh has authored research papers in leading AI and NLP venues, including EMNLP, COLING, and LREC.

Acknowledgement

I would like to sincerely thank my family and friends for the constant support and encouragement they provided during the journey of writing this book. I am especially grateful to my wife, Richa, my brother, Dinesh, my sister-in-law, Rajashree, and my friends Ram and Aparna, whose presence and support made this effort possible.

I am also thankful to BPB Publications for their guidance and professional expertise in shaping this book. The process involved multiple rounds of revision and involved constructive feedback and collaboration of reviewers and editors throughout the journey.

Over the years of working in the technology industry, I have had the opportunity to learn from many colleagues, co-founders, and domain experts. While it is not possible to acknowledge everyone individually, I remain sincerely grateful to all who have contributed to my learning and growth.

Writing my first book was a significant learning experience, and those insights have been carried forward into this book. Feedback and suggestions from many readers played an important role in shaping the work, and I am grateful to all of them for their contributions.

Preface

The global industry is rapidly adopting generative AI to achieve its business goals. AI professionals who understand how GenAI solutions are designed, developed and deployed are in great demand. Developing GenAI applications requires a sound understanding of the available models and the various GenAI engineering techniques.

This book is designed to provide a comprehensive guide to building enterprise GenAI applications. It covers multiple aspects of enterprise GenAI solutions, including the engineering, business and governance.

In this book, you will learn about the key GenAI engineering techniques such as prompt engineering, finetuning, RAG and agentic workflows. You will learn to develop enterprise AI applications using these techniques through five example projects. You will also understand how to ensure that the solutions are scalable, high-performing and optimized, with an eye on benefits, costs and risks.

This book is intended for the newer members of the AI engineering teams working on building enterprise AI applications. It will also be useful to experienced developers who have built machine learning or deep learning applications and want to venture into the GenAI practice.

With this book, you will gain the knowledge and skills to become a proficient developer in the field of enterprise AI development using GenAI engineering techniques. I hope you will find this book informative and helpful.

Chapter 1: Introduction to Transformer Models — This chapter lays down the foundations for the entire book by introducing the reader to the core ideas in GenAI, especially in **large language models** (**LLMs**). It presents the basics of language processing using various models, focusing on the working of transformer models such as GPT, including hands-on text generation using the OpenAI API.

Chapter 2: The SOTA GenAI Models — This chapter provides an overview of the current state-of-the-art foundation models. Builds on the foundations provided earlier to include non-transformer models and models capable of handling images and audio. This chapter presents a classification of the GenAI models based on the size, openness, modalities and architecture that is useful in selecting models for practical applications. It discusses the implications of model selection on parameters such as deployment, cost and performance.

Chapter 3: GenAI in Industry — This chapter connects the GenAI preliminaries to real life industry applications. The chapter explores the benefits that enterprises derive from GenAI implementations. It further discusses the capabilities of AI models that power the industrial use cases. It also outlines the process through which organizations identify and select GenAI use cases. A variety of such use cases are described, grouped by functions such as human resources and business development.

Chapter 4: Prompt Engineering — This chapter introduces prompt engineering, the critical skill needed for effectively working with GenAI models. The chapter highlights the general-purpose nature of GenAI models and prompt engineering as the techniques that guide them to perform specific tasks. It discusses various prompting techniques, beginning with simple instruction prompting and covering important methods such as chain-of-thoughts and tree-of-thoughts. The final part of the chapter is dedicated to a tutorial on developing a Marketing Assistant using various prompt engineering techniques.

Chapter 5: Fine-tuning Generative Models — This chapter discusses fine-tuning as an important technique to overcome the limitations of generative models in specialized applications. The chapter explains the basics of fine-tuning and how this approach enhances model performance without having to train from scratch. Various fine-tuning techniques such as adapters, LoRA and prompt fine-tuning are discussed, along with the use of a GPU for the training. The chapter includes a tutorial on developing a GenAI-based HR Assistant that leverages the power of fine-tuning.

Chapter 6: Enhancing GenAI with RAG — This chapter addresses RAG, the powerful alternative to fine-tuning for incorporating enterprise-specific knowledge in the GenAI application. In this chapter, RAG is shown as a technique that combines retrieval methods with the generation capabilities of the models. The core components of the RAG pipeline—chunking, indexing, retrieval and prompting- are discussed in detail. The chapter introduces LangChain, the popular framework for building RAG applications and illustrates its use in building a contract intelligence system through a tutorial.

Chapter 7: Advanced RAG in Action — This chapter explains how certain advanced techniques can help to overcome the limitations of the naïve RAG approach described in the previous chapter. The chapter examines the improvements possible across all parts of the pipeline, with particular focus on the retrieval part. Techniques such as hybrid retrieval, reranking and query enhancement are discussed, with a special mention of the role of the knowledge graphs. The tutorial in this chapter is dedicated to the development of a Customer Success Navigator that utilizes many of the advanced RAG techniques.

Chapter 8: Agentic Workflows — This chapter is dedicated to a class of GenAI systems that goes beyond generation to perform action. The chapter explores critical concepts in agentic systems such as reasoning, planning, tool use and memory with the help of ReAct and Reflexion, the well-known frameworks for designing agents. It introduces LlamaIndex, the popular agent building frameworks and presents a tutorial to build an IT Operations Assistant that automates routine tasks.

Chapter 9: Deploying GenAI Systems — This chapter shifts the focus from development to real-world use by examining how GenAI systems are deployed in production environments. The chapter outlines the key requirements of production-grade systems such as performance, cost, availability and security. It discusses the use of various types of architectures to fulfill these requirements, with special attention to cloud-based deployment. An example describing a GenAI system deployment illustrates how the concepts are applied in practice.

Chapter 10: AI Governance and Ethics — This chapter addresses the risks, ethical considerations and governance challenges associated with enterprise deployment of GenAI systems. The chapter shows how ignoring these critical aspects can undermine trust, compliance and organizational stability. It explores the evolving field of AI regulations across the globe and examines the impact of AI on society, particularly on the future of jobs and workforce transformation.

Chapter 11: Future of Generative AI — This chapter looks beyond the current practices to explore the future trajectory of GenAI. The chapter discusses the key trend in architectures, scaling, efficiency and capabilities of GenAI models. Going beyond technology, the chapter examines the societal and economic implications of generative AI. It concludes on a forward-looking note, emphasizing responsibility, adaptability, and human-centered design. This final chapter invites the readers to continue engaging with a field that is still rapidly unfolding.

Code Bundle and Coloured Images

Please follow the link to download the
Code Bundle and the ***Coloured Images*** of the book:

https://rebrand.ly/6f3671

The code bundle for the book is also hosted on GitHub at **https://github.com/bpbpublications/Building-Generative-AI-for-Enterprise.** In case there's an update to the code, it will be updated on the existing GitHub repository.

We have code bundles from our rich catalogue of books and videos available at **https://github.com/bpbpublications**. Check them out!

Errata

We take immense pride in our work at BPB Publications and follow best practices to ensure the accuracy of our content to provide an indulging reading experience to our subscribers. Our readers are our mirrors, and we use their inputs to reflect and improve upon human errors, if any, that may have occurred during the publishing processes involved. To let us maintain the quality and help us reach out to any readers who might be having difficulties due to any unforeseen errors, please write to us at: **errata@bpbonline.com**

Your support, suggestions and feedback are highly appreciated by the BPB Publications' Family.

At **www.bpbonline.com**, you can also read a collection of free technical articles, sign up for a range of free newsletters, and receive exclusive discounts and offers on BPB books and eBooks. You can check our social media handles below:

Instagram

Facebook

LinkedIn

YouTube

Get in touch with us at: **business@bpbonline.com** for more details.

Piracy

If you come across any illegal copies of our works in any form on the internet, we would be grateful if you would provide us with the location address or website name. Please contact us at **business@bpbonline.com** with a link to the material.

If you are interested in becoming an author

If there is a topic that you have expertise in, and you are interested in either writing or contributing to a book, please visit **www.bpbonline.com**. We have worked with thousands of developers and tech professionals, just like you, to help them share their insights with the global tech community. You can make a general application, apply for a specific hot topic that we are recruiting an author for, or submit your own idea.

Reviews

Please leave a review. Once you have read and used this book, why not leave a review on the site that you purchased it from? Potential readers can then see and use your unbiased opinion to make purchase decisions. We at BPB can understand what you think about our products, and our authors can see your feedback on their book. Thank you!

For more information about BPB, please visit **www.bpbonline.com**.

Join our Discord space

Join our Discord workspace for latest updates, offers, tech happenings around the world, new releases, and sessions with the authors:

https://discord.bpbonline.com

Table of Contents

Chapter 1
Introduction to Transformer Models

Introduction

Generative **artificial intelligence** (**AI**) is changing the way people live and work. It is likely that you have already used generative AI through chatbots such as *ChatGPT* or *Gemini*. But as a programmer, you might want to create these tools yourself. This book provides the essential techniques to build generative AI solutions for industries, people, and governments. These solutions will solve important problems in the areas of productivity, services, healthcare, education, and so on.

Before creating an AI application, however, a good understanding of the technology is necessary. This chapter will give you an insight into how things work in generative AI.

AI is the pursuit of understanding and replicating human intelligence. AI scientists and engineers try to build machines that imitate what humans can do, such as seeing, hearing, using language, and solving problems. Generative AI is a branch of AI that deals with generating content. It includes models that can generate text, images, speech, and other types of content. After its introduction in late 2022, this technology quickly became popular in industries across various fields. It especially proved useful in areas that involve knowledge and language processing. Generative AI techniques, such as the **large language models** (**LLMs**), can process language with an ease that was never experienced before. This introductory chapter will focus on language processing to understand how generative AI works. In literature, generative AI is referred to as GenAI or GAI; this book will use the term GenAI.

Structure

This chapter covers the following topics:

- Language processing with GenAI
- Recurrent neural networks to transformers
- Training the transformer
- Learn text generation with code

Objectives

By the end of this chapter, you will have a good understanding of how transformer models work. You will understand why the generative AI models have transformed the language processing field and how they have progressed from the early models, such as **recurrent neural networks** (**RNNs**), to the latest transformer models. You will learn important concepts such as attention, pre-training, **supervised finetuning** (**SFT**), and **reinforcement learning with human feedback** (**RLHF**). You will be able to write simple programs to use the GenAI model API for text generation.

Language processing with GenAI

GenAI models make language processing tasks very easy. Here is a short example code that detects whether a given statement is positive or negative:

```
classifier = pipeline("text-classification")
classifier("The flavors were well-balanced, but the portion size was too small
for the price.")
```

Output:

```
[{'label': 'NEGATIVE', 'score': 0.9889463782310486}]
```

The preceding code is just a snippet that demonstrates the power of GenAI's language processing. The following is an explanation of the code:

- The variable `classifier` is initiated with a GenAI model using the **Hugging Face library Transformers**. The type of model used here is a transformer, about which you will learn more in this chapter.
- The transformer is then used to classify the given text. Note that the sentence given here is not very obviously negative. Still, the model is able to correctly classify it.

It is a very simple example, but you must have noticed the impressive capability shown by the model. Creating machines that can process human language has been a long-time ambition of scientists. The field of **natural language processing** (**NLP**) is quite old, but so far, understanding and generating human language has always remained challenging for machines.

Processing human language using computers is difficult because although language adheres to some rules, such as vocabulary and grammar, it contains many peculiarities. The following are some of the things that make the processing of human language by computers difficult:

- **Context**: No part of a text is isolated. One sentence is connected to another and words within a sentence also depend on each other. For example, pronouns (he, she) in one part of a text refer to some noun in another.

- **Mixed vocabulary**: The language we encounter in everyday life rarely uses words from a single language. This happens very often in countries with multi-lingual communities such as Canada, South Africa and India. After smartphones became popular, people even started using symbols like emoticons while writing texts, adding to the complexity.
- **Ill-formed language**: In casual conversations, people sometimes use grammatically incorrect sentences. For instance, *You going?* is an accepted communication in a text message.
- **Humor and sarcasm**: The intended meaning of a sentence can be different from the literal one. For example, *This is great!* might not always be used in a positive manner.

Software programs use a sequence of rules (called an algorithm) to process input. However, human language contains many exceptions to rules, making it hard for programs to understand and process it with complete accuracy.

GenAI offered another approach, which had already brought transformation in processing images, to crack the language problem. This approach was to use neural networks to process data such as images and text. Around 2010, it became known that neural networks with many layers (called **deep learning networks**) are effective in image processing. Like language, images are also difficult to process using rule-based methods. This gave AI researchers the idea that deep learning can also solve the NLP challenge.

The first real breakthroughs came in 2014 with the introduction of embeddings and sequence-to-sequence networks. The research on using deep learning for NLP gathered speed, and a significant milestone was the introduction of the transformer architecture in the now iconic research paper *Attention Is All You Need* in 2017. This architecture gave rise to LLMs. These models, as you saw in the code snippet earlier, do an incredible job of handling language processing tasks.

Recurrent neural networks to transformers

This section covers the evolution of language models from RNNs to transformers and LLMs. RNNs are the simplest type of neural network that can be used to process language effectively. It has certain shortcomings, especially when it comes to long text. **Long Short-Term Memory** (**LSTM**) is an improvement over RNN. Transformers use many of the principles of LSTM, but utilize a unique method of processing the text. Before starting with RNN, two fundamentals are covered first: embeddings and the processing of text by neural networks.

Embedding

Machine learning algorithms, such as regression or clustering, work on numbers. To use neural networks (which are machine learning algorithms), language must be converted into numbers. There are many ways to achieve this, but the most common and popular method is called **embedding**.

Embedding converts words into vectors. Since vectors are sets of numbers, this makes them suitable for use by machine learning models. Understanding embedding is essential to using transformer models; hence, the major aspects will be explored here. There are two ways in which embedding can be done for any language:

- **Use existing embedding**: There are available embedding libraries, which come in the form of an API or a model. The following is an example of using the OpenAI Ada embedding:

```
import openai
# Replace with your actual OpenAI API key
openai.api_key = "YOUR_OPENAI_API_KEY"

def get_ada_embedding(text):
  response = openai.embeddings.create(
      input = [text],
      model = "text-embedding-ada-002"
  )
  embedding = response.data[0].embedding
  return embedding


#Get embedding for a word
word = "school"
embedding = get_ada_embedding(word)
print(embedding)
```

  Output:

```
[0.002107415348291397, 0.001848519197665155, -0.002626933855935931,…]
```

  In the preceding example, a vector for the word *school* is created by using the OpenAI library provided by OpenAI, the company that created ChatGPT. The **`Embedding.Create`** API call is used to create the vector. Notice the following argument:

```
model="text-embedding-ada-002
```

  OpenAI provides many options for embedding, and the **`ada-002`** model has been chosen, which returns the vector for the given word.

- **Creating your own embedding**: For special purposes, you can create your own embedding for a language. To do this, the right type of neural network and a big enough training dataset will be needed. However, for this book, existing embedding will be used, and thus, the creation of your own embedding will not be explored.

Tokens

Rather than converting words into vectors, most embedding methods prefer to break the words into smaller parts. For example, the word *misunderstand* can be broken into two tokens: *mis* and *understand*. This turns out to be better than using vectors for words, as one token can give rise to many words, so the number of token vectors is less. Tokens also make it possible to convert new words into vectors. For instance, if the word *bitcoin* was not initially present in the embedding set. However, as the tokens *bit* and *coin* are available, this vector can be represented with these two tokens.

Let us now see an example of how a sentence can be broken into tokens:

```
from transformers import AutoTokenizer

# Load a pre-trained tokenizer for gpt2
tokenizer = AutoTokenizer.from_pretrained("gpt2")

# Example sentence
sentence = "It is better to be careful than sorry"

# Tokenize the sentence
inputs = tokenizer(sentence)

# Get the token IDs
token_ids = inputs["input_ids"]

# Convert token IDs to tokens
tokens = tokenizer.convert_ids_to_tokens(token_ids)

print("Tokens:", tokens)
print ("Token ids:", token_ids)
```

Output:

```
Tokens: ['It', 'Ġis', 'Ġbetter', 'Ġto', 'Ġbe', 'Ġcareful', 'Ġthan', 'Ġsorry']
Token ids: [1026, 318, 1365, 284, 307, 8161, 621, 7926]
```

Once again, the transformers library from Hugging Face has been used here. The code is quite simple to understand, except for the part about **`token-ids`**. Embedding is like a dictionary, and every entry in this dictionary is a token associated with a vector. Every entry is also given a unique number, called a **token ID**. These numbers are passed to the GenAI model while processing text. In the code example, the tokens are printed so that you can inspect them.

Most literature on GenAI refers to tokens, instead of words, while discussing text processing. This book will also adhere to this practice.

Note: **Just keep in mind that tokens are nothing but words, sometimes broken for embedding purposes.**

Dimension

Embedding is a set of vectors, and all the vectors in an embedding are the same size. The size is called the **dimension** of the embedding and is a significant property since it impacts the model's behavior. In the preceding example, you can find out the dimension by simply adding the following line to the code:

```
dimension = len(embedding)
```

Embedding represents the real-world

Before concluding the discussion on embedding, it is important to mention an interesting property. Embedding vectors are correlated with the real-world meaning of the words that they represent. Let us see this with an example.

Consider the words *school* and college. These words are close to each other in meaning. The following code converts them into embeddings:

```
import openai

# Replace with your actual OpenAI API key
openai.api_key = "YOUR_API_KEY"

def get_embedding(text, model="text-embedding-ada-002"):
 response = openai.Embedding.create(
      input=[text],
      model=model
  )
  return response["data"][0]["embedding"]

# Define the words to be converted
words = ["school", "college"]

# Get embeddings for each word
school_embedding = get_embedding(words[0])
college_embedding = get_embedding(words[1])
```

```
print("School embedding:", school_embedding)
print("College embedding:", college_embedding)
```

Now, check how close the two vectors are. To do this, calculate the angle between them using the following code:

```
import numpy as np

cosine_similarity = np.dot(school_embedding, college_embedding) /          (np.
linalg.norm(school_embedding) * np.linalg.norm(college_embedding))

print ("Similarity:", cosine_similarity)
```

Output:

```
Similarity:  0.9216369004437915
```

Instead of the angle, this code gives the cosine of the angle between the vectors. The value is a good indicator of how close the vectors are. If the value is close to 1, the vectors are close. In the preceding example, you can see that the vectors are close to each other, just like their word counterparts.

You can try calculating the cosine for some other words, like *bus* and *memory*. You will get a value that is much smaller than one, indicating that the vectors are far away.

This property of embedding is key to understanding the way transformers work. Before transformers, how neural networks work on text will be discussed.

Text processing by neural networks

Text is made up of tokens, which can be converted into vectors. A **neural network** (NN) is very good at processing vectors.

NNs are made of many layers, each of which can be thought of as a matrix followed by a non-linear function. Consider the first layer, where the input vector is received and multiplied by the matrix. The output of this multiplication is another vector (which is a non-linear function). This vector becomes the input to the next layer, which is also a matrix that multiplies this incoming vector. This chain continues till the last layer is reached. The output of the last layer is the output of the NN. The NN can be considered a big matrix converting the input vector into the output vector.

Without the non-linear function, all the layers would be equivalent to just one layer. Such a network can convert the input vector into the output vector only in a *linear* way. To achieve the desired results, the input must be related to the output in more complex ways, which is possible only if the calculations involve non-linear functions.

When the token vectors are given as input to the NN, it will produce another vector. This vector can be another token, but some additional processing is required to ensure that it is a vector. Some explanation is required to understand why it is so.

In the following figure, V1 (the output of a NN) and other word vectors can be seen. For ease of explanation, 2D vectors are assumed, though they are of a much bigger size in reality.

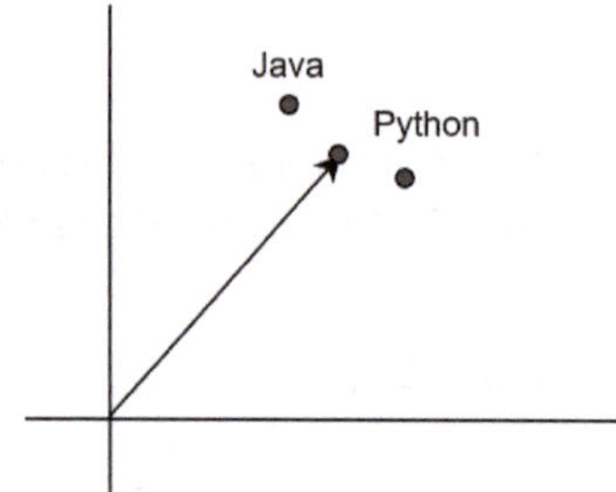

***Figure 1.1**: Output vector of a neural network*

In the preceding figure, V1 does not precisely fall on any of the token vectors. However, it is quite close to some of the tokens, and any of these closely placed tokens can be treated as the output.

Once any of the possible tokens is assigned, the NN can be said to take a token as the input and give another token as the output. The NN, thus, becomes a token processing and, by the same logic, a text processing system.

This view of the NN as a text-processing system is very basic, as only a single token has been processed. The following section will explore how NNs can process entire blocks of text.

Sequence processing

Text can be considered a sequence of words grouped by sentences. Text can contain paragraphs, sections, etc., which are nothing but groups of sentences. A text is not just a collection of words, as the words and sentences have a particular order, which is equally important in understanding the meaning of the text.

Words can be converted to tokens and tokens to embedding vectors. So, for an NN, the input text is a sequence of vectors. There can be two types of output:

- A single vector
- Another sequence of vectors

Consider the first possibility, where an input sequence of token vectors is converted to a single vector. This vector can represent a token, but it can also represent a **class**. Consider the use case where the NN is given one or more sentences taken from a news item. The NN classifies it as *politics, sports, business, technology,* or *other.*

Input:

```
Apple unveiled its latest flagship smartphone, featuring a revolutionary new camera system and a significantly improved processor.
```

Output:

```
Technology
```

The output vector here represents one of the five possible classes. This task is called **classification** in machine learning, and it will be used for some of the discussions in this chapter.

NNs process a sequence of token vectors to produce a meaningful output, such as the class vector in the preceding example. Two features of the sentence need to be considered while making sense of a sentence:

- Words (or tokens) in the sentence
- The order in which the words appear

However, there is one more factor that adds to the complexity of the task. The meanings of the words depend on each other. The following are some examples:

- Words refer to other words; for instance, the word *its* in the preceding input refers to *Apple*.
- Words can have two or more meanings; for instance, in the preceding example, *Apple* is a company, not a fruit.

Thus, the impact of words on each other must be considered while processing a sentence. This impact is called *context* and is the most important aspect of text processing. So, an NN used for processing text must be able to process the following:

- The meaning of tokens
- The order in which the tokens appear
- The context

In the last few years, many architectures of neural networks capable of text processing have been developed. The most basic one is the RNN, which will be explored in the following section.

Recurrent neural network

Text processing requires the ability to process the tokens, their positions, and the context. Let us begin with the position; RNNs are special types of NNs that process one token at a time in the order they appear in the sentence. They contain just one layer, which sequentially processes the input tokens. This means that the order of the tokens is considered while processing.

A layer of an NN is a matrix followed by a non-linearity. Every token vector gets multiplied by the matrix with the non-linearity applied. In the RNN, tokens get processed one after the other in this manner, and all the vectors come together to create the final output vector.

In the last section, it was mentioned that context must be used while processing any word. RNNs create context by keeping it as a type of internal memory. Every time a new token is processed, the context memory gets updated.

The RNN layer contains two matrices instead of one. One matrix is used to multiply the current token, and the other one multiplies the context. When written as a program, the calculations will look like the following:

```
context_vector = non-linearity(multiply(context_matrix, context_vector) +
(token_matrix, token_vector))
```

In the preceding code, **context_matrix** and **token_matrix** are the two matrices in the layer, and **context_vetor** is the context memory. The code can be better understood with the help of the following schematic:

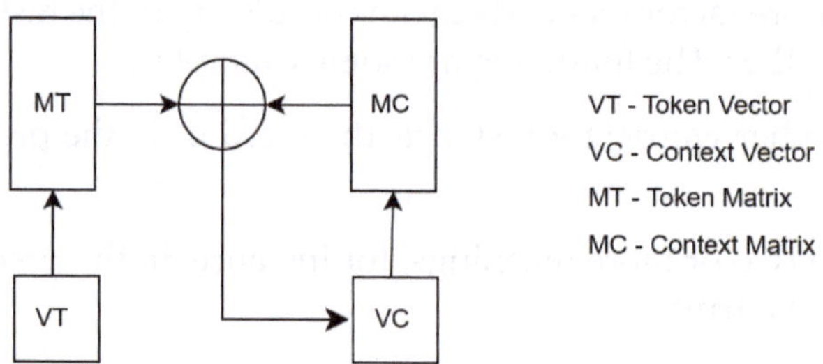

Figure 1.2: *Context calculation of a recurrent neural network*

In fact, the RNN layer contains one more matrix, which is used only when all the tokens in the text are processed. The context vector is multiplied by this matrix to get the final output:

```
output_vector = non-linearity(multiply(output_matrix, context_vector))
```

Using RNN for sentiment analysis

Sentiment analysis is one of the best-known problems in language processing. It involves categorizing the given text as *positive* or *negative*. This helps in analyzing reviews of a product, judging the response to a movie, or estimating the popularity of an electoral candidate. An example of this was given at the beginning of this chapter, where a transformer model was used. RNN can be used for this task by giving it the following statement:

```
S='The film fizzles out in its later part, leaving the viewer bored and
frustrated.'
```

RNN processes one word at a time, starting with *the*, and finishing with *frustrated* and the period (.). For every token, it will consider the token vector and the context accumulated so far. The final vector will contain the essence of the sentence. This can be considered the meaning of the sentence, packed in a vector, and is called the **representation** (**R**) of the sentence. The following figure illustrates the creation of representation by the RNN:

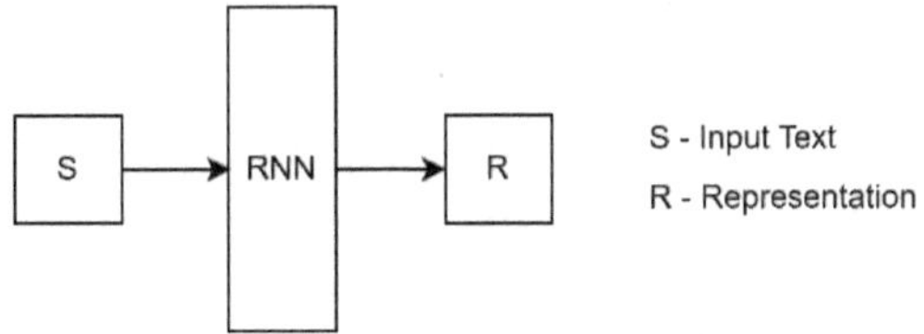

***Figure 1.3**: Representation layer of RNN*

For classification (such as that required in sentiment analysis), another operation is required. `R` should be converted into `1` (positive) or `0` (negative). This is achieved by another simple NN layer. *Figure 1.4* shows the classification layer added to the network.

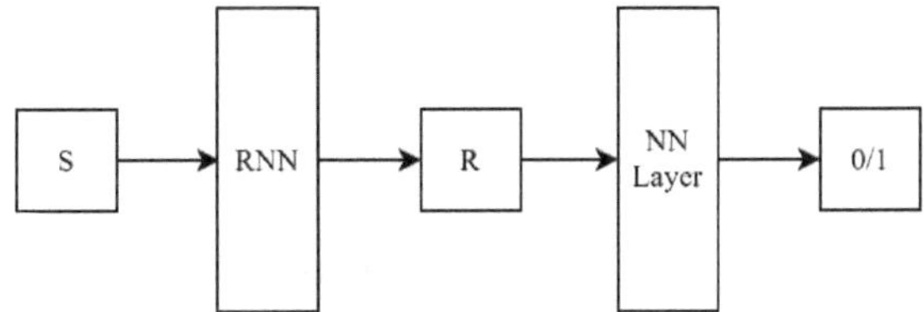

***Figure 1.4**: RNN with classification layer*

Converting a vector in the NN layer into `1` or `0` is done in three steps:

1. The matrix of the layer converts `R`, the representation vector, into a number. The matrix that achieves this has dimensions (1 x n) where *n* is the dimension of `R`.

2. A non-linearity called *Sigmoid* converts the number to another number between 0 and 1. This number is `P`. For example:

```
P = Sigmoid(0) = 0.5
P = Sigmoid(4) = 0.98
P= Sigmoid(-4) = 0.017
```

   Figure 1.5 shows the graph of the Sigmoid function. Notice that the output of the function always remains between 0 and 1.

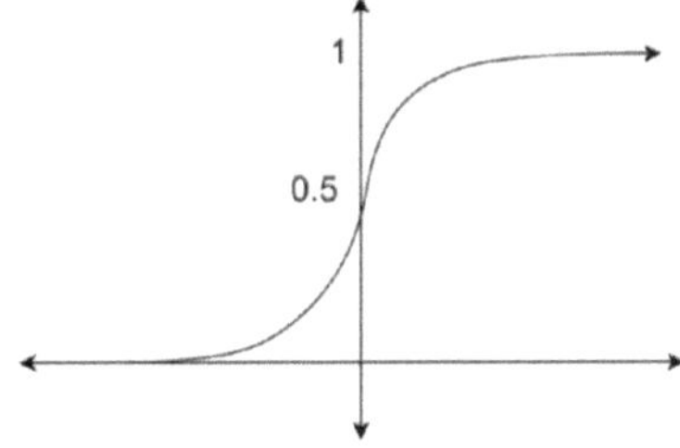

***Figure 1.5**: The Sigmoid function*

3. The number `P` is the probability of `S` being positive. For example, if `P` is `0.9`, there is a high probability that `S` is positive. To get `1` or `0` from `P`, simply apply a threshold `T`. For example, if `T` is `0.75`, the output of the classification layer will be `1` for all values of `P` above `0.75`.

In RNNs, a part of the network is dedicated to creating a representation. This part is called the **representation layer**. Another part takes the representation created and uses it for the task demanded from the network. This part is called the **task layer**. In the preceding example, the task layer accomplished classification, but it can be used for any task required by the problem statement. This will be useful when learning about sequence-to-sequence networks.

RNNs opened a new vista in text processing, as applications such as sentiment analysis could now be built for production. The machine learning approach to text processing proved to be more effective than the previous rule-based approach.

However, RNNs had some limitations. They could not be used when the text was long, say a few paragraphs. An improved architecture was developed to overcome this limitation, called LSTM networks.

Long Short-Term Memory model

Language processing depends on models creating better context. RNNs create context by adding contributions of each word to an accumulated vector in the memory. The context contribution is computed using a matrix.

When the input text gets longer, this simplistic method is no longer effective. It is easy to understand this by imagining the process of creating context for yourself. When reading a long text, you have to remember the text you have read so far to make sense of what you are reading right now. However, this can also lead to confusion. Suppose you come across the word *it*, which refers to a noun that appeared previously. If you remember all the nouns used previously, you might be confused about which noun is being referred to. The more you remember, the easier it is to get confused.

This is called the problem of long context. You need the memory of previous text, but it can lower the quality of the context. LSTM architecture is an attempt to solve this problem.

Long Short-Term Memory architecture

A simple solution to the problem of long context is to keep a limit on the length of text to be kept in the context memory. When moving forward through the text, the words that go out of the context window are removed. In the following figure, you can see the context window applied to a piece of text:

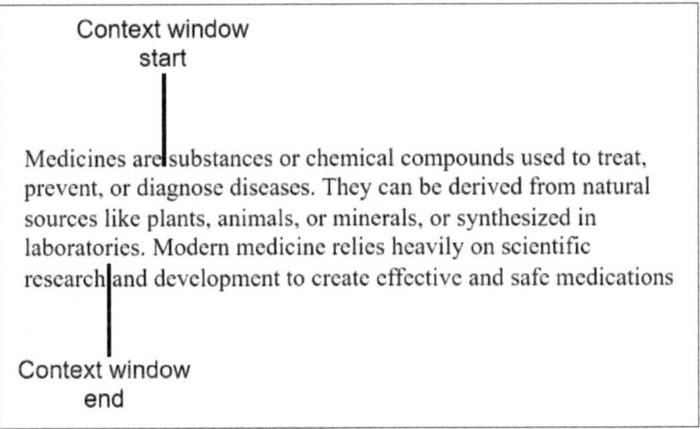

***Figure 1.6**: The context window*

This solution is called the **short-term memory** architecture, as it remembers only the most recent tokens in the text. However, this solution raises another problem. The words that are removed from the context may be important. Thus, a challenge arises, which is the need to remember the important words but forget the others. This is what the LSTM achieves.

LSTM does this by using two different layers for context creation instead of the one layer used in RNN. These layers are called **gates**. One of the gates is given the current context, and it provides a vector to be forgotten, which is removed from the context. The **remember** gate is given the new word, and it gives the vector that should be added to the context. This dual operation at each step helps maintain a context that remembers everything that is important. The following figure shows the architecture of the LSTM model with the remember gate and forget gate:

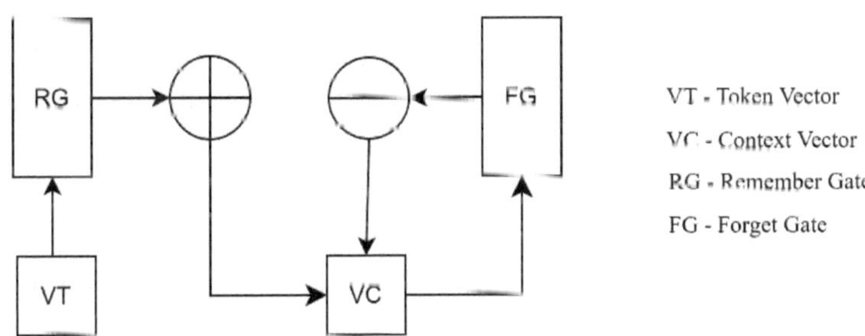

***Figure 1.7**: LSTM architecture*

The preceding explanation raises the question of how the gates (in other words, layers) know what should be remembered and what should be forgotten. The answer lies in the training of the model.

LSTMs can be trained for a particular task. For instance, to train the LSTM model for the classification task mentioned in the section about RNN, training data must be created. The training data is made up of several sentences. For each sentence, the expected output of the model, `1` or `0`, is specified. When using the untrained model to classify sentences, the model will make mistakes in the classification. These mistakes are used to adjust the network.

A neural network is made up of layers, which are matrices that are made up of elements, also called **parameters**. While adjusting the network, these parameters are given values so that fewer mistakes are made. When the network makes the fewest mistakes, the model is considered to be trained.

More technical details will be looked at when transformers and finetuning are discussed. For now, a basic understanding of how LSTM gates *know* what to remember and what to forget is enough. Since gates are also network layers, they learn the correct parameters during training on a specific task.

After looking at how NNs process text to create one vector, the second possibility of processing a sequence of tokens to create another sequence of tokens will be discussed. The models that perform this task are called **sequence-to-sequence** (**seq-2-seq**) networks.

Sequence-to-sequence models

The most popular application of sequence-to-sequence tasks is machine translation, in which the model is given one or more sentences in a language, and the output is one or more sentences in another language.

A model that performs this task should support at least two features:

- The input sequence can be of any length. Data in the form of text, unlike images, has no fixed size. The seq-2-seq model should be able to accept variable length input, though it can place an upper limit on the length.
- The input and output sequence lengths can be different. Take the example of a machine translation task. The text in one language can be long, while its translation can express the same meaning in fewer tokens.

LSTM architecture can process any length of input, so it satisfies the first requirement. To use the LSTM model to generate a sequence of tokens, an innovative architecture that can achieve the generation of a sequence was proposed in 2014. Since then, it has been the cornerstone of sequence generation. This is the **encoder-decoder** architecture.

Encoder-decoder architecture

The encoder-decoder architecture uses two LSTM models, one is used as the encoder and the other as the decoder. The two parts work together to generate a sequence of tokens.

The encoder is the same as the LSTM, except that it has a task layer. It processes all the tokens in the input sequence and produces a final context vector at the end. This context vector represents all the important tokens in the sentence, taken in the right proportion and processed with non-linearities. It thus embodies the entire input text. This can be written in a code format as the following:

```
context_vector = Encoder(input_token_sequence)
```

The decoder is also an LSTM model, but it is used in a different manner. Consider only the first step of the decoder LSTM. Usually, the LSTM steps receive the previous context and an input token. But there is no input token now, as the input has already been processed. Instead, the first step of the decoder receives a special token called the **start** token.

The first step of the decoder contains two layers to process the inputs. The first layer produces an output vector, the second one creates a context.

In code, it can be written as:

```
decoder_output[0] = decoder_output_layer (encoder_context, <start>)
```

It is possible to write this code in terms of the actual matrices and non-linearity, but it is avoided for the sake of clarity. You can refer to the RNN section and rewrite it yourself.

Similarly, for context:

```
decoder_context = decoder_context_layer (encoder_context, <start>)
```

> Note **that this is the first step of LSTM, therefore, the input is encoder context and output is decoder context. From the second step onwards, the decoder context will keep getting modified.**

Unlike the encoder, where only the context is used, the output is most important in the decoder. This is a vector generated by the decoder, and it is necessary to turn it into a token. To do this, classification is used. The first step of the decoder contains a third classifier layer that performs this operation.

```
token[0] = decoder_classfier_layer (decoder_output[0])
```

Figure 1.8 shows the generate of the decoder output as well as the decoder context:

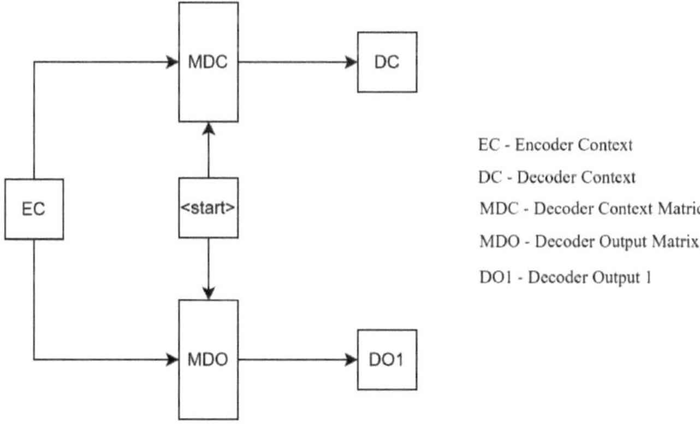

***Figure 1.8:** First step of the decoder*

The second step and the steps after that are very similar to the first one, but the inputs received are a little different. Let us look at the code for the second step:

```
decoder_output[1] = decoder_output_layer (decoder_context, token[0])
decoder_context = decoder_context_layer (decoder_context, token[0])
token[1] = decoder_classfier_layer (decoder_output[1])
```

The second step receives the decoder context created and the token generated by the first step. In general, for any step *n*:

```
decoder_output[n] = decoder_output_layer (decoder_context, token[n-1])
decoder_context = decoder_context_layer (decoder_context, token[n-1])
token[n] = decoder_classfier_layer (decoder_output[n])
```

The decoder tries to predict the next token by looking at the previous token and the context. If it does this repeatedly, a sequence of tokens will be generated. In due time, the **end** token is generated, which stops this process.

Seq-2-seq models and GenAI

Till the introduction of seq-2-seq models, machine learning models were used to analyze data for prediction or classification. The output in these applications is a number or a vector. The ability of seq-2-seq models to generate text opened a new world of possibilities. The applications of these models were quite different from the earlier analytical ones. They were given the name **generative** applications, as opposed to the earlier **discriminative** ones. This book mentions translation as one such application, and you will see more in the upcoming chapters. In the decade following the introduction of seq-2-seq models, generative applications became popular. The term GenAI was coined to describe the models and the applications of this nature.

The most important model in the generative category is the **transformer**, which you will learn about in the next section.

Transformers

GenAI applications can be created using seq-2-seq models. Initially, seq-2-seq models were built using LSTM networks. However, LSTM-based models suffer from a problem. LSTMs process their input sequentially, one token at a time. This means that the time taken to process lengthy text is quite long. In 2017, a new architecture was introduced that used an innovative method of building seq-2-seq models. This architecture was called **transformer**. Since then, the popularity of transformer models has grown. Today, it is the architecture of choice for GenAI applications, especially for language generation.

Transformers are essentially seq-2-seq networks, so they adhere to the method of sequence generation described previously. Let us describe this method again to help us to get started:

- Process a variable length input text to create context. The context should take into account the tokens, their positions, and the dependencies between them.
- Use the context of the input to predict the first token of the output sequence.
- Take the previously generated token and the updated context to predict the next token. Repeat this process till the **end** token is generated.

Transformers work in the same way, but they introduce the following two innovations:

- Transformers process all the input tokens together. This saves a lot of time, but the order of the tokens is lost. To restore the importance of order, transformers use a technique called **positional encoding**.
- Transformers employ **attention**, a novel method of creating context.

Context creation by attention

LSTMs and RNNs use a sequential accumulation method of creating context. Thus, they always have one context vector in memory, no matter how long the text is. Transformers use a different approach. They process all the tokens together and create one context per token. See *Figure 1.9* for a diagrammatic representation of the transformer context creation:

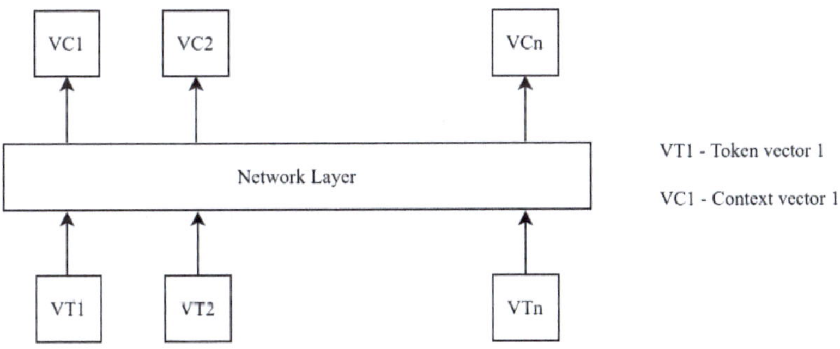

Figure 1.9: *One context vector per vector in transformers*

The flip side of this method is that transformers need to put a maximum limit on the length of the input that they can process. This limit is called the **context window**. Strictly speaking, the context window includes both input and output sequences. Here are the context windows of some well-known models:

Model	Context window (tokens)
Bert	512
GPT-3	2048
GPT-4	32000

Table 1.1: *Context windows of well-known models*

Transformers process all the tokens together, so they can employ a different method to consider the relationships between the tokens. Context creation requires consideration of the impact tokens have on each other. Since transformers create one context vector for each token, the impact of all the other tokens should be contained in this vector.

```
current_token = token[n]
other_tokens = token[0,…,n-1,n+1,…]
token_context[n] = compute_context (current_token, other_tokens)
```

The preceding code assumes that the function **compute_context** can create the context vector. This function is given the current token whose context is being computed, and all the other tokens. For instance, if the transformer is processing the following sentence:

```
S = "The best parties in life are the ones you throw for yourself."
```

If **throw** is the token that is being processed:

Note: That tokens can be slightly different from words. However, for the sake of clarity, we will assume that they are the same.

```
current_token = token[9] = 'throw'
other tokens = ['The', 'best', 'parties', 'in', 'life', 'are', 'the', 'ones',
'you','for', 'yourself', '.']
```

The most important and interesting thing here is that the impact of certain tokens on the current token is more than that of others. In the preceding example, the impact of **parties** on **throw** is much more than **The** or **best**. The word **throw** has many meanings, and **parties** is the word that gives it the right context here. Similarly, the word **life** and **throw** give the right meaning to the word **parties**, which can also mean political parties.

The **compute_context** function must make sure that it considers the right contribution of each token while computing the context for the current token. It should give more weight to the token **parties** and much less to the token **best**. In other words, the context creation should give the right amount of *attention* to the tokens in the sequence. This is why the mechanism is called context creation by *attention*.

The following calculation looks at how the attention creation function (**compute_context**) works:

```
current_token = token[n]
other_tokens = token[0,…,n-1,n+1,…]
for each tk in other_tokens
      token_context[n] = token_context[n] + Weight(tk, current_token) * tk
```

For the current token, the context vector is a combination of contributions from all other tokens and the contribution from each token is in proportion to its weight.

Some tokens are more important when making meaning of the current token. There is a simple way to calculate the importance or weight of a token. This is done by finding how close the two vectors are; the closer the vectors are, the higher their importance to each other. The closeness of vectors is measured by calculating the cosine of the angle between them, which is the same as their dot product, as can be seen in the following:

```
Weight(token1, token2) = Dot_product(token1, token2)
```

Transformers do not directly use the two tokens. They use vectors that are derived from the tokens. The following is what it looks like:

```
current_token = token[n]
other_tokens = token[0,…,n-1,n+1,…]
current_key = Multiply (key_matrix, current_token)

for each tk in other_tokens
      value_tk = Multiply(value_matrix, tk)
      query_tk = Multiply(query_matrix, tk)
      token_context[n] = token_context[n] +
            Dot_product(current_key, query_tk) * value_tk
```

Instead of the tokens **`current_token`** and **`tk`**, the code now uses three vectors: **`current_key`**, **`value_tk`**, and **`query_tk`**. They are created by multiplying the token vectors by three matrices, which are part of the transformer layer. These matrices are collectively called the KQV matrices.

The earlier code did not have any learnable parameters. The context contribution of a pair of tokens will always be fixed. However, the introduction of the three matrices brings parameters, which are learned during the training of the transformer.

Multi-head attention

Practical transformers create more than one context per token. Each such computation is called a **head**. Suppose a transformer has three heads, then it will have three sets of KQV matrices and will compute three contexts per token.

One token in a sentence impacts another token, and this impact can be significant or less so. However, two tokens can be related in more than one way: they can be strongly related in some sense and weakly related in another. For example, the token **`parties`** and **`are`** are weakly related from the **`meaning`** point of view but are strongly related in the grammatical sense. Multi-headed attention takes these different aspects of token relation into account.

Positional encoding

In sequence processing, one aspect is that the order of the tokens in the text must be considered while processing. In the case of RNN and LSTM, this happens automatically, as the tokens are processed sequentially. However, in transformers, all the tokens are processed together.

The designers of the transformer architecture employed a trick to include the position of the tokens in the context calculations. After the token vectors are received at the input, they are multiplied by a certain factor, which depends on the position of the token.

```
factor[n] = Get_position_factor(n)
```

The **Get_position_factor** is a function that calculates the factor for the given position. The typical functions chosen for this purpose are combinations of trigonometric functions like sin and cos.

Feed-forward network

In the preceding section, you saw how transformers create multiple contexts per token. These contexts are brought together through a multi-layer neural network. As you know, neural networks are like matrices. The matrices in the **feed-forward network** (**FFN**) are used to multiply all the contexts of the token and bring them together to form one context vector per token.

Transformer block

The architecture that has been discussed so far makes up one block of a transformer. *Figure 1.10* shows a schematic of the transformer block:

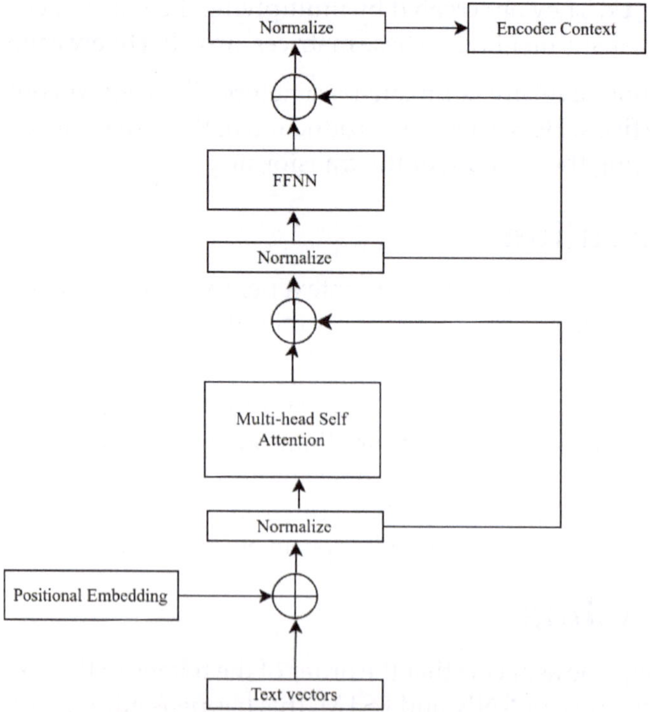

***Figure 1.10**: Architecture of transformer block*

Notice the two **add** and **normalize** blocks in the schematic. It was found that normalizing the vectors and adding the original vector to the output produces much better results.

Multiple blocks

The preceding schematic describes a transformer block. Real-life models like GPT-3 use many such blocks connected in series. The output of one block becomes the input for the next block. This allows the transformer to detect complex relationships in the text, such as a part of the text influencing another part. The multi-block architecture is shown in *Figure 1.11*:

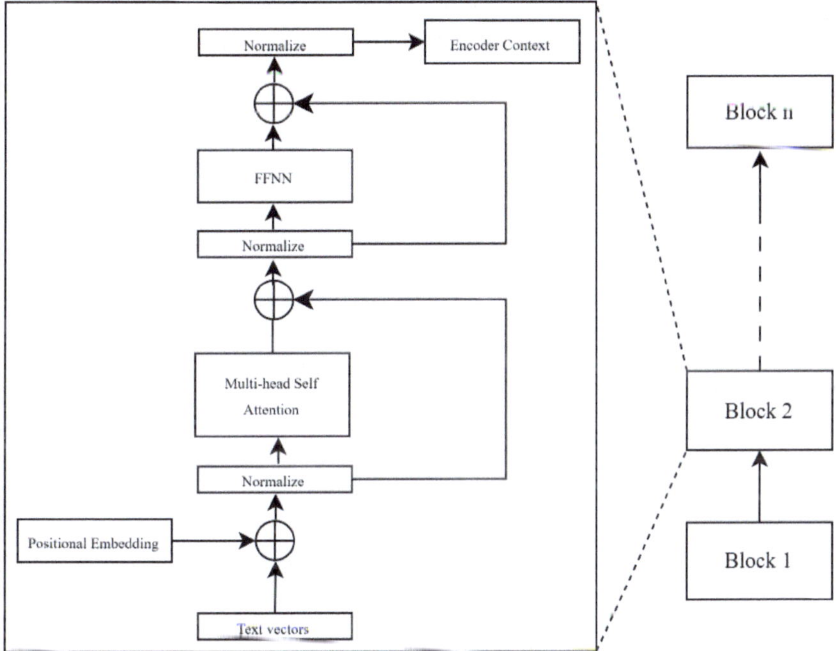

***Figure 1.11**: Multi-block architecture*

Encoder and decoder blocks

A transformer creates context vectors from input tokens using the component called the **encoder**. The section on encoder-decoder architecture mentioned that another component called the **decoder** is required for text generation. Transformers also contain the decoder component.

The decoder in a transformer has a slightly different design from the one that was discussed in the encoder-decoder section. This difference comes from the fact that transformers create one context vector per token, unlike RNNs or LSTMs. The first step of the decoder is given the `start` token, but it has to use the context from all the outputs of the encoder, instead of just one.

```
decoder_output[0] = decoder_output_layer (encoder_context[], <start>)
```

All the encoder contexts are being passed as a collection to the decoder output layer.

The actual output token has to be generated through a classifier.

```
token[0] = decoder_classfier_layer (decoder_output[0])
```

For the second token onwards, the decoder has to attend to two sets of tokens:

- **The input tokens**: This type of attention is called **cross-attention.**
- **The output tokens generated so far**: This is called **self-attention.**

The encoder contains only self-attention heads, while the decoder contains both self-attention and cross-attention. *Figure 1.12* is a representation of how the two types of attention are used in a decoder:

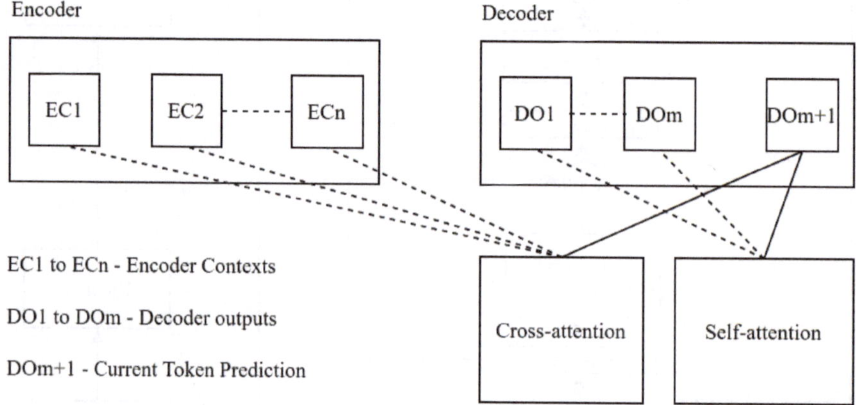

***Figure 1.12**: Architecture of transformer decoder*

Summary of transformer architecture

The transformer is made up of:

- Encoder blocks
- Decoder blocks

Each encoder block contains:

- Positional encoding
- Add and normalize
- Self-attention heads
- Feed forward network

Each decoder block contains:

- Self-attention heads
- Cross-attention heads
- Add and normalize
- Feed forward network
- Token classifier

Transformer architecture is complex as there are many components. The components create a great mechanism for learning language capabilities, but for learning to happen, transformers have to be trained in a certain way.

Training the transformer

Transformers are made up of NNs, and the training of a model involves:

- Task
- Training data
- Loss function
- Adjustment of parameters

Before the training, the **training data** is prepared, which contains both the inputs and the expected output. Then the untrained model performs the **task** on the training data. The **loss function** helps to measure how many mistakes the model is making. Then **the adjustment of parameters** of the model is done using an algorithm called **backpropagation**. This is done repeatedly until the loss value drops to a minimum.

The task

The task used in transformer training involves completing or correcting the given text. For example, if the model is given the following sentence:

```
input_text = "To be or not to be, that is the"
```

Training data

This task does not require the expected output to be specified. As you can see, the previous sentence has been created by hiding one token from the sentence:

```
S = "To be or not to be, that is the question"
```

The input is from *Shakespeare's* text, *Hamlet*. Thus, we already know the expected output. This idea makes transformer training scalable as it saves the effort of manually creating the expected outputs, called **labels**, as in the case of tasks like classification. This type of training is called **self-supervised** training.

The loss function

The loss function calculates the mistakes made in predicting the tokens. In the example given, the model should have predicted the vector for the token **question**. Suppose it predicts the token **choice**. The loss function calculates the difference between these two tokens. The closeness of vectors is indicated by the dot product between the vectors, and this principle is used to design the loss function. For mathematical convenience, the logarithm of each dot product is taken. The loss for all such predicted tokens is added. The loss function thus looks like the following:

```
Loss = Sum(Log( Dot_product (expected_vector, predicted_vector)))
```

The loss functions used in actual training are a lot more complicated. However, the example should give you the basic principles behind them.

Adjustment of parameters

A transformer contains a very large number of parameters. Even a smaller model like Bert has millions of parameters. These parameters are distributed over the various components of the transformer:

- K, Q, and V matrices for each head in each block
- Feed forward network
- Classifier

During parameter adjustment, the backpropagation algorithm allocates the loss to each of the parameters. The parameters are then given new values proportional to the allocated loss. This involves a large number of calculations. Special hardware, such as **graphics processing units** (**GPUs**), is required to complete the training in a reasonable time.

Layers of transformer training

The training described in the preceding section uses a self-supervised method to train the transformer over a large training data set. Typical data sets used for training current transformers contain billions of tokens. After this training, the model acquires excellent language capabilities. Specifically, the model becomes good at completing sentences. This stage of training is sometimes called **base** training.

This capability, although powerful, is of limited use. To make the model useful, further layers of training are added to the model. Two such layers that are currently popular are SFT and RLHF.

Supervised fine-tuning

SFT training uses properly labeled training data instead of the masked sentences used in base training. A typical example of such data looks like the following table:

Input (prompt)	Output(response)
In which year was the Indian Constitution adopted by the constituent assembly?	1949

Table 1.2: Typical example of training data for SFT

The loss function and the adjustment of parameters are similar to base training. Due to the explicit instructions given, the model becomes capable of following instructions from the user, especially for answering questions. A model that is given SFT is called the **instruct model**.

Reinforcement learning with human feedback

SFT teaches the model what to do, but it cannot teach it what not to do. SFT also guides the model to determine which of the possible responses is better than others. This is achieved through the RLHF training method based on the reinforcement learning principle. The training data for this contains multiple possible responses for each prompt. The data also specifies the rank given to each answer.

RLHF is used to train the model to produce responses that are preferred by humans and to avoid objectionable responses. The model, after adding the RLHF training layer, is called a **chat model**.

Learn text generation with code

Transformers have a complex structure made up of various NNs. They are trained through multiple layers of training. As a result, transformers become very good at language processing.

However, a transformer is not the only type of NN that can generate content. Another type of NN, called the **autoencoder**, can generate images. The working of autoencoders has not been explored, but image generation is also a very useful capability.

We will now see some examples of both text and image generation. The information in this section is only for the basic introduction. We are going to study many advanced scenarios of text and image generation later, but the introduction here will give us an opportunity to witness the power of the models that we studied earlier.

Language generation tasks

The transformers built and trained for language generation are called LLMs. They are capable of many language-related tasks, such as the following:

- **Question-answer**: They can understand a user query and provide an answer. During training, LLMs acquire a vast amount of knowledge about the world, which they use while answering the question.
- **Summarization**: LLMs can create a summary of the given text. They can limit it to a certain length, give more importance to certain points, and write in a particular style.
- **Content generation**: LLMs can produce stories, essays, poems, and other types of content. It is possible to tailor the output to your needs. For example, you might want the story to follow the style of O. Henry or PG Wodehouse.
- **Translation**: Some LLMs are trained on multiple language datasets. They can translate the given text from one language to another.
- **Comprehension**: This is another variation of the question-answer ability. LLMs can answer questions based on the provided text.

Apart from the previously mentioned language tasks, transformers trained with large text data sets can also perform tasks such as classification and reasoning and demonstrate mathematical abilities. The uniqueness of GenAI models, such as transformers, is that they are general-purpose, unlike earlier models, which had to be trained for one specific task.

Prompt-response method

No matter the task you want the LLM to perform, there is a general-purpose way to achieve it, which is called the **prompt-response** method. The method consists of the following:

- The user submits a text to the LLM. This text is called the **prompt,** and the activity is called **prompting**.
- The model returns another piece of text called the **response**.

The simplicity of this method is splendid. One can think of many complicated tasks that an LLM can perform, but the way to use it is always going to be standard. This fact has contributed a lot to the quick adoption of LLMs.

Let us see an example of using LLMs for language generation tasks. For any developer using LLMs, there is a choice between using the API of a public, closed model like the GPT family from OpenAI or using an open-source model in the code itself. Both methods will be used in the examples, but first, a prerequisite for coding the given examples will be discussed, which is using Google Colab.

Using Google Colab

In the following examples, any front end will not be developed. Instead, a convenient tool for coding will be used. Google Colab is a cloud service that allows users to write and execute Python (and other languages) code in their web browser. It also offers access to GPUs if needed.

To use Colab, go to the URL:

https://colab.research.google.com

You will need a Gmail account to use this service. Once you log in with your Gmail account, you can use the application. If you have used Jupyter Notebook before, you will find Colab very similar (in fact, Colab uses Jupyter notebooks). But even if you have not, it is really simple to use Colab. Look at the following figure:

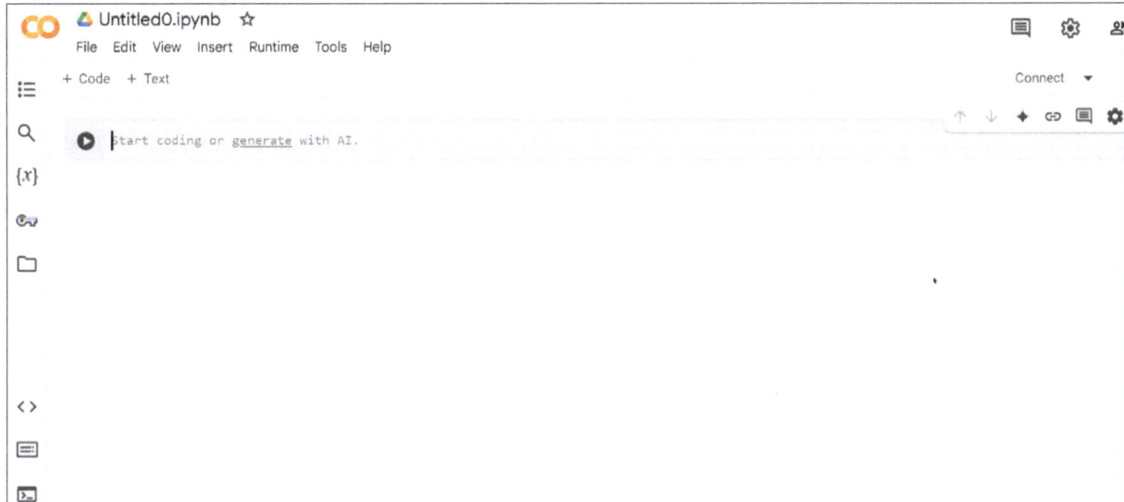

***Figure 1.13:** Google Colab*

When you start, a Python environment is automatically created for you. To start coding, click on the **+Code** at the top left. This will add a new code block where you can start entering the code. To run a block, click on the arrow in the black circle beside the block.

Question-answering

Suppose you are building a chatbot for financial literacy. Your chatbot will allow anyone to ask simple questions about investments, taxes, and other matters related to personal finance and provide them with answers. Here is the code:

```
import openai
# Set OpenAI API key
openai.api_key = "YOUR_OPENAI_API_KEY"

def qa_financial(prompt):

        # Call the OpenAI GPT-4o-mini model
        response = openai.chat.completions.create(
```

```
            model="gpt-4o-mini",
            messages=[
            {"role": "system", "content": "You are an expert in financial
domain. Provide clear and concise answers to questions about investments,
taxes, and personal finance."},
            {"role": "user", "content": prompt},
            ],
            temperature=0.2,
            max_tokens=350,
            n=1,
        )
        return response.choices[0].message

#Get the question from the user and call the qa function

print("Ask me a question about investments, taxes, or personal finance.")

user_query = input("\nAsk you question: ")
answer = qa_financial (user_query)

print(f"\nAnswer: {answer}")
```

A sample run of the preceding code should look like:

```
Ask me a question about investments, taxes or personal finance.
Ask your question: What are ETFs?
Answer: An Exchange-Traded Fund (ETF) is an investment fund that trades on stock
exchanges, just like individual stocks. It is a basket of securities—such as
stocks, bonds, commodities, or a mix of these—that tracks the performance of a
specific index, sector, or asset class…
```

Let us discuss the code. As the OpenAI Python library is being used, it provides convenient access to OpenAI models from Python code. The **ChatCompletion** class and its **create** method were used to generate the response. The model used here is the GPT-4o (o for **omni**) from OpenAI.

The standard way to interact with an LLM is to send a prompt and receive a response. Here, the prompt is divided into the following two parts:

- **System prompt**: This part of the prompt tells the model about the background of the task. The role of the model, the rules of the tasks, and any other information can be included. This part of the prompt is provided by the code.

- **User prompt**: This is the query by the user. As you can see, a placeholder has been put here that will be replaced by the user query at runtime.

Apart from the system and user prompts, certain parameters are supplied to the completion function. These parameters are called **decoding parameters**. There are many such parameters, and their impact depends on the model being used. The following is a brief explanation of the ones that have been used:

- **temperature:** You can assign a value between 0 and 1 to this parameter. Temperature influences randomness in the responses. Higher temperatures will result in more creative responses, but the risk of getting wrong information is also greater. Lower temperatures lead to more deterministic answers. In the examples, a lower temperature has been kept to ensure that users get fact-based answers as the chatbot is giving finance-related information.

- **max_tokens:** This tells the model the maximum number of tokens to generate. The decoder of the transformer model stops when this number is reached.

- **n (number of responses)**: This specifies the number of responses the model should generate. Each response will contain at most `max_tokens`.

A very simple method of prompting has been used. A separate discipline called **prompt engineering** that contains innovative prompting methods has evolved in the last few years. Some of these methods will be discussed later in the book.

Conclusion

This chapter explored the fundamentals of language processing using transformers, the most prominent models of GenAI. It started with the basics of how language is converted into vectors and how neural networks are used to process them. Some early text processing models like RNN and LSTM were also discussed. The GenAI game starts with seq-2-seq networks, which were visited briefly. After these fundamentals, the chapter then focused on the transformer architecture in some detail. The training of the transformers that make them so effective in text processing was also discussed. Finally, simple coding was done to generate text using a large language model, the most popular form of the transformer.

Text generation is only one type of content that GenAI models can generate. They can also create images, audio, and video. In fact, there are models other than transformers (such as variational autoencoders) that are used to generate images and other content. However, the discussion in this chapter focuses only on transformers and text generation.

In the next chapter, we will explore some of the practical models utilized in the GenAI industry. These models will include some non-transformer models, too. It will also discuss some of the fundamentals that were not addressed in this chapter.

Chapter 2
The SOTA GenAI Models

Introduction

The last chapter discussed the use of neural networks such as **recurrent neural networks (RNNs)**, **Long Short-Term Memory (LSTMs)**, and transformers for language processing. Transformers take the generative approach to language processing. In recent years, generative models have witnessed a surge in popularity driven by their effectiveness in processing diverse data modalities beyond language, such as images and audio. While transformers have emerged as a prominent architecture, alternative approaches have also proven successful in handling these non-textual domains. Models designed to generate data through various architectural implementations are collectively referred to as GenAI models.

Since the introduction of the first GenAI models in 2018, an incredible variety of models has become available through the contributions of both the academic and industrial communities. A GenAI solution developer now has a problem of plenty in selecting the right model for their solution. Though GenAI systems contain many different components, such as databases and coding layers, the GenAI model is the central and most important component. The success of the system depends, to a large extent, on selecting the right model.

This chapter introduces the readers to the various GenAI models available for system development. The pace of research and development in the AI industry is rapid, and no book can hope to cover all the models. The approach taken in this chapter is to explore how the universe of GenAI models can be divided into categories. In each category, some well-known models will be discussed. In the case of non-transformer models, some explanation of their architecture is also included.

Structure

This chapter covers the following topics:

- Categorizing GenAI models
- Open-source and closed-source models
- Modality of the models
- Large and small models
- Model architectures
- Learning image generation with code

Objectives

By the end of this chapter, you will understand the landscape of GenAI models, the diversity of models, and important models in each category. You will add to your understanding of architectures like autoencoders and **generative adversarial networks** (**GANs**) to your knowledge of transformers. You will also be able to write code to generate images using text prompts.

Categorizing GenAI models

The number of available GenAI models is truly staggering. Hugging Face, the repository of open-source generative AI models, hosts more than 1.3 million models as of January 2025. Navigating through this vast landscape can be very confusing for GenAI solution developers. Hence, it is necessary to partition the vast number of models into smaller sections.

The partitioning of models can be done based on certain *aspects*. An aspect is a property that GenAI models possess, such as size, type of data processed, and architecture used. Each aspect will give rise to model categories. For example, the size aspect will lead to the categories of small models and large models. While this section discusses some important aspects, subsequent sections treat each of the aspects in detail, with associated categories and examples of models.

Public availability

The genesis of neural network research can be traced to academic institutions. In accordance with the established norms of academic inquiry, researchers rigorously reported their findings, including comprehensive details of the employed models. Pivotal breakthroughs in deep learning, such as backpropagation, **convolutional neural networks** (**CNNs**), **RNNs**, and groundbreaking models like AlexNet were readily accessible to the broader scientific community through peer-reviewed publications and publicly available code repositories.

When a new model is introduced, the innovators publish important details about it, including:

- Model architecture
- Training data
- Model parameters (also called **model weights**)
- Training algorithm
- Evaluation results

These details together are called **model source**. The availability of the model source enables other researchers to replicate the implementation and add further improvements to it. This process drives advancements in the field.

Over time, research in neural networks and deep learning moved to industrial organizations such as *Google*, *Microsoft*, and *Meta* (formerly Facebook). These organizations continued the tradition of publishing the model source. In 2018, BERT (*Google*) and GPT-1 (*OpenAI*) became the first GenAI models to be introduced. They were called **open-source** models as the inventors made all the details publicly available through papers, technical reports, and code repositories.

However, as the research progressed, some of the model makers decided not to publish the model source. Instead, they hosted the models themselves and offered their services in the form of an **application programming interface** (**API**). OpenAI was the first company to do so, with its GPT-3 model that was only available as an API. Many models that followed GPT-3 adopted the same strategy. Some examples of such **closed-source** models are GPT-4, Gemini, and Claude 3.

After the launch of ChatGPT in November 2022, a clear pattern was seen. Closed-source models were more capable and could be used in production applications, while open-source models were smaller and experimental. That situation soon changed with the introduction of models like Llama and Mistral. The *Open and closed source models* section will explore both types of models in detail.

Modality

At their core, GenAI models operate under the principle of sequence-to-sequence processing. They function by accepting an input sequence and subsequently generating an output sequence. As defined in *Chapter 1, Introduction to Transformer Models*, a sequence is characterized as an ordered arrangement of numbers or vectors. While the preceding discussions primarily focused on the processing of text sequences, it is important to recognize that GenAI models possess the capability to process other types of sequences, such as images and audio.

In GenAI parlance, the type of data processed by a model is called the **modality**. Some common modalities are:

- Text
- Image
- Audio
- Video

The modality of the GPT3.5 model (which powered the first version of ChatGPT) is text. The input and output modalities of a model can be different. For example, the Vision Transformer accept images as input and produce text as output. Models can also accept text as well as images as input, such models are called **muti-modal**.

The *Modality of the models* section will discuss models that cater to various modalities. It will also explore a variation of the transformer used for processing images: the Vision Transformer.

Model size

Like any neural network, the functioning of a GenAI model is intricately linked to its parameters. These parameters serve as the repository for the model's learned knowledge. Consequently, a model's capacity for learning is directly correlated with the number of parameters it possesses. This parameter count is frequently referred to as the model's **size**.

Researchers noticed that once the size crosses a certain critical threshold, models start demonstrating impressive capabilities such as language understanding and basic reasoning. This discovery led to a constant growth in model size.

However, the increase in size comes with a cost. Training and deploying larger models demand significant computational resources, translating to increased time and financial expenditure. This has spurred a parallel line of research aimed at achieving comparable performance with more compact models. Notably, researchers have successfully developed models with fewer than five billion parameters while still demonstrating commendable capabilities across a range of tasks.

Contemporary GenAI model development embraces a multifaceted approach, with researchers actively exploring both the potential of large-scale models and the development of smaller, resource-efficient alternatives. A common practice involves releasing a single model architecture in a series of variants with varying sizes. For instance, Meta's Llama 3 model is offered in multiple configurations, including eight billion, 70 billion, and 405 billion parameter versions, where **8B** signifies eight billion parameters.

Model size has many implications for GenAI system developers, including cost, accuracy, and latency. These will be discussed in detail in the *Model size* section.

Model architecture

GenAI models operate by processing sequences of data. Internally, they employ two key subprocesses:

- Process the input to create context.
- Use the context to predict the next token.

In *Chapter 1, Introduction to Transformer Models,* it was shown that the next token prediction can give rise to sequence generation. It also introduced the transformer architecture that achieves the preceding two subprocesses to generate text.

Since the introduction of the transformer, many variations of the original architecture have emerged, each building on the fundamental principles while exploring innovative designs to improve performance. While the original architecture incorporated both encoder and decoder components, some of the transformer models, such as the GPT family, follow a decoder only architecture. To enhance efficiency and resource utilization, researchers have explored innovative techniques, such as the **mixture of experts** and **multi-token prediction**, aiming to accelerate the generation process while minimizing computational demands.

The transformer architecture has been applied to other modalities as well. The **Large Vision Transformer** mentioned in the discussion on modality is a good example. Newer transformer architectures are also capable of processing multiple modalities together.

While transformer architectures have garnered significant attention in recent years, it is crucial to acknowledge the contributions of other architectural paradigms. Architectures such as **autoencoders** and **GANs** have demonstrated remarkable efficacy in generating images and audio.

The *Model architectures* section will discuss various models based on some of these architectures. This section will also include a concise overview of key architectures, such as autoencoders and GANs, to provide a better understanding of the models.

The exploration of models begins with the variety of open-source and closed-source models.

Open-source and closed-source models

The trajectory of GenAI model development has oscillated between open-source and closed-source approaches. Initially, GenAI models were exclusively open-source. However, the commercial success of ChatGPT led major technology companies to prioritize the development of proprietary, closed-source model APIs. Despite this trend, open-source development persisted, and thanks to the contributions of organizations such as Meta, Mistral, and DeepSeek, open-source models have regained prominence and now rival their closed-source counterparts in popularity.

From the perspective of a GenAI system developer, there are important differences between the two types of models. The following are the main points of comparison:

- **Accessibility**: Open-source models offer users a significant degree of control, as they are freely accessible and allow for independent decisions regarding deployment, customization, and security. In contrast, closed-source models restrict user access to the model itself, offering only interaction through APIs provided by the model developers.
- **Customization**: Developers can customize open-source models through fine-tuning, leveraging the complete model architecture and weights. Even though closed-source models also offer varying degrees of fine-tuning capabilities, these capabilities are often restricted and controlled by the model providers, limiting the extent of user customization.
- **Performance**: Initially, open-source models generally exhibited lower performance on benchmarks compared to their closed-source counterparts. However, recent advancements have seen many open-source models achieve comparable, and in some cases superior, performance. It is crucial to note that not all open-source models are created equal, and developers must carefully evaluate the capabilities of each model before selection.

- **Cost**: While open-source models are available to developers without licensing fees, they incur costs associated with hosting and infrastructure. For large models, these operational expenses can be substantial. Conversely, closed-source models typically operate on a usage-based pricing model, which can also become expensive at scale. Therefore, the optimal cost strategy depends on a variety of factors, including usage patterns and model size.
- **Data security and confidentiality**: The reliance on APIs for accessing closed-source models necessitates the transmission of input data outside the user's organizational network, raising concerns regarding data confidentiality. Open-source models, conversely, can be hosted locally, thereby mitigating this risk.
- **Ease of getting started**: For initial explorations and proof-of-concept projects, the readily available APIs of closed-source models offer a convenient starting point, eliminating the overhead of deployment. This ease of access makes them a potentially more attractive option for such preliminary work compared to open-source alternatives.
- **Deployment flexibility**: Open-source models offer deployment flexibility, accommodating a wide range of environments, from on-premises servers and private cloud instances to edge devices like mobile phones. Closed-source models, however, lack this versatility.

The following table summarizes the comparison between the two types of models:

Point	Open-source	Closed-source
Accessibility	Freely accessible; allows full control over deployment, customization, and security.	Restricted access; interaction only through APIs provided by the developers.
Customization	Complete access to model architecture and weights for fine-tuning.	Limited fine-tuning capabilities controlled by model providers.
Performance	Historically lagged behind, but now many achieve comparable or superior performance.	Generally high performance, often optimized with proprietary advancements.
Cost	No licensing fees, but incurs hosting and infrastructure costs	Usage-based pricing. Costs can become high at scale.
Data security and confidentiality	Can be hosted locally, reducing the risk of data exposure.	Requires data transmission to external servers via APIs, raising confidentiality concerns.
Ease of getting started	Requires setup and deployment, which can be complex.	APIs provide easy access, making them more convenient for initial exploration.
Deployment flexibility	Can be deployed on-premises, in private clouds, or on edge devices.	Limited deployment options, usually restricted to cloud-based access.

Table 2.1: Comparison of open-source and closed-source models

Llama family of models

Having examined the comparative advantages and limitations of open-source and closed-source GenAI models, the following discussion will focus on Meta's Llama family of models. This exploration will encompass their architecture, capabilities, and significance within the broader open-source AI ecosystem.

Background

Meta (formerly *Facebook*) released the first model in the Llama family, Llama 1 (called LLaMA at the time), in February 2023. While open-source, Llama 1's availability was initially restricted to the research community, excluding commercial use. The model's release, in sizes ranging from seven billion to 65 billion parameters, was met with considerable enthusiasm, enabling researchers to experiment with a powerful language model using comparatively modest resources. Llama 1's introduction significantly invigorated open-source model research.

Following the successful launch of Llama 1, Meta released Llama 2 in July 2023. This iteration, also offered in a range of sizes, demonstrated significant improvements in both performance and efficiency. Critically, Llama 2 removed the previous licensing restrictions, permitting commercial use. This change spurred considerable industry interest, with AI solution providers and users alike customizing the model through fine-tuning and developing applications around it. Llama 2 thus emerged as a viable alternative to prominent closed-source models of the time, such as the GPT family.

The most recent iterations of the Llama models, Llama 3 and Llama 3.1, were released in April and July 2024, respectively. These versions incorporate several enhancements over previous models, including an expanded context window, improved reasoning abilities, and support for a broader range of languages. The Llama family of models has now garnered significant support within the AI community, encompassing startups, users, and service providers

The following discussion of architecture and related details will primarily reference Llama 3. Any notable features or differences present in earlier versions will be explicitly highlighted.

Technical details

Llama is a transformer-based large language model that builds upon the foundational transformer architecture, incorporating several key innovations for enhanced performance and efficiency. However, Llama's design diverges from the general architecture discussed in *Chapter 1, Introduction to Transformer Models,* in one significant aspect: it employs a decoder-only architecture, omitting the encoder component. This design prioritizes tasks such as text generation and summarization.

While Llama is an open-source model, certain architectural details remain undisclosed. For instance, the number of decoder blocks and the token embedding size have not been publicly released. The following table presents the technical specifications that *have* been published:

Specification	Value
Architecture	Decoder only transformer
Model sizes	8B, 70B 405B (for Llama 3.1)
Vocabulary	128,000 tokens
Context window	32,000 (Llama 3) 128,000 (Llama 3.1)

Table 2.2: Technical specifications of Llama models

Model variants

Llama 3.1 is offered in three sizes: 8B, 70B, and 405B (where *B* denotes billions of parameters). This range of options allows GenAI solution developers to select the most appropriate variant for their specific requirements. The following are the key considerations for variant selection:

- **Performance and accuracy**: The 8B variant exhibits comparatively lower performance on standard language task benchmarks. The 70B model performs well on a wide range of common tasks. Finally, the 405B variant excels in more complex tasks, particularly those requiring logical reasoning.
- **Speed**: While the smallest variant offers the advantage of rapid response times due to its reduced size, the larger variants exhibit significantly slower processing speeds.
- **Computational requirements**: The 8B model is suitable for execution on mobile devices. Running the 70B model requires substantial computational resources, typically involving two to four high-performance **graphics processing units** (**GPUs**), such as the NVIDIA A100. The largest variant, the 405B model, demands significantly greater computational power.
- **Suitable applications**: In applications where computational power and speed are paramount, such as real-time translation on a mobile device, the 8B model is the most suitable choice. The 70B model offers strong performance for a variety of applications, including chatbots and coding assistants, while typically requiring GPU server-based computation. Finally, advanced applications like intelligent agents and decision-making systems will necessitate the capabilities of the 405B model.

Comparison with other models

For comparison, we will consider the 70B variant of Llama 3.1. This model can be compared with models such as:

- Closed-source models

  - GPT-4o
  - Gemini 1.5
- Open-source models
  - DeepSeek V3
  - Qwen 2.5 Max

Direct performance comparisons between models are challenging due to the continuous nature of model upgrades. System developers must base their evaluations on the models available at the time of design. However, some general observations can be made from comparisons of the models discussed:

- Closed-source models, such as GPT-4, exhibit marginally superior performance in language understanding tasks, although the difference is slight.
- More recent open-source models, including DeepSeek V3 and Qwen 2.5 Max, outperform Llama 3.1 70B, likely due to advancements in architecture and training data.
- While Llama 70B provides satisfactory performance in reasoning tasks, it lags behind models like Qwen. Reasoning is a rapidly evolving area, and newer models often benefit significantly from the latest algorithmic developments.

Performance comparisons can also consider the speed of input processing and token generation. While this metric is dependent on both the underlying infrastructure and model configuration, Llama models generally offer a balanced performance in terms of speed and accuracy. However, newer models such as Qwen and DeepSeek demonstrate faster processing and generation capabilities.

The key takeaway from this comparative analysis is that Llama models offer performance comparable to similarly sized models currently available. However, for specific applications, developers should conduct their own evaluations using the latest models accessible to them.

Llama models at a glance

In summary, the discussion of the Llama family of LLMs highlights the following key points:

- Llama models employ a decoder-only transformer architecture and are available in a variety of sizes.
- These models are open-source, although certain technical specifications remain proprietary.
- Llama models offer deployment flexibility, ranging from mobile devices to multi-GPU server clusters. As open-source models, they require deployment on user-managed infrastructure.

- These versatile, general-purpose models deliver performance comparable to other models of similar size.
- Llama models are applicable to a wide range of tasks, including classification, translation, chatbot development, coding assistance, decision support, and reasoning.

Modality of the models

Many real-world applications require the processing of diverse data modalities. Examples include the following:

- Text-to-speech and speech-to-text applications, which involve interconversion between textual and audio data.
- Document understanding applications, which require the conversion of scanned document images to text.
- Image generation tools, which create images based on textual descriptions.
- Music generation applications, which generate music from user instructions.

These examples illustrate the need for GenAI models capable of converting one data modality (e.g., image, text) into another (e.g., text, audio). Such models are termed **multi-modal models (MMMs)**.

Text modality has already been discussed in the earlier material. This section will focus specifically on image and audio modalities, discussing four model types:

- **Image-to-text**: image understanding
- **Text-to-image**: image generation
- **Speech-to-text**: speech recognition
- **Text-to-speech**: speech generation

The architectures of these models differ from the transformer architecture previously discussed. These architectures will be briefly outlined, and a representative model of each type will be examined.

Image understanding models

Image understanding models, also known as **image-to-text** or **image captioning** models, receive an image as input and generate a textual description as output. The **Vision Transformer (ViT)** architecture is currently the most prevalent architecture for these models.

Architecture of ViT

Vision Transformers adhere to the encoder-decoder structure of the traditional transformer architecture. A key concept in their operation is image tokenization. The input image is partitioned into patches, typically 16x16 pixels in size (though patch size can be adjusted). Each patch is then flattened into a vector, which is subsequently tokenized using a trained network.

Following tokenization, positional embeddings are applied to the tokens, encoding the original 2D location of each patch within the image. The subsequent process of context creation mirrors that of text transformers. The encoder generates a context vector for each patch token.

Note: **The original ViT architecture was encoder-only and primarily employed for image classification tasks. For image captioning, the decoder component was subsequently integrated.**

The decoder of the ViT is virtually the same as the text transformer. It uses the context from the image encoder to generate tokens in an autoregressive manner, as described in the section on transformer architecture.

Vision Transformers have significantly impacted the field of **Optical Character Recognition** (**OCR**), revolutionizing the conversion of images to text. They are rapidly displacing earlier image processing-based and LSTM-based OCR technologies. Microsoft's **Transformer-based Optical Character Recognition** (**TrOCR**) is a prominent example of a ViT model in this domain, which will be discussed next.

TrOCR model

Microsoft Research introduced the TrOCR model in 2021, marking a substantial advancement over existing CNN or LSTM-based approaches. Prior models lacked explicit training on textual data. TrOCR, in contrast, is trained on large image and text datasets. It is an end-to-end model directly encoding the image and generating text through a decoder. Furthermore, TrOCR's architecture facilitates fine-tuning for specialized tasks, such as handwriting recognition.

The fully open-source release of TrOCR has demonstrated the efficacy of this approach. Since its release, numerous contributors have fine-tuned TrOCR for specific applications, making these fine-tuned models publicly available. The following are examples of such models and their respective use cases:

Model	Training data	Purpose
`trocr_base_handwritten`	IAM Dataset	Handwriting recognition
`trocr_base_printed`	SROIE Dataset	Printed text recognition
`trocr_base_str`	IC13, IC15, IIIT5K, SVT	Single-line image text recognition

Table 2.3: Finetuned TrOCR models with use cases

Numerous additional fine-tuned TrOCR models are available through repositories such as Hugging Face, enabling developers to select a model appropriate for their specific needs.

The **base** designation in TrOCR model names indicates the medium-sized variant of the underlying transformer architecture. Other available sizes are designated as **small** and **large**. In terms of parameter count, these sizes correspond to:

- **Small**: 65 million
- **Base**: 334 million
- **Large**: 558 million

As these figures illustrate, TrOCR models are significantly smaller than LLMs like Llama and GPT. This relatively modest size contributes to their popularity by enabling execution with more readily available computing resources.

Image generation models

Automatic image generation is a significant industrial application, with use cases including:

- **Content creation**: Generating visuals for marketing materials, blog posts, and other content.
- **Video game development**: Creating graphical assets for video games.
- **Design**: Conceptualizing ideas for interior, architecture, and apparel design.

Image generation models employed various technologies over the last few years. While variational autoencoders were preferred during the early 2010s, the introduction of GAN architecture brought a transformation in image generation in the latter half of the decade. Since 2020, diffusion models have become popular. In the following subsection, we will focus on the diffusion architecture.

Architecture of the diffusion models

The diffuser image generation models have three components: diffuser, denoiser, and text encoder:

- **Diffuser**: The diffuser component iteratively adds noise to an input image. Repeated application of this process progressively degrades the image until it approximates pure noise. It is important to understand that the diffuser component is non-trainable.

  Note: **The noise introduced consists of random values sampled from a normal distribution. These values are then added to the pixel values of the image.**

- **Denoiser**: The denoiser component is trained to remove noise from a noisy image. Typically implemented as a neural network, such as a CNN, it learns to predict the appropriate amount of noise to be removed in a single step.

- **Text encoder**: The text encoder is a standard encoder component derived from the text transformer architecture. Many models utilize a pre-trained encoder, such as BERT. This encoder takes a text prompt as input and generates a corresponding context vector as output.

Training of the diffuser

The training dataset comprises pairs of text prompts and corresponding images. For example, a prompt might be *Generate an image of a red car parked beside a lake*, and the paired image would be a visual representation of that description. The training process proceeds as follows:

1. The image is input to the diffuser, which iteratively adds noise until the image is almost entirely obscured.
2. The text prompt is input to the text encoder, which generates encoded context vectors.
3. The noisy image from *Step 1* and the context vectors from *Step 2* are then input to the denoiser. The denoiser employs cross-attention on the context vectors to predict the noise to be removed from the image.
4. The predicted noise is compared to the noise added in *Step 1*. The difference between these noise values is used to calculate the loss.

Steps 3 and *4* are repeated until the original image is reconstructed by iteratively removing the added noise.

This training process is iterated over a large corpus of prompt-image pairs. Through this iterative training, the denoiser learns to effectively remove noise conditioned on the provided text prompt. The process is shown in the following figure:

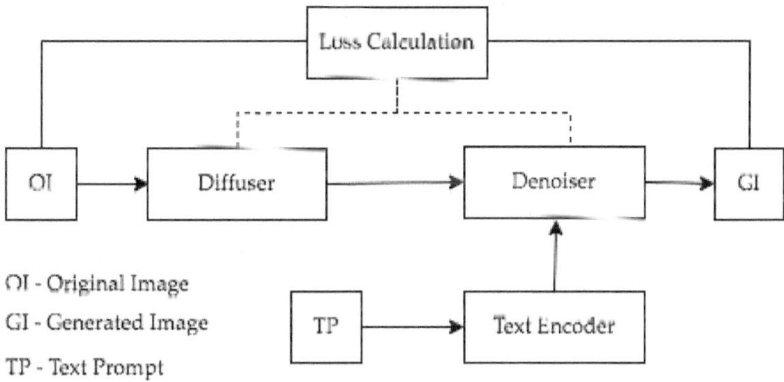

***Figure 2.1**: Training of a diffuser model*

Image generation

During image generation, only the denoiser and text encoder components are active. The denoiser receives pure noise as input, along with the encoded prompt vectors. Following the learned process from training, the denoiser predicts the noise to be removed from the image in a step-by-step manner, guided by the context of the prompt through cross-attention. In this generative phase, the denoiser creates a novel image that, due to its training, closely corresponds to the description provided in the text prompt.

While practical implementations of diffusion models incorporate additional complexities, the preceding explanation should serve as a sound conceptual understanding of the core principles underlying image generation using diffusion.

The following section will examine Stable Diffusion, a prominent and widely used model for image generation.

Stable Diffusion model

Stable Diffusion, an open-source image generation model, was released in August 2022. Developed by *Stability AI*, a UK-based AI company, in collaboration with other organizations, it rapidly gained widespread adoption across various industries due to its powerful image generation capabilities and relatively low deployment costs.

Stable Diffusion employs the diffusion architecture described earlier but incorporates an additional component: an autoencoder. This autoencoder compresses the image into a smaller representation during the training phase. The remaining training and generation processes are consistent with the standard diffusion model. The image generated by the denoiser is subsequently decompressed by the autoencoder to restore it to its original dimensions.

Since the initial release of Stable Diffusion, *Stability AI* has continued to develop the model, culminating in the release of Stable Diffusion 3.5 in October 2024. These subsequent versions have incorporated numerous architectural advancements aimed at addressing limitations and enhancing overall performance. Stable Diffusion 3.5 is now offered in three variants: Medium (with 2.5 billion parameters), Large Turbo (with 3.5 billion parameters), and Large (with eight billion parameters).

Accessing Stable Diffusion

Stable Diffusion models are accessible through various means. Users have the option of deploying the models on their own infrastructure. Stability AI, the developer of Stable Diffusion, provides APIs for model serving. Third-party platforms, such as Hugging Face, also host the models and offer corresponding APIs. Furthermore, Stable Diffusion's integration into numerous web and mobile applications provides convenient access for image generation.

Typical applications

Stable Diffusion models find application across a wide range of industries where image generation is crucial. The marketing and advertising sectors are particularly prominent users, leveraging these models for content creation. Design-related fields, including interior design, apparel design, and product conceptualization, also utilize Stable Diffusion. It is important to note that, in design applications, these models primarily serve as idea generators rather than producing final designs. The entertainment industry also employs Stable Diffusion to generate storyboards and visuals for comics and other media.

In summary, Stable Diffusion represents a significant advancement in the application of GenAI for image generation. Its open-source nature and ease of access have contributed to its widespread adoption and popularity within industry.

Speech recognition models

Speech-to-text (**STT**) functionality is essential for numerous industrial applications. The automated transcription of audio files offers significant efficiency gains in business operations, enabling professionals to record thoughts and subsequently transform these recordings into document drafts. Such applications are called **automatic speech recognition** (**ASR**) applications. Several prominent ASR applications include the following:

- **Medical transcription**: Physicians record patient notes, which are then transcribed into medical records using STT.
- **Legal**: Court proceedings, statements, and depositions can be automatically converted to written documents.
- **Customer service**: Service calls are transcribed for quality assurance and training purposes.
- **Meeting minutes**: Recorded meetings can be automatically converted into minutes and action items.

Over the past two decades, various technologies have been developed to address the challenges of ASR. Early approaches utilized techniques such as **Hidden Markov Models** (**HMMs**) and **Gaussian Mixture Models** (**GMMs**). In the 2010s, deep learning emerged as the preferred methodology for STT applications. Later in that decade, RNNs and LSTMs gained prominence in speech processing due to their inherent suitability for sequential data. Currently, in the 2020s, transformers have become the dominant technology for STT models.

STT models fall under the broader category of audio modality processing. The following discussion will examine the architecture of the Audio Spectrogram Transformer, followed by an analysis of Whisper, a prominent and widely used STT model.

Architecture of the Audio Spectrogram Transformer

The **Audio Spectrogram Transformer** (**AST**) enables the application of conventional transformer architectures to the processing of audio signals. AST can be specifically trained for speech recognition tasks. Introduced in 2021, this architecture was rapidly adopted for the development of numerous speech-to-text models.

The architecture of the AST closely resembles that of the ViT, comprising both an encoder and a decoder. However, audio signals require specific pre-processing before they can be input to the encoder. This conversion is achieved through the following three steps:

1. The audio signal is segmented into patches of a specific duration, for example, 30 seconds.
2. Each patch is transformed into its frequency spectrum. This process is analogous to converting an image to JPEG format, and the resulting representation is termed the **spectrogram**.
3. The spectrogram of each patch is converted into an embedding using an embedding model.

These embeddings are then input to the encoder, which employs self-attention mechanisms to generate context vectors.

The decoder component of an AST is adapted from text transformer models, such as GPT-2. While typically derived from existing models, the decoder can also be specifically trained for certain applications. Following the established auto-regressive process and guided by cross-attention to the encoder's context vectors, the decoder generates text corresponding to the input audio signal. This generated text represents the transcription of the audio.

Practical STT models often employ variations of the AST architecture described. One such model, Whisper from OpenAI, will be discussed in the following section.

Whisper model

Whisper, an open-source STT model, was released by OpenAI. Its initial version was released around the same time as ChatGPT, with a subsequent, improved version released a year later, in November 2023. Whisper's versatility in transcription and translation across a wide range of languages has contributed to its widespread adoption and popularity.

Technical details

Whisper employs the same AST architecture previously described, with one key modification. Prior to encoding, the spectrogram is processed through two convolutional layers. This pre-processing step aids in the detection of local dependencies within the audio signal, leading to improved transcription accuracy.

The most recent iteration of Whisper, designated **Whisper Large-V3**, has been trained on approximately five million hours of audio data. Another variant called **Whisper Large-V3 turbo** is also available for faster transcription with minimum degradation in quality. This model offers multilingual support, encompassing transcription, translation, and language identification of the audio input.

Availability

As an open-source model, Whisper is readily available for download from popular repositories such as Hugging Face. Its relatively modest size (1.5B parameters) allows for hosting on systems with less powerful GPUs. Furthermore, Whisper is accessible via APIs offered by OpenAI, Microsoft Azure, and other providers, providing solution developers with deployment flexibility.

Comparison

While Whisper is recognized for its versatility, encompassing transcription, translation, and language identification, as well as its flexible deployment options, other models may be more suitable for specific requirements. For instance, models like Universal-2 from *AssemblyAI* are known for higher accuracy, particularly in recognizing proper nouns. Regarding processing speed, Whisper performs slightly below models such as wav2vec 2.0 from Meta. Solution developers should consider these alternatives when specific performance characteristics are prioritized.

Adoption in industry

Whisper finds application in numerous critical STT use cases across diverse domains, including healthcare, law, customer service, and others previously mentioned. Its widespread adoption is attributable to its accessibility, low cost, and generally good accuracy. Whisper exhibits robust performance in transcribing multiple languages and handling diverse accents and background noise, all common challenges in industrial audio settings. However, Whisper is not immune to occasional transcription errors. Therefore, solutions employing Whisper often incorporate a quality control step to validate the output before it is utilized.

In summary, Whisper serves as a representative example of current speech-to-text GenAI models. Based on the AST architecture, it provides robust STT capabilities suitable for addressing industrial challenges, even if other models may offer superior performance in specific areas. This combination of factors contributes to Whisper's widespread popularity as an STT model.

Speech generation models

Speech generation has a longer history than other types of generation, pre-dating the rise of modern AI. However, generating natural-sounding speech has consistently posed a significant challenge. Natural speech is characterized by elements such as intonation, expression, and pauses. The absence of these features results in speech that sounds robotic and unnatural. Recent advancements in GenAI models have now made it possible to synthesize speech that approaches naturalness.

Speech generation, also known as **text-to-speech** (**TTS**), has a wide range of industrial applications, including the following:

- **Accessibility**: Providing auditory access to text for visually impaired individuals.
- **Virtual assistants**: Enabling interactive assistance by providing information and instructions through speech.
- **Content generation**: Automating the creation of audio content, such as podcasts.
- **Language learning**: Facilitating language acquisition through auditory learning aids.

The field of TTS models is characterized by significant diversity, with numerous technologies employed in their construction. Commonly used architectures include the following:

- **Sequence-to-sequence with LSTM**: An encoder-decoder architecture implemented using LSTM networks.
- **Transformer**: It is similar to the AST architecture discussed previously, but with reversed roles for the encoder and decoder components.
- **Diffusion**: A diffusion-based approach employing a denoiser to generate spectrograms conditioned on a text prompt.

Key parameters to consider when selecting a TTS model include:

- **Language support**: The model must support the required language(s), including any necessary accents and dialects.
- **Natural speech quality**: The generated speech should exhibit naturalness, incorporating elements such as intonation, modulation, and expressive qualities.
- **Voicepacks**: The model should be capable of generating diverse speaking styles, often referred to as voicepacks and typically identified by human names.
- **Licensing**: Models may be proprietary or open-source. The licensing model should align with system requirements.

Practical TTS solutions typically integrate with services provided by established platform providers rather than directly utilizing models. The following is a list of commonly used services:

TTS service	Provider	Languages supported	Common uses
Google Cloud Text-to-Speech	Google	40+	Voiceovers, podcasts, multilingual applications
Amazon Poly	Amazon AWS	Multiple	Real-time applications, accessibility tools, content creation
Microsoft Azure TTS	Microsoft Azure	75+	Accessibility features, customer service bots, content narration

TTS service	Provider	Languages supported	Common uses
Watson Text-to-Speech	IBM	Multiple	Customer engagement, accessibility solutions, educational tools
Bark	Suno AI	Multiple	Voice assistants, multilingual applications, sound effects, and music generation

Table 2.4: Commonly used TTS services

Large and small models

Model size presents a trade-off for both model developers and users. The following factors are influenced by model size:

- **Training data requirements**: Larger models necessitate substantially more training data to achieve optimal performance.
- **Training computational resources**: Training large models requires significant computational resources, often involving multiple GPUs operating in parallel.
- **Training time**: Even with parallel processing across multiple GPUs, larger models require longer training times.
- **Hosting computational resources**: Hosting larger models demands greater computational resources, including memory, GPU memory, and storage.
- **Fine-tuning resources**: Fine-tuning larger models requires more computational resources and time.
- **Inference speed**: Larger models typically exhibit slower token generation speeds.
- **Accuracy**: Large models perform better at various tasks than their smaller counterparts.

Model creators, thus, have to plan the number of parameters carefully. For GenAI solution builders, model size is a critical parameter. They have to balance between the accuracy and speed required by their solution and the hosting demands of the model.

Computation requirements of GenAI models

The preceding sections have examined various architectures employed in constructing GenAI models, including RNNs, transformers, and diffusion models. A common characteristic of these architectures is their reliance on neural networks. Neural network operations inherently involve extensive matrix multiplications. For a model with one million parameters, the computations are equivalent to multiplying a series of matrices with a combined total of one million parameters.

Central processing units (**CPUs**) are inefficient at matrix multiplication, necessitating the use of specialized processors known as GPUs. Originally designed to accelerate computer graphics for applications like video games, GPUs have become essential for AI computing due to their efficient matrix processing capabilities. GPUs are utilized in both the training and inferencing stages of GenAI models. The following discussion will focus specifically on inferencing.

To illustrate computational requirements, consider the Llama 3 8B model, which contains eight billion parameters. Each parameter is represented as a **single-precision floating-point number** (**FP32**). The memory required to store the entire model is calculated as follows:

```
bytes_per_parameter = 4
model_size = 8
memory_required =  bytes_per_parameter * model_size

print ('Memory required:', memory_required, 'GB')
```

Output:

```
Memory required =   32 GB
```

Executing this model will need a GPU with a minimum of 32 GB of RAM. Applying the same calculation, the GPU memory requirement for the Llama 3.1 405B model is 1620 GB. Given that the NVIDIA A100 GPU possesses 80 GB of **Video RAM** (**VRAM**), deploying the Llama 3.1 405B model would require 21 A100 GPUs. As GPUs are a costly resource, this example demonstrates the substantial expense associated with hosting large models.

Optimizing computation requirements

Due to the substantial computational costs associated with hosting large models, numerous techniques have been developed to mitigate these resource demands. These techniques generally fall into two categories: optimizing existing large models and constructing lightweight models.

Parameter pruning

Parameter pruning reduces computational requirements by eliminating non-essential parameters from a trained model. SparseGPT is an example of such an algorithm, operating in three stages:

1. Each layer of the model is partitioned into blocks of a defined size.
2. Within each block, the algorithm identifies the parameters that contribute the least to the model's output.
3. These identified parameters are then removed from the layers in a single operation.

Pruning algorithms can achieve up to a 50% reduction in model size without significantly impacting accuracy, resulting in substantial savings in computational resources.

Quantization

Quantization of large models centers on reducing the precision of model parameters. For instance, if the original model parameters are represented with 32-bit precision (requiring 4 bytes of memory each), quantizing them to 8 bits results in a four-fold reduction in model size. However, it is crucial to ensure that this reduction in precision does not negatively impact model accuracy beyond acceptable thresholds. Quantized versions of many popular models, including Llama 3, are available on repositories like Hugging Face, often with varying levels of quantization. The following are examples of quantization levels available for the Llama 3 model on Hugging Face:

Model	Quantization	Model file name
Llama 3 8B	8 bit	Meta-Llama-3-8B.Q8_0.gguf
Llama 3 8B	4 bit	Meta-Llama-3-8B.Q4_0.gguf
Llama 3 70B Instruct	8 bit	Meta-Llama-3-70B-Instruct-v2.Q8_0-00001-of-00003.gguf

Table 2.5: Examples of quantized models available on Hugging Face

The way of optimizing computation requirement is to construct lightweight models. There are two ways to do it, mixture of expert models and small models.

Mixture of experts models

Mixture of experts (MoE) models, while possessing a full complement of parameters, utilize them selectively. These models comprise smaller subsets of parameters, termed **experts**, that are specialized for particular tasks or domains. During inference, a routing mechanism, often called a **gate**, assigns the appropriate expert to the current task. Consequently, only a subset of the total parameters is active during any given execution, thereby reducing the computational demands. The following schematic illustrates the MoE mechanism:

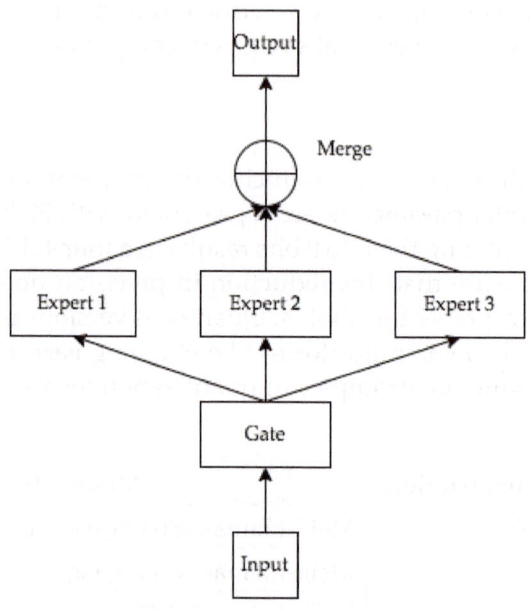

Figure 2.2: Schematic of MoE mechanism

The following are some examples of models utilizing the MoE architecture with details:

Model name	Total parameters (billions)	Number of experts	Active experts	Active parameters (billions)
Mixtral 8x7b	46.7	8	2	11.7
DBRX	132	16	4	36
DeepSeek V3	671	NA	NA	37

Table 2.6: Examples of MoE-based models

Small models

Early applications of generative AI, such as classification and sentiment analysis, utilized smaller models like BERT (110 million parameters) and GPT-1 (117 million parameters). As previously discussed, text generation capabilities demonstrated significant improvements with increasing model size, which spurred the trend toward larger models. This trend was particularly pronounced in language models, which, in turn, motivated research into the development of smaller, more specialized models. The introduction of **small language models** (**SLMs**) like Microsoft's Phi and Google's Gemma in 2023 marked the beginning of a trend toward creating smaller models optimized for a narrower range of tasks.

Importance of training data quality

While the capacity to leverage training data is correlated with the number of parameters in a model, enabling larger models to potentially train on more data, recent research suggests that training data *quality* is a more significant factor than sheer *quantity* in determining model performance. Key aspects of data quality to consider include the following:

- **Data diversity**: The data should encompass a broad range of examples, avoiding over-representation of limited subsets. It should also span diverse topics, linguistic structures, and contexts.
- **Minimal duplication**: Duplicate data negatively impacts model performance. Removing duplicates not only reduces data volume but also improves overall performance.
- **Correctness**: Accurate and coherent data contribute to enhanced model performance. This includes minimizing errors, ambiguities, and poor construction.

This finding suggests that investing in data cleaning, correction, and sanitization can yield benefits in two primary ways:

- Removing duplicate, incorrect, and redundant information from the training dataset reduces its size, making it suitable for models with fewer parameters.
- The improved training data quality leads to enhanced performance of the trained model. Consequently, smaller models can achieve satisfactory performance on their designated tasks.

Domain-specific training

Another approach to reducing the volume of training data while preserving its quality involves focusing the dataset on one or more specific topics, such as a particular discipline within the medical, legal, or technical fields. The resulting model becomes specialized, or expert, in the chosen topic(s). However, its performance in other domains may be suboptimal.

Qwen2.5 model

Qwen2.5 is a good example of a small model. As a large language model, it leverages the traditional transformer architecture with a number of innovations. The 0.5B, 1.5B and 3B parameter variants of Qwen-2.5 is of particular interest in the context of smaller model development.

The training of Qwen-2.5 exemplifies the principles outlined in the previous section. The pre-training data underwent several enhancements, including:

- **Data filtering**: Low-quality data was removed from the training set using the previous Qwen model (Qwen2-Instruct) as a filter.

- **Domain-focused data**: Data from two earlier models, Qwen2.5-Math and Qwen2.5-Coder, was incorporated into the Qwen-2.5 training set, significantly improving its performance on mathematical and coding tasks.
- **Use of synthetic data**: High-quality training samples were generated using previous Qwen models and further refined through filtering algorithms, such as reward models.
- **Improved data mix**: Using the Qwen2-Instruct model, the training data samples were classified, revealing overrepresentation in domains like e-commerce and entertainment, and underrepresentation in science and technology. A careful update process was implemented to create a more balanced dataset.

The Qwen-2.5 models also underwent extensive post-training. **Supervised fine-tuning (SFT)** and **reinforcement learning (RL)** techniques were employed to enhance specific capabilities, including mathematical and logical reasoning, coding proficiency, cross-lingual functionality, and long sequence generation. Consequently, the Qwen models achieve comparable performance to significantly larger models on several standard benchmarks. A comparison of these smaller models with their larger counterparts is of particular interest. The following table presents a comparison of scores on some key benchmarks:

Benchmark	Qwen2.5 0.5B	Qwen2.5 1.5B	Qwen2.5 3B	Qwen2.5 7B	Qwen2.5 72B
MMLU (General tasks)	47.5	60.9	65.6	74.2	86.1
GPQA (Maths and science)	24.8	24.2	26.3	36.4	45.9
HumanEval (Coding)	30.5	37.2	42.1	57.9	59.1
Multi-exam (Multi-lingual)	30.8	47.9	54.6	59.4	78.7

Table 2.7: Comparison of Qwen model variants on common benchmarks

As the data indicates, the performance of the smaller models is generally lower, but the difference is not drastic. Specifically, the 3B variant offers a viable alternative, often without significant compromises in performance compared to its larger counterparts.

Qwen-2.5 models are available open-source, enabling user deployment on local infrastructure. Their smaller size facilitates deployment on edge devices, such as mobile phones. These smaller Qwen models find application in several areas, including:

- **Mobile applications**: The smaller variants are suitable for deployment on mobile devices, making them well-suited for edge computing applications.
- **Coding assistance**: Due to their specialized training, Qwen models demonstrate expertise in coding tasks, making them valuable assistants for programmers.
- **Customer service**: The scalability requirements of customer service applications align well with the low resource demands of Qwen models.

- **Education**: Qwen models can be deployed locally within educational institutions to support teachers and students in answering questions and preparing materials.

In summary, the Qwen-2.5 model's smaller variants underscore the significance of training data quality for achieving effective performance in smaller-scale models. The reduced resource requirements of these models enable deployment on readily available computing resources, including edge devices such as mobile phones, thus facilitating a wide range of practical applications.

Model architectures

This chapter has introduced several GenAI model architectures employed for diverse applications. The following table provides a concise summary of the architectures discussed:

Architecture	Purpose	Example model
Decoder Transformer	Text generation	Llama 3
Vision Transformer	Image-to-text	TrOCR
Diffusion-Denoiser	Image generation	Stable Diffusion
Audio Spectrogram Transformer	Speech-to-text Text-to-text	Whisper SpeechT5

Table 2.8: Summary of model architectures

It is important to note that the preceding list is not exhaustive. Researchers and developers are continually exploring novel architectures and combinations of existing architectures to create models with enhanced performance and efficiency. The following subsections will examine additional architectures, including some that are currently in the experimental phase.

Autoencoders

Autoencoders belong to the broader category of self-supervised learning networks, a group that also includes the diffusion networks discussed earlier in this chapter. These networks learn by attempting to reconstruct their input. Autoencoders are commonly used for image generation.

Autoencoders consist of two components: an encoder and a decoder. During training, the encoder transforms an input image into a lower-dimensional vector representation. Subsequently, the decoder attempts to reconstruct the original image from this compressed vector. The reconstructed image is then compared to the original, and the difference is used to calculate a loss value. The parameters of both the encoder and decoder are adjusted based on this calculated loss.

Both the encoder and decoder components of autoencoders can be utilized during inference. The encoder, having learned effective image representations, can be employed for image classification tasks. The decoder, conversely, can be used for reconstructing noisy images. They do not have the capability to generate new images.

A variant of the autoencoder, known as the **variational autoencoder** (**VAE**), is frequently employed for image generation tasks. VAEs incorporate probabilistic elements into the encoding and decoding procedures. Specifically, the VAE encoder generates two values for each dimension of the compressed vector representation:

- μ: the mean of a normal distribution
- σ: the standard deviation of the distribution

In other words, the encoder represents each dimension of the compressed vector as a probability distribution rather than a single value. VAEs incorporate an additional component, the **Latent Space Sampler**, which generates a vector by sampling from these distributions. This sampled vector, called the **latent vector**, is then used by the decoder to reconstruct the original image. The training process for VAEs remains analogous to that of traditional autoencoders. The process is illustrated in the following figure:

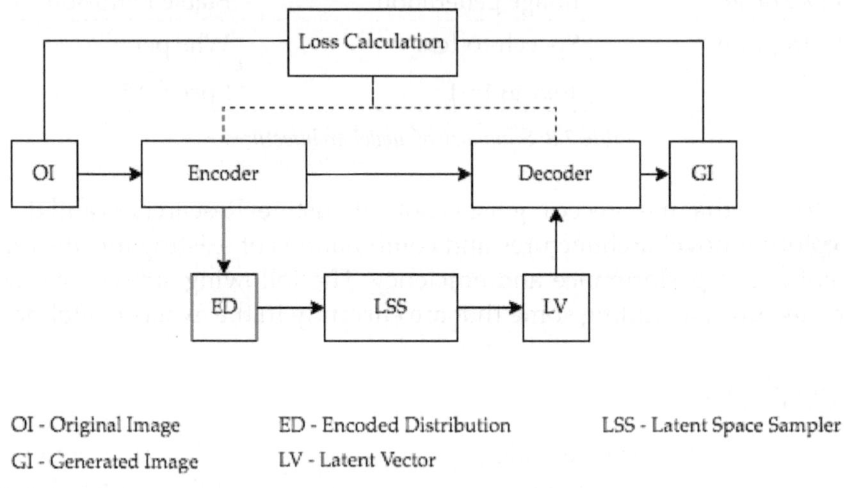

Figure 2.3: *Training of the VAE*

The probabilistic nature of the encoded parameters enables VAEs to generate novel images not present in the training set. For image generation, a latent vector is sampled from the prior distribution. Due to the probabilistic encoding, the latent vector will differ from any vector generated during training. Consequently, the image reconstructed by the decoder using this novel vector will also be a novel creation.

The **conditional variational autoencoder** (**CVAE**) is another variant employed for generating images based on textual prompts. A text encoder, such as the encoder component of a transformer model, generates a context vector from the input text prompt. This context vector guides the latent vector sampling process during both training and generation. During training, prompt-image pairs are used, where the prompt describes the corresponding image, enabling the network to learn the relationship between text and visual content. In the generation phase, the provided prompt is used to generate a latent vector. Through the learned associations, the decoder then produces an image that aligns with the description provided in the prompt.

The initial version of DALL-E, released by OpenAI in 2021, was based on a CVAE architecture. While subsequent versions transitioned to diffusion-based methods, they retained the VAE as a component of the encoder. Although diffusion models have largely become dominant in the image generation field, VAEs continue to be incorporated as architectural elements in many models.

Generative adversarial networks

Generative adversarial networks (**GANs**) predate the transformer architecture, having been first proposed in 2014. While initial GAN implementations utilized simpler neural networks and CNNs, subsequent architectures have incorporated transformers. GANs gained popularity for image generation, particularly following the development of Conditional GANs in 2016, which enabled image generation based on textual descriptions. However, after 2020, competing architectures, such as diffusion models and text-to-image transformers, began to supplant GANs as the preferred models for image generation. Currently, GANs remain relevant for specific applications, including real-time applications and facial reconstruction, where they sometimes offer advantages over diffusion models.

Like autoencoders, GANs also belong to the class of self-supervised learning networks, learning by attempting to reproduce the training data. However, GANs achieve this through an adversarial process. A GAN model comprises two components: a generator and a discriminator.

The discriminator is trained independently to classify images as either real or fake. The generator, on the other hand, is trained in conjunction with the discriminator. Its objective is to generate images that can deceive the discriminator. Thus, if the discriminator classifies a generated image as fake, this misclassification contributes to the generator's loss.

Through numerous iterations, the generator progressively improves its ability to produce realistic images. Once trained, the generator can be used independently for image generation. When coupled with a text encoder, such as an LSTM or transformer encoder, the generator can produce images that correspond to a given textual description.

A notable case study within the GAN architecture is the StyleGAN model family, introduced by NVIDIA in 2018. These models utilize a CNN-based architecture and achieved significant popularity in the early 2020s for image and video generation. NVIDIA's release of the complete source code and datasets facilitated extensive experimentation and adaptation of these models for a broad range of applications. While largely superseded by diffusion models for general image generation tasks, StyleGANs continue to be employed for specialized applications.

While VAEs and GANs are not currently the dominant architectures for generative tasks, it is important to remember that previously less-favored architectures can regain prominence through modifications that enhance their capabilities beyond current state-of-the-art models. Therefore, understanding VAEs and GANs remains valuable for comprehending the evolving landscape of generative AI architectures.

This concludes the discussion of various model categories. The following section will provide practical experience using image generation models through code examples.

Learning image generation with code

Earlier in this chapter, we explored how models like diffusion models, VAEs, and GANs can generate images from text prompts. These image synthesis capabilities of GenAI models are now widely applied across various domains, including content creation, video game development, and industrial design. This section will demonstrate how to generate images using GenAI models through code.

Image generation capabilities

Image generation mostly follows the process of creating an image that matches the description provided. This method is also called text-to-image generation. Two types of text-to-image capabilities are most commonly used:

- **New image creation**: The provided prompt describes a desired image, and the model generates the image from scratch.
- **Image editing**: The prompt specifies modifications to an existing input image. The model then generates an updated image reflecting these changes. In some cases, two input images may be used, with one serving as the background in the generated output.

Models used for image generation

Modern image generation models often integrate various architectures, such as diffusion models, transformers, and VAEs, to achieve optimal performance. Developers can select from two primary types of models:

- **Open-source models**: These models can be downloaded and deployed within the developer's own environment. The specific model variant must be chosen based on available computing resources. Stable Diffusion is a representative example of this category.
- **Closed-source models**: These models are not available for download. Instead, providers offer an API that developers can utilize. This approach allows access to significantly larger models without the need to manage the associated computational requirements. OpenAI's DALL-E 3 model is a prominent example.

This discussion will use the Dall-E 3 API for demonstrating text-to-image generation.

New image generation with DALL-E 3

An HR manager is planning an event to honor the best employees in the team. They take help from the IT team to build a small python program that can generate images for creating the posters for the event. The posters should be personalized, with a different design for every employee being honored. The following code will run in a Google Colab Notebook:

```
import openai
import requests
from PIL import Image
from IPython.display import display
from io import BytesIO

# Set your OpenAI API key
openai.api_key = "YOUR_API_KEY"

#This prompt will generate a personalized employee poster
prompt = "Create a vibrant, celebratory, modern corporate poster designed to
honor the employee of the month. The image should feature dynamic abstract
shapes, a bright and energetic color palette, and visual symbols of success
and achievement—such as abstract trophies, rays of light, or upward curves—
evoking a sense of celebration and recognition in a sleek, professional style.
The design should be entirely visual with no text present."

# Call the OpenAI API to generate the image
response = openai.images.generate(
    model='dall-e-3',
    prompt=prompt,
    n=1,
    size="1024x1024"
)

# Extract the image URL from the API response
image_url = response.data[0].url
print("Generated Image URL:", image_url)

# Open the image using PIL and display it
```

```
response = requests.get(image_url)

# Open the image with PIL using a BytesIO stream
img = Image.open(BytesIO(response.content))

display(img)
```

Output:

```
Generated Image URL: https://oaidalleapiprodscus.blob.core.windows.net/private/… (truncated)
```

Refer to the following figure:

Figure 2.4: Image generated by DALL-E 3

The code uses the OpenAI library used in the code example in *Chapter 1, Introduction to Transformer Models*. To handle images, it uses the PIL library along with the io library. You can see that the prompting of the models is almost identical to the text prompting, with a few of the following additional parameters:

- **n**: this parameter indicates the number of images that should be generated. While DALL-E 3 allows the generation of only one image at a time, the earlier DALL-E 2 allowed up to 10 images. The developer should check the documentation at the time of coding for any changes.
- **size**: The *size* parameter specifies the resolution of the images to be created.

The **`images.generate`** function returns a URL that points to the OpenAI server. The image is shown using three functions:

- The **`io.BytesIO`** class converts the URL into a bytes stream.
- The **`PIL.Image`** class is constructed from this bytes stream.

- The **IPython.display.show** method is used to display the image in the Colab Notebook.

The HR manager can generate different images by running this code multiple times. They can also change the prompt to create more personalization.

Conclusion

This chapter has aimed to bridge the gap between the fundamentals of GenAI models and their practical business applications. It introduced various model categories, classified by source availability, modality, size, and architecture. Within each category, common architectures and applications of subcategories were explored.

The discussion of the comparative advantages and disadvantages of different model types will benefit developers of GenAI applications. The chapter provides guidance on choosing between open-source and closed-source models or selecting a smaller model over a larger one based on specific project needs. Furthermore, it informs developers about the diverse capabilities of GenAI, such as image and audio generation, that can be integrated into their applications.

While this chapter has covered a range of model architectures, it is important to acknowledge that GenAI model architecture is an active area of research. Readers should anticipate the emergence of new architectures even as this book is being read. However, the fundamental principles discussed herein should provide a solid foundation for readily understanding these future developments.

The preceding chapters have provided a comprehensive overview of the technological foundations of GenAI models. The next chapter will transition from theory to practice, initiating the exploration of industrial applications. It will focus on the preliminary considerations for GenAI adoption, establishing a foundational framework for the examination of real-world projects that will follow.

CHAPTER 3
GenAI in Industry

Introduction

The integration of AI into industrial processes is not a recent development, as enterprises have utilized AI techniques for over half a century. However, the pace of AI adoption has accelerated with the emergence of **generative artificial intelligence** (**GenAI**). Estimates indicate that between 55% and 70% of the *Fortune 500* companies are currently implementing or planning to implement GenAI in the near future. This represents a remarkably high adoption rate for a technology that has only been available for a few years.

This chapter will examine the high-level aspects of GenAI implementation within industrial settings, focusing on the motivations driving companies to adopt AI and the anticipated benefits. This discussion is essential as developers become involved after a project has been approved and sponsored, thus rendering high-level strategic considerations outside their immediate purview. Nevertheless, it is crucial for GenAI developers to possess a comprehensive understanding of the rationale behind their work to enhance effectiveness. They should understand the motivations driving their company's GenAI implementation, anticipated benefits, and the process by which GenAI use cases are identified and prioritized.

It is important to examine GenAI's applications within industrial tasks and processes, which involve complex tasks such as decision-making, design, and troubleshooting. Therefore, understanding how GenAI models can facilitate and streamline these tasks is essential. When groundbreaking technologies emerge, industries undergo a series of transformations that progress through stages of initial interest, rapid expansion, and disruptive change. For companies, it is crucial to capitalize on the growth phase and mitigate the risks associated with disruptive change. Generally, enterprises integrate new technologies in three phases: basic applications, specialized tasks, and development of competitive differentiators.

The success of GenAI implementations is influenced by the selection of appropriate use cases. Decision-makers must consider a range of parameters when evaluating potential GenAI applications. The chapter will present illustrative use cases from various organizational functions. To ensure broad applicability, the discussion will focus on common areas such as human resources and customer service.

Structure

This chapter covers the following topics:

- Capabilities of GenAI models
- Impact on industries
- Example use cases
- Introduction to projects

Objectives

By the end of this chapter, you will get an understanding of the applications of GenAI models in the industry. You will learn the various capabilities of GenAI models that contribute to practical applications. You will get an insight into the phased proliferation of GenAI technology in the industry and a solid understanding of the common use cases of GenAI in organizations.

Capabilities of GenAI models

The preceding chapters of this book have primarily examined GenAI models from a technical standpoint. While model capabilities were discussed, the focus was largely on illustrating their underlying mechanisms. This section shifts the perspective to explore these capabilities specifically in the context of addressing real-world industrial challenges.

From an industrial problem-solving perspective, the capabilities of GenAI models can be broadly categorized into two distinct areas:

- Task capabilities
- Skills

Task capabilities are useful in building solutions, while skills are instrumental in putting the task capabilities to work.

This section begins by examining task-specific capabilities. These capabilities stem from the sequence-to-sequence nature of GenAI models, as detailed in *Chapter 1, Introduction to Transformer Models*. Variations in the input and output sequence formats lead to diverse task functionalities. The first task capability explored is **description**.

Description

As the name implies, description tasks involve generating an output that provides a descriptive representation of the input. While the output is typically textual, description tasks are particularly valuable when the input is non-textual, such as images or audio. However, there are also notable applications of text-to-text description. Examples of description tasks include information extraction, image description, audio transcription, comprehension, and classification.

Information extraction

Information extraction is a highly valuable text-to-text task. It involves identifying and extracting specific data points from a given text or document. In some cases, pre-defined data points are targeted, while in others, all available relevant information is extracted. Examples of information extraction include the following:

- Extracting entities such as people, dates, and locations from news articles.
- Extracting contractual details such as parties, monetary amounts, and terms from legal contracts.
- Extracting pertinent data from financial statements.

Structured output: A critical aspect of information extraction involves presenting the extracted data in a structured format. Many models are capable of generating output using notations such as JSON or XML. This structured representation facilitates efficient utilization of the extracted information for subsequent processing steps.

Producing structured data can serve a very useful function. It can actually create data set for training other machine learning models for prediction, classification and other tasks. Thus, GenAI models can contribute to the implementation of other types of AI as well.

Image description

Image description involves transforming a given image into a corresponding textual representation, which can be highly beneficial in various contexts. Short descriptions can be used for image captioning, while longer, more detailed descriptions can serve as input for further analytical processes. Examples of image description applications include the following:

- Object counting within an image.
- Verification of image content against specific criteria, such as confirming worker compliance with safety regulations (e.g., helmet usage).
- The generated textual description can be used as input for subsequent classification tasks.

Audio transcription

Audio transcription, analogous to image description, involves converting audio input into a textual representation. However, audio transcription typically demands higher fidelity, as it often entails converting spoken language into written text. Additional complexities arise due to factors such as multiple speakers, multilingual content, and background noise. The following are examples of audio transcription applications:

- Generating meeting notes.
- Creating call transcripts.
- Producing automatic subtitles.

Comprehension

Comprehension tasks involve GenAI models answering questions based on provided textual input. This capability underpins **retrieval-augmented generation** (**RAG**) solutions, which have gained significant traction in industry.

> Note: **While comprehension involves question answering, it differs from the question-answering (QA) ability associated with translation tasks.**

Examples of comprehension applications include the following:

- Chat with your document applications.
- Natural language querying of spreadsheet data.

Classification

Classification, a text-to-text task, involves assigning a given text to one of a set of predefined categories. The output is typically a single word or phrase representing the assigned class. Examples of classification tasks are as follows:

- **Sentiment analysis**: Determining the emotional tone of a text (e.g., positive, negative, neutral).
- **Topic detection**: Identifying the subject matter of a text (e.g., sports, politics, technology).
- **Image classification**: Categorizing an image based on its textual description.

Translation

Translation tasks involve transforming the input to produce an output that is adapted for a specific purpose. Typically, the input and output modalities remain consistent. Translation capabilities facilitate the adaptation of source material to better suit a given context. Key translation abilities include language translation, image editing, voice dubbing, and summarization.

Language translation

Language translation, a core capability of AI systems since their inception, has achieved a high level of sophistication with the advent of GenAI models. This text-to-text task involves converting textual content from one language to another. Examples of language translation applications include the following:

- Translating import or export documentation for multinational corporations.
- Providing real-time audio translation during international events.
- Translating court documents to enhance citizen access to justice in multilingual countries.

Image editing

Image editing, a form of image-to-image translation, utilizes models to modify images based on textual prompts. Examples of image editing capabilities are as follows:

- Background removal.
- Applying visual filters to images.
- Modifying or altering the stylistic presentation of an image, such as transitioning from a classical to a modern aesthetic.

Note: **The ability to specify the changes through a prompt is due to the instruction following capability of the GenAI models, which will be discussed later.**

Voice dubbing

Voice dubbing, while related to audio translation, presents distinct challenges. Dubbing typically involves replacing the audio track of a video, such as a film or advertisement. Maintaining temporal alignment between the audio and the video's visual content is crucial, as the audio must synchronize with the on-screen action. Furthermore, the dubbed audio should strive to preserve the emotional nuances and expressive qualities of the original audio. Examples of voice dubbing applications are as follows:

- Dubbing films and advertisements for international audiences.
- Localizing video games for different linguistic markets.
- Dubbing training videos for multinational enterprises with geographically dispersed teams.

Summarization

Summarization, a widely utilized text-to-text task, condenses content for improved readability. This capability is also applicable to audio and video content. The following are some examples of summarization applications:

- Summarizing financial reports.
- Generating summaries of court judgments.
- Producing concise summaries of project documentation.

Generation

GenAI models possess the ability to generate novel content, a capability known as the generation task. This generation process is typically guided by textual prompts, leveraging the models' instruction-following capabilities. These models can produce a variety of content types, including text, images, audio, and video. Some examples of generation capabilities include question answering, content generation, idea generation, and code generation.

Question and answer

Question-answering (**QA**) involves GenAI models generating textual responses to provided questions. This is arguably the most recognized capability of these models. The models generate answers based on the knowledge acquired during their training. Consequently, models are sometimes specifically trained to answer questions within particular domains.

Note: **The QA capability functions without requiring external reference material. When relevant context is provided to the model alongside the question, it becomes a comprehension task, as discussed previously.**

Content generation

Content generation, alongside QA, is a widely recognized and utilized GenAI task. Elaborate prompts can be employed to guide the generation process, ensuring the relevance and appropriateness of the output. Examples of content generation applications include the following:

- Generating essays, stories, and poems.
- Creating suitable images for digital posts and articles.
- Generating audio training materials.
- Composing instrumental and vocal music.
- Creating video content.

Idea generation

A frequently overlooked capability of GenAI models is their capacity to generate novel ideas, thereby assisting individuals and teams in their endeavors. These models can often propose concepts that are not readily apparent, including those drawn from diverse and seemingly unrelated domains. These ideas can be leveraged for various purposes as follows:

- Developing brand names.
- Generating product designs.
- Planning projects and travel itineraries.

- Facilitating problem-solving.
- Generating creative writing ideas.

Code generation

Code generation is a significant and extensive activity within the information technology industry. GenAI models, trained on vast repositories of existing code, are capable of generating code in response to developer-provided problem descriptions. Applications of this capability include the following:

- Writing functions in programming languages such as Python and Java.
- Creating test cases for software applications.
- Building website structures and components.
- Generating SQL queries for database interactions.

This concludes the examination of the task capabilities of GenAI models. The following discussion will focus on the skills that contribute to these task capabilities. Two crucial skills are **instruction following** and **reasoning**.

Instruction following

While GenAI models can generate content, the output may not always align with the intended purpose. For instance, a generated essay might be excessively lengthy or employ language that is too difficult for the target audience. Therefore, it is essential to guide the model towards producing suitable content.

To achieve this, GenAI models undergo specialized training known as **supervised fine-tuning (SFT)**, as discussed in *Chapter 1, Introduction to Transformer Models*. This training equips the models with the ability to interpret and execute user instructions, thereby enabling them to modify generated content appropriately. This ability to adhere to user directives is termed **instruction following**. This skill is always applied in combination with some task capability, such as description or generation, to create suitable content.

The following table describes some of the commonly used instructions with examples:

Instruction	Example
Length	`Generate a 300-word essay` `Create a summary in 2-3 lines`
Level	`Explain to a five-year-old child` `Write a report for a senior finance executive`
Style	`Create the image in the impressionist style`

Instruction	Example
Dos and don'ts	`Avoid using names of people and companies`
Structure	`List the items as a table with the following columns…`

Table 3.1: *Model instructions with examples*

Reasoning

GenAI models perform all tasks through the prediction of subsequent tokens. From this perspective, they do not inherently *understand* the input or output they process. Nevertheless, these models exhibit certain capabilities that closely resemble cognitive processes such as thinking and understanding. These collective abilities are termed **reasoning**. While reasoning abilities are primarily associated with language models, it is important to note that multimodal models also incorporate text-processing components, extending the applicability of reasoning in most of the GenAI models. Reasoning enables models to analyze information in a structured manner and derive inferences. Various types of reasoning abilities exist, and the most significant are common-sense reasoning, mathematical reasoning, and logical reasoning.

Common-sense reasoning

GenAI models acquire a substantial understanding of everyday life, including situational awareness, interpersonal relationships, and social conventions. This knowledge is derived from the vast datasets on which these models are trained. They effectively learn and internalize these principles from the patterns present in the data. GenAI models can then apply common sense reasoning during various tasks, such as content generation.

Mathematical reasoning

GenAI models exhibit the capability to perform basic mathematical operations, including addition, subtraction, and squaring, as well as more complex calculations through the combination of these operations. The precise mechanisms by which these mathematical abilities emerge are not fully understood, and instances of simple errors in mathematical reasoning have been observed. Nevertheless, this capability proves valuable in specific application domains.

Logical reasoning

Logical reasoning entails the application of formal logical rules to input data to derive conclusions. These logical operations encompass processes such as induction, deduction, and syllogism. Logical reasoning abilities are essential for controlling operational flow, similar to that of software programs.

Enhancing reasoning abilities

The reasoning capabilities of GenAI models are subject to several limitations. However, these limitations can be mitigated, and the reasoning abilities themselves can be enhanced through the application of specific techniques, such as **chain-of-thought** (**CoT**) prompting. The synergistic combination of reasoning abilities with instruction following and task-specific capabilities yields particularly powerful results.

The following table summarizes the GenAI model capabilities:

Capability	Type	Abilities
Description	Task	Information extraction Image description Comprehension Transcription Classification
Translation	Task	Language translation Image editing Summarization Voice dubbing
Generation	Task	Question answering Content generation Idea generation Code generation
Instruction following	Skill	Length Style Level Structure
Reasoning	Skill	Common-sense Mathematical Logical

Table 3.2: Summary of GenAI model capabilities

Activities in enterprises

Enterprises engage in a diverse range of operational activities, including manufacturing, service delivery, personnel management, customer support, and regulatory compliance. These industrial activities are inherently complex, often involving multiple individuals and teams over extended periods.

Most enterprise activities can be further separated into a set of fundamental components. These include the following:

- **Decision-making**: Selecting from a range of available options.
- **Data collection**: Extracting relevant information from various sources.
- **Execution**: Implementing a sequence of instructions to achieve a specific outcome.
- **Troubleshooting**: Identifying and resolving problems encountered during execution.
- **Design**: Planning new projects, products, or operational processes.
- **Innovation**: Developing novel and valuable solutions.

Typical daily operations within an enterprise consist of combinations of these fundamental activities. For instance, the process of hiring a new employee involves data collection, decision-making, and execution.

Fundamental activities provide a framework for understanding the integration and utility of GenAI models within industrial operations. This relationship will be explored in the subsequent section.

Using model capabilities

GenAI models provide value by facilitating and streamlining fundamental industrial activities. Consequently, a direct correlation exists between these activities and the capabilities of GenAI models. Examples illustrating this connection include the following:

- **Information extraction**: This capability can aggregate data points from diverse sources, such as documents, databases, and web pages. These extracted data points can then be summarized to simplify decision-making processes.
- **Content generation**: This can be employed to create materials containing product information, competitive analyses, frequently asked questions, and other relevant content. This material can be utilized by sales personnel to effectively convince potential clients.
- **Comprehension and reasoning**: These capabilities can be combined to identify historical records that are analogous to a current problem, thereby significantly aiding in troubleshooting.

Numerous additional examples can be provided to demonstrate the link between model capabilities and fundamental activities. Given that most industrial operations are composed of these fundamental activities, GenAI models offer substantial potential for operational improvement.

The following figure represents this connection between model capabilities and fundamental activities:

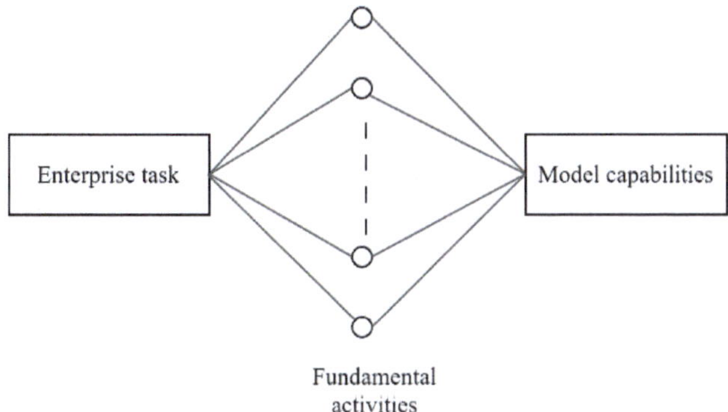

***Figure 3.1**: Connection between model capabilities and industrial activities*

Impact on industries

All transformative technologies exert a profound influence on industry, leading to a lifecycle of adaptation within enterprises. This lifecycle typically manifests in three distinct phases:

- **Curiosity**: During the nascent stages of a technology, there is significant industry-wide enthusiasm. Companies initiate experimentation and share their findings. Applications identified in this phase tend to be innovative and ambitious, aimed at large-scale transformations. However, the realized benefits are often limited due to the immaturity of both the technology and its users.
- **Establishment**: Following the initial wave of experimentation, industries begin to integrate the technology into practical operations. Expectations become more realistic and refined. The technology is employed to optimize various operational processes, resulting in productivity gains, improved profitability, enhanced customer satisfaction, and overall growth. This phase can also lead to employment shifts, which may become a concern. Established companies that adopt the technology early tend to be the primary beneficiaries of this phase.
- **Disruption**: As the technology becomes increasingly prevalent, new market entrants discover innovative applications. This leads to the development of novel products and services, fostering industry expansion and creating new opportunities. Conversely, established incumbents may become less competitive due to the emergence of new operational paradigms. These new entrants eventually become established, and the cycle repeats with the arrival of subsequent technological advancements.

It is important to note that the progression through these technology adoption phases is not uniform across all sectors of industry. Different segments, such as companies within specific regions, may exist in varying stages of adoption. For example, while some segments remain in the curiosity phase, others may have transitioned into the establishment phase. The evolution of information technology and the internet serves as a pertinent illustration of this phenomenon. While industries like finance rapidly leveraged information technology for establishment and subsequent disruption, others, such as agriculture and education, experienced a more gradual adoption curve.

These principles of technological adoption are equally applicable to the integration of GenAI. Currently, most industries are in the curiosity phase, actively exploring potential applications and seeking to transition into the establishment phase. The following section will examine the diverse ways in which companies are leveraging GenAI in this phase.

Establishment phase

The establishment phase can be characterized as a period of *operational optimization*. In this phase, companies deploy technologies like GenAI to enhance the efficiency of their existing operations. This typically involves a detailed analysis of current processes and the strategic application of technological capabilities to specific process components. This phase can be further divided into two distinct sub-phases as follows:

- **Directly applicable capabilities**: As previously discussed, business activities can be decomposed into fundamental components. Some of these components directly correspond to the capabilities of GenAI models. For instance, composing email correspondence directly aligns with the rephrasing capabilities of **large language models (LLMs)**. These directly applicable capabilities are typically the first to be implemented during the establishment phase.
- **Compound and specific capabilities**: Activities such as decision-making and planning are inherently complex and do not directly correspond to a single model capability. When targeting these complex activities for improvement, specialized applications are developed. These applications combine multiple model capabilities in a tailored manner. Such applications are generally implemented after users have become familiar with the directly applicable capabilities.

Disruption phase

During the disruption phase, the technology is leveraged to develop entirely new products and services, driven by significant innovation. This phase, unlike the establishment phase, is less structured and more characterized by a series of iterative successes and failures. GenAI is already disrupting sectors such as content creation and media and is anticipated to induce substantial transformations across numerous industries.

In essence, the impact of GenAI on organizations is contingent upon their current stage of adoption. During the establishment phase, organizations typically realize gains in operational efficiency. Conversely, the disruption phase may propel them into entirely new market positions and strategic trajectories. The nature of GenAI use cases also evolves with the adoption phase, progressing from simple, directly applicable implementations to increasingly complex, integrated applications.

Example use cases

While the specific implementation of GenAI varies across organizations, discernible patterns can be identified. The preceding sections have established two key principles:

- GenAI utilization is influenced by the company's adoption phase, with the establishment phase emphasizing operational optimization.
- Business operations can be categorized into fundamental activities, which can then be enhanced through the application of specific GenAI model capabilities.

These principles provide a unifying framework for understanding GenAI use cases across diverse organizational contexts.

This section will explore a range of GenAI use cases designed to enhance business operations within organizations. These use cases are categorized as follows:

- **Use cases in common functions**: Despite industry variations, certain fundamental functions, such as finance, human resources, and legal, are universally present across organizations. Use cases pertaining to these common functions will be examined first.
- **Use cases in specific functions**: Each organization also possesses specialized functions tailored to its unique business activities. For example, a financial institution may have a lending department, while a manufacturing firm will have a production function. Use cases related to these specialized functions, which are inherently industry-specific, will be discussed subsequently.

Use cases in common functions

Common functions typically provide support to the core business operations. While the processes within these functions are generally well-established, they can exhibit variations depending on the company's industry and specific organizational structure. For instance, marketing, a common function, will have distinct processes in a consumer goods company compared to a company specializing in large-scale projects.

Use cases for marketing

Marketing plays a critical role in driving revenue and fostering growth within organizations. The following discussion will examine key processes within the marketing function and explore how GenAI can be leveraged to enhance its effectiveness:

- **Market study and competitor analysis**: These are essential components of the marketing function, enabling organizations to monitor market dynamics and competitor activities. The insights gained from these analyses inform branding, content creation, and product planning processes.

  GenAI can be employed to analyze information published across various websites and online forums pertaining to specific markets. It can also process and analyze industry reports. The comprehension and summarization capabilities of GenAI models can be utilized to generate concise, insightful reports on market trends and competitive landscapes.

- **Branding**: Branding encompasses a range of processes, including messaging, communication, traditional and digital advertising, and campaign management. These processes are designed to ensure that the company's image and market positioning are accurately conveyed to its target audience.

  The idea generation capabilities of GenAI models can be used to suggest brand names, taglines, and other creative assets. Image generation can also be employed to produce multiple visual options for marketing content. In essence, the content generation capabilities of GenAI are instrumental in optimizing and enhancing branding processes.

- **Lead generation**: It is a core responsibility of the marketing team, focused on identifying potential customers for the sales team to engage. This process involves both inbound and outbound strategies. Inbound lead generation centers on creating valuable content that attracts the target audience and facilitates their discovery of the company's offerings. Outbound lead generation involves direct communication with potential prospects through channels such as email, social media, and telephone calls.

  GenAI can aggregate lead-related information from diverse sources, including websites and databases. It can efficiently generate relevant content designed to attract the target audience. Furthermore, GenAI facilitates the personalization of communication with potential leads, which improves response rates. GenAI enabled automated calling has also been shown to be an effective lead generation tool.

Use cases for sales

While marketing establishes the brand identity and market positioning of a company's offerings, the sales function bears the direct responsibility for customer acquisition and order closure. Key sales processes are outlined as follows:

- **Sales outreach and communication**: The sales team engages with prospective customers through various channels, including meetings, emails, calls, and messaging. These interactions include providing information about the company and its products and services, delivering demonstrations, and presenting proposals. Consistent follow-ups and maintaining regular contact are essential for successful sales conversions.

GenAI can significantly enhance the sales enablement process by providing sales teams with pertinent information. The comprehension and summarization capabilities of GenAI can generate relevant sales materials, facilitating effective communication. Furthermore, its rephrasing ability can be employed to personalize emails and messages, thereby improving engagement with prospective customers.

- **Objection handling and negotiations**: The sales team has to handle concerns about pricing, quality and so on. The clients also need information about what infrastructure and resources will be needed to use the company's product, and about the comparison with other providers. Sales teams must provide the right answers to the queries in a timely manner.

  For larger projects, the sales process also involves negotiating the pricing and terms. For projects such as engineering and construction, complex contracts have to be negotiated before the sale is closed.

  GenAI can efficiently address customer queries by analyzing past records, product catalogs, and data sheets. It can also integrate market and competitor analysis data collected by the marketing team. Real-time assistance is achievable through live call transcription. The transcribed call data can be utilized to analyze concerns and sentiments expressed during meetings, enabling GenAI to provide actionable insights. Furthermore, GenAI can analyze contract terms under discussion and suggest modifications, drawing upon the analysis of past projects and contracts.

- **Upselling and cross-selling**: These are critical strategies for maximizing revenue from existing customer relationships. Acquiring new customers is a resource-intensive process, making it advantageous to increase business from current clients by offering higher-tier versions of existing products (upselling) or related products and services (cross-selling). This strategy necessitates strong customer relationships, a thorough understanding of customer needs, and knowledge of complementary offerings.

  GenAI can leverage historical data to provide recommendations on which products or services to offer to specific existing customers, utilizing its reasoning capabilities. If more specialized recommendation models are required, GenAI can generate datasets for training these models. Additionally, GenAI can create content, such as newsletters and informative messages, to nurture and maintain customer relationships.

Use cases for human resources

The **human resources** (**HR**) function is responsible for critical processes related to personnel, including recruitment, employee management, and training. As human capital represents an organization's most valuable asset, the significance of the HR function is paramount. The efficacy of HR processes directly impacts the performance of all other organizational functions. The following list explores key HR processes and the potential applications of GenAI:

- **Talent acquisition**: Identifying and hiring suitable candidates is vital for the success of all organizational functions. This process encompasses defining requirements, crafting job descriptions, screening and matching resumes, conducting interviews, and selecting qualified individuals.

  GenAI can enhance every stage of the talent acquisition process. It can generate job descriptions based on discussions with relevant business functions. The description and reasoning capabilities of GenAI are utilized to match available resumes with job requirements, facilitating candidate shortlisting. Furthermore, multimodal generation capabilities can be employed to conduct automated preliminary interviews.

- **Employee management**: Encompasses a range of critical processes, including payroll and regulatory compliance, performance evaluation, salary adjustments, and internal transfers. It also involves initiatives aimed at enhancing employee morale, reducing attrition, and fostering a positive work environment. Addressing ethical considerations, such as diversity and inclusion, and preventing workplace harassment are also within the purview of HR processes.

  While processes such as leave management and payroll are often automated through software, GenAI can provide valuable insights by analyzing comprehensive employee data. Its description capabilities can generate summaries to facilitate performance management. GenAI can contribute to boosting employee morale by creating personalized appreciation messages and suggesting ideas for events and initiatives tailored to the current organizational context. Chatbots can provide employees with easy access to information and streamline the reporting of issues.

- **Employee training**: The training processes, often managed by a dedicated **learning and development** (**L&D**) department, encompass the dissemination of knowledge regarding the company's operations, products and services, customer base, values, and policies. Specialized training modules are designed to address the specific needs of various functional areas, such as manufacturing or logistics. Training programs are typically structured into initial onboarding and ongoing professional development phases. These programs ensure consistent resource quality, particularly during periods of rapid growth or employee attrition.

  GenAI can facilitate the development of effective training modules by synthesizing information from diverse sources. Training materials can be presented in easily digestible formats, such as concise text segments or short audio clips. For companies with a multilingual workforce, GenAI can seamlessly translate training materials into multiple languages. Furthermore, GenAI can generate quizzes and assessment tools to evaluate trainee comprehension and ensure effective knowledge transfer.

Use cases in specific functions

Industry-specific functions typically represent the core operational activities of a business. The processes within these functions are often the culmination of years of domain-specific expertise and experience. Consequently, even within the same functional area, significant process variations can exist between companies. For example, the methodologies employed for managing software development projects can differ substantially between two software development firms.

While GenAI applications for common functions are frequently productized and widely available, those for specific functions are often highly customized. These customizations reflect the unique process details that have evolved within each company. This section will explore selected industry-specific functions and their associated GenAI use cases, focusing on generally known information.

Use cases in financial lending

Financial services companies engage in the lending of capital to both individuals and businesses. This encompasses a range of loan products, including home loans, personal loans, vehicle loans, business loans, and overdraft facilities. For financial institutions such as banks and **Non-Banking Financial Companies** (**NBFCs**), lending constitutes a core revenue-generating business function. Key processes within the lending function are outlined as follows:

- **Customer acquisition and onboarding**: These are crucial processes in lending, involving clear communication of loan requirements and terms to prospective borrowers. Typically, a range of documents must be submitted for loan processing. Lending company officers interact with potential customers to ensure they select appropriate loan products and meet all necessary criteria. This process is essential for driving business growth and ensuring customer satisfaction.

  Front-line staff can leverage personalized materials generated by GenAI to enhance customer interactions. Prospective borrowers can utilize self-service chatbots, specifically designed to provide accurate advice and inform them of required documentation. GenAI can also automate document verification, highlighting any missing information. Furthermore, data entry for loan applications (loan origination) can be automated using GenAI's information extraction capabilities.

- **Loan approval**: The loan approval process encompasses several sub-processes, including document verification, credit assessment, and fraud detection. This process is inherently complex due to the diverse nature of loan applications and requirements. Lenders aim to minimize lending to high-risk applicants while simultaneously capitalizing on business opportunities. This necessitates a delicate balancing act.

  While loan approval already integrates various digital techniques, including machine learning, GenAI can further enhance automation. It can extract and synthesize data from multiple sources, including applicant-provided documents and external, publicly available information such as social media and websites. GenAI's reasoning abilities can be particularly valuable in fraud detection and risk assessment.

- **Loan monitoring**: This process is particularly relevant for business loans, which typically involve substantial loan amounts and a heightened risk of default. Business borrowers are required to submit various business-related documents throughout the loan servicing period. These documents undergo audits by both internal and external auditors to identify potential future defaults. In the event of such findings, borrowers receive appropriate guidance and warnings.

  The volume of collected documents, such as bank statements and inventory records, can be extensive, even for a single business. GenAI can efficiently compile and analyze this information, pinpointing records that raise suspicion and warrant further investigation. It can also help to automatically generate reminders and other notifications for the borrower.

Use cases for pharmaceutical research

The research function within pharmaceutical companies is primarily dedicated to the discovery and development of novel drug candidates for manufacturing. This research may involve identifying entirely new drug molecules or creating variations of existing drugs. While the discovery of novel molecules is typically undertaken by a limited number of organizations, the development of variations, known as formulations, is a more prevalent practice. The following encompasses processes involved in both categories of pharmaceutical research:

- **Drug discovery**: The discovery of novel molecules involves a multi-stage process: selecting a target disease, identifying potential candidate molecules, and evaluating the molecule's efficacy in treating the disease. This is an extended, uncertain, and expensive endeavor that can span years of research without guaranteed success, a primary reason for the infrequent introduction of new drugs.

  GenAI can significantly expedite the process by analyzing extensive databases of existing and historical drugs, thereby identifying suitable candidates. Often, the discovery of new molecules involves repurposing existing molecules for novel applications with slight modifications. While other AI techniques, such as **reinforcement learning**, are employed for specialized tasks like protein analysis, GenAI can support these techniques by generating the necessary training datasets.

- **Pre-clinical trials**: The initial phase of drug testing involves laboratory and animal studies to assess the drug's safety and efficacy. This stage focuses on evaluating potential toxicity and examining pharmacokinetic properties, such as drug absorption, distribution, and excretion. A substantial portion of these studies is conducted using in vitro simulations.

A key advancement in pre-clinical trials is the reduction of animal testing. GenAI, in conjunction with other computational tools, facilitates the performance of extensive in-silico (laboratory-based) experiments. The description, translation, and reasoning capabilities of GenAI are utilized to generate datasets and analyze experimental results. Furthermore, GenAI aids in the preparation of regulatory reports for submission to relevant authorities.

- **Clinical trials**: Clinical trials, which involve testing drugs on human subjects, are complex and require meticulous execution. In addition to clinical considerations, this process involves navigating numerous legal and regulatory compliance requirements. Sub-processes include patient and partner recruitment, the actual testing procedures, statistical analysis of results, and submission of reports to regulatory authorities such as the **Food and Drug Administration** (**FDA**).

  GenAI can significantly streamline the extensive documentation requirements associated with clinical trials. It can also aid in patient matching, record maintenance, and reducing the time required for report generation.

More examples from other domains

A number of use cases of GenAI in industry-specific functions can be explored. Some more examples are as follows:

- **Equipment maintenance**: Manufacturing facilities rely on a diverse array of equipment, and the troubleshooting and repair of this equipment are typically handled by a dedicated function. Timely equipment maintenance is crucial for minimizing machine downtime, which can negatively impact production schedules and revenue streams.

  Engineers can leverage GenAI to obtain assistance with equipment-related inquiries. A GenAI system populated with relevant data, such as equipment manuals and historical repair records, can provide targeted suggestions and diagnostic guidance. Furthermore, GenAI can integrate with inventory management systems to determine the availability of required spare parts.

- **Electronic design**: Design engineers in electronics companies utilize available components to develop electronic systems, such as controllers and sensing modules. A critical aspect of their work involves selecting the appropriate components that meet design specifications. This process necessitates referencing extensive manuals and scrutinizing detailed technical specifications, which can be a time-consuming and challenging task.

  By integrating comprehension and reasoning capabilities, GenAI can provide valuable assistance to design engineers. A GenAI system, capable of processing component manuals, can efficiently identify and recommend suitable component choices, thereby saving engineers significant time and effort.

This section has presented a range of illustrative GenAI use cases across both common and industry-specific functions within organizations. While the potential applications of GenAI are extensive, companies must strategically select appropriate use cases to initiate their GenAI implementation. The subsequent section provides guidance on how to effectively choose the most suitable use cases.

Selecting use cases

Organizations evaluate potential GenAI use cases based on a set of defined criteria. Use cases that demonstrate strong performance across multiple criteria are prioritized for early implementation. While each organization must determine its own specific evaluation criteria, certain factors are commonly considered. Examples of these criteria are presented as follows:

- **Alignment with business objectives**: Organizations pursue specific overarching goals, such as revenue growth, profitability, customer satisfaction, and employee well-being. A proposed GenAI use case should demonstrably contribute to one or more of these objectives. Management can further prioritize these objectives and evaluate the use case's alignment with the highest-priority goals.
- **Impact of implementation**: Successful implementation of a GenAI use case should yield tangible benefits, such as time savings or quality improvements. The magnitude of this impact should be substantial. For instance, a 50% reduction in task completion time may be achieved, but if the task represents only 5% of the overall process, the overall impact will be minimal. Therefore, only use cases with the potential for significant impact should be prioritized.
- **External vs. internal impact**: GenAI use cases can have varying impacts. Some may focus on internal operational improvements, such as waste reduction, while others may directly enhance customer-facing aspects, such as service quality. Although organizational preferences may differ, there is often a general inclination towards prioritizing use cases that yield external, customer-perceptible benefits.
- **Ease of implementation**: As previously discussed, GenAI models possess a range of capabilities. Certain use cases align more closely with these capabilities than others, resulting in easier implementation. Another critical factor is the potential impact on employees and the required change management effort. Use cases that minimize disruption and require less extensive change management should be given higher priority.

The preceding list gives an idea of how the evaluation criteria for use cases can be chosen. As mentioned before, organizations will develop their own unique set of criteria and assign varying weights to them during the evaluation process.

The subsequent chapters of this book will explore the implementation of specific GenAI use cases through project-based examples. The concluding section of this chapter provides an introduction to the five projects that will be developed.

Introduction to projects

The following five chapters detail the development of GenAI solutions for enterprise applications, presented in the format of individual development projects. Each chapter will encompass the project's background, requirements specification, coding and integration procedures, and necessary optimization strategies. Furthermore, each chapter will provide comprehensive explanations of the specific GenAI techniques employed.

The selected use cases are designed to familiarize the reader with diverse facets of enterprise GenAI development. The key factors considered in their selection include:

- **Technology phase of the company**: The example companies are assumed to be in the establishment phase, ensuring a primary focus on improving operational processes.
- **Type of function**: The use cases are selected from both common and industry-specific functions. Furthermore, specific considerations within common use cases are incorporated. The detailed descriptions of these use cases will familiarize the reader with pertinent aspects of business processes across various industries.
- **Business objective**: An effort has been made to align each use case with diverse business objectives, including revenue generation, profitability enhancement, quality improvement, customer satisfaction, and employee well-being.
- **GenAI technique**: The use case projects are structured in a progressive order of complexity, starting with prompt engineering and culminating in agentic workflows. Concepts introduced in earlier projects serve as foundational knowledge for subsequent ones.
- **Model capabilities**: An emphasis has been placed on showcasing a wide range of GenAI model capabilities through the various solution features developed within the projects.

The following section introduces the projects. The introduction contains the use case description, business objective, and impact, and the GenAI technique used.

Creating a Marketing Assistant

This project focuses on the development of a GenAI assistant designed to support the marketing team. The assistant will facilitate content generation, enable content translation for global audiences, assist in campaign design, and provide decision support. Content generation will encompass materials such as email copy, social media posts (including images), and sales pitch scripts. Campaign design will involve tasks such as target audience identification, material design, and marketing channel selection. Strategic support will include assistance with company and product positioning, product planning, and business partnership development. The assistant will provide support through both direct question answering and proactive suggestions for various problem-solving aspects.

Business objective and impact

The Marketing Assistant developed in this project is anticipated to have a substantial impact on business operations. By streamlining content generation, the assistant will enhance the efficiency of the marketing team. Content localization will enable broader audience reach, and improved campaign design and strategy will drive increased lead generation. These factors are expected to positively influence the company's revenue streams and strengthen its brand image.

GenAI technique used

The Marketing Assistant project employs prompt engineering as its primary GenAI technique. Prompting represents the most straightforward method for utilizing GenAI model capabilities. The system will leverage advanced prompting techniques, such as **chain-of-thought** and **tree-of-thought** prompting, to effectively utilize model capabilities such as content generation and translation. These methodologies will ensure that the model's reasoning abilities are properly applied to achieve optimal results.

Creating an HR Assistant

This project focuses on the development of an assistant to support the HR function within an organization. The assistant will streamline various HR activities, including recruitment, performance management, training, and personal development. Specifically, it will be capable of generating job descriptions, scanning and matching resumes to relevant positions, providing learning resources, and suggesting topics for personal growth. The assistant will also be able to generate and analyze employee surveys, providing actionable recommendations for enhancing employee morale.

Business objective and impact

The HR Assistant is designed to enhance the efficiency of the HR team by automating tasks such as job description preparation and resume screening. This automation will accelerate the talent acquisition process, directly impacting company operations. Furthermore, the assistant will contribute to a better-trained and more satisfied workforce, both of which are critical factors for organizational success.

GenAI technique used

The assistant relies on models that require extensive knowledge of the company's skill requirements, job roles, and other proprietary information. To ensure these models possess this knowledge, the fine-tuning technique will be employed. Locally hosted language models will be utilized for this purpose, and various fine-tuning methods, such as **Low Rank Adaptation** (**LoRA**), will be implemented.

Building a contract intelligence system

This project focuses on developing a GenAI solution for use by a company's legal team. The legal team typically manages two primary areas: contract management and litigation. This system, designated **contract intelligence**, will concentrate on the contract management processes, which are typically more voluminous and time-sensitive than litigation. The system will empower the legal team to analyze existing contracts, draft new agreements, and ensure contract compliance with relevant legislation and regulations.

Business objective and impact

Contract management plays a crucial role in regulating interactions with external stakeholders. From a risk mitigation standpoint, thorough contract analysis is essential. Furthermore, readily accessible contracts facilitate efficient project execution and billing processes, thereby contributing to revenue growth.

GenAI technique used

The contract intelligence system utilizes the **retrieval-augmented generation** (**RAG**) technique to facilitate its operations. The RAG approach involves a structured, multi-stage process. Information retrieval, prompt augmentation, and model-based generation constitute the three primary steps within the execution pipeline. Core model capabilities, such as description and translation, will be leveraged to develop the system's functionalities.

Developing a Customer Success Navigator

This project focuses on the development of a solution, designated as the Customer Success Navigator, designed to assist customer service teams. These teams are responsible for processing incoming support tickets, providing responses to clients, and resolving reported issues. Customer service interactions occur through various channels, including telephone calls and online chats. The navigator will enhance these activities by providing ticket summaries, suggesting responses, and identifying similar past issues.

Business objective and impact

The Customer Success Navigator is designed to enhance the productivity of customer service agents, thereby reducing agent workload and stress. Customers will benefit from faster and more accurate responses, leading to increased customer satisfaction. Elevated customer satisfaction will subsequently drive upselling and cross-selling opportunities, contributing to revenue growth.

GenAI technique used

The Customer Success Navigator is constructed using advanced RAG techniques, including query rewriting, retrieval reranking, and knowledge graph integration. These techniques are employed to minimize errors, enhance answer quality, and address limitations inherent in basic RAG implementations. Notably, the system demonstrates the construction and utilization of a knowledge graph, a powerful technique that can be independently applied across a wide range of applications.

Developing an IT Operations Agent

The project aims to develop a solution for the IT team of an organization called the IT Ops Agent. The ops agent will help the team in activities such as incident management, code review, configuration management, predictive maintenance and change management. Some of these tasks will involve autonomous, unattended monitoring to predict or detect problems.

Business objective and impact

The ops agent system enhances the operational efficiency of IT teams through the automation of both routine and complex tasks. This leads to improved maintenance of IT systems, resulting in reduced downtime for users. Streamlined change management processes enable faster system implementation and upgrades, providing a competitive market advantage. Furthermore, autonomous monitoring enhances system security.

GenAI technique used

The IT Ops Agent leverages agentic workflows to achieve self-directed, autonomous functionality. Agentic workflows have gained considerable popularity due to their inherent autonomous capabilities. The ops agent integrates these workflows with human intervention to mitigate execution errors.

Conclusion

This chapter served to bridge the theoretical understanding of GenAI, acquired in previous chapters, with the practical applications to be developed in subsequent chapters. It explored the capabilities of GenAI models from an application-centric perspective, focusing on functionalities such as description, translation, generation, reasoning, and instruction-following. Furthermore, the chapter examined the transformative impact of GenAI implementation on industry, acknowledging the progression through curiosity, establishment, and disruption phases. The chapter then concentrated on the establishment phase, presenting a range of enterprise-level GenAI use cases. These use cases spanned both common and industry-specific functions. Finally, this chapter introduced the five development projects that will be detailed in the following chapters. The next chapter will start the project-based exploration with the development of the Marketing Assistant use case.

CHAPTER 4
Prompt Engineering

Introduction

Generative AI (**GenAI**) models are like versatile Swiss Army knives. They possess a remarkable breadth of capabilities, encompassing text, image, and audio generation, text summarization and classification, and sophisticated reasoning tasks. However, this general purpose nature necessitates explicit instruction to guide the models toward desired outputs. The input provided to elicit specific responses is termed a **prompt**.

The significance of crafting effective prompts has increased dramatically in recent years, leading to the development of numerous prompting techniques and the emergence of prompt engineering as a distinct discipline.

Early model prompting used simple methods, matching the limited abilities of early GenAI models. As models advanced with in-context learning and reasoning, more complex techniques like few-shot, chain-of-thought, and tree-of-thought prompting emerged. This shift highlights the need for prompt engineering skills and a deep understanding of both techniques and model capabilities. As GenAI adoption grows across industries, the demand for skilled prompt engineers is rising, and employee proficiency in prompt engineering is becoming crucial for maximizing efficiency and productivity.

For GenAI system developers, a strong command of prompt engineering is essential, even though prompting is often performed internally by the system. Selecting and implementing the most appropriate prompting technique is crucial for achieving accurate and reliable results.

This chapter introduces core and advanced prompting techniques with code examples, culminating in a hands-on project: building a GenAI-powered Marketing Assistant to apply the concepts in practice.

Structure

This chapter covers the following topics:

- Basics of prompt engineering
- In-context learning
- Chain-of-thought prompting

- Tree-of-thought prompting
- Development of Marketing Assistant

Objectives

By the end of this chapter, you will develop a strong understanding of various prompt engineering techniques. You will be able to apply the appropriate method, such as few-shot, chain-of-thought, or tree-of-thought prompting, based on the specific requirements of a problem statement. Additionally, you will explore the development of a practical GenAI applications that incorporate different prompting techniques.

Basics of prompt engineering

Sending a prompt affects a GenAI model in numerous ways. Understanding how these models work internally, as discussed earlier in this book, helps us see how prompts have these various effects.

As discussed in *Chapter 1, Introduction to Transformer Models,* transformers generate text through the prediction of subsequent words, effectively *completing* the given text sequence. Consequently, they need an initial text input to start the generation process, which is referred to as a **prompt**. This represents the most basic effect of prompting.

> Note: **Some GenAI models, such as variational autoencoders (VAs), do not need a prompt to generate an image. However, they need a text prompt to create a useful image.**

Another aspect of prompts is their utility in instructing the model. Because GenAI models are designed for general-purpose use and are capable of diverse tasks, prompts are essential for specifying the precise task to be executed.

For the next aspect, refer to the *attention mechanism* described in *Chapter 1, Introduction to Transformer Models*. The models create context for the words they have been provided using attention. The context guides the generation of the output sequence, thus greatly determining the model's output.

The following subsections will examine the completion, instruction, and context aspects of prompts, accompanied by illustrative examples.

Completion

The most fundamental capability of **large language models** (**LLMs**) is to complete the text given to them. Early models possessed this capability only. This aspect of prompting is now rarely used, but it is useful to get started with prompt engineering. The following code gives an example:

```
import openai
# Set OpenAI API key
openai.api_key = "YOUR_OPENAI_API_KEY"

prompt = "The meaning of life is"

# Call the OpenAI GPT-4o-mini model
response = openai.chat.completions.create(
    model="gpt-4o-mini",
    messages=[
    {"role": "user", "content": prompt},
    ],
    temperature=0.7,
    max_tokens=50,
    n=1,
)

reply = response.choices[0].message
print("Response: ", reply.content)
```

The output is as follows:

```
Response:  The meaning of life is a profound and often philosophical question that has been contemplated by thinkers, theologians, and individuals throughout history. Different cultures, religions, and philosophies offer various interpretations, and many people
```

The code is developed using Google Colab. For help on how to use Colab for coding, refer to *Chapter 1, Introduction to Transformer Models*. OpenAI library is used in this example to prompt the model GPT 4o-mini. For the present, ignore the parameters **temperature**, **max-tokens**, and **n**. The prompting is done through the following parameter:

```
{"role": "user", "content": prompt}
```

This is a dictionary with two members. The **role** member refers to the fact that this prompt is sent by the user to the model. Other roles are used in more advanced prompting. The most important part is the **content** member, which carries the prompt to the model. In this example, we use the following completion prompt:

```
prompt = "The meaning of life is"
```

The model will try to complete the sentence. You can see the response of the model in the output, which is a meaningful completion of the prompt.

Completion can achieve a limited range of tasks. For practical prompting purposes, other aspects need to be added to the prompt.

Instruction

The instruction component of a prompt conveys the specific task that a model is intended to perform. Given the general-purpose nature of GenAI models, a mechanism is required to enable them to execute particular functions. This mechanism is realized through two distinct phases: instruction tuning and instruction prompting, which are described as follows:

- **Instruction tuning**: Instruction tuning refers to the specialized training added to GenAI models after their base training, enabling them to follow instructions and execute specific tasks. Models that have undergone this training are designated as **instruct models**. Instruction tuning is a form of supervised learning conducted using a labeled dataset that includes both prompts and corresponding responses.
- **Instruction prompting**: Instruct models can be directed through instructions embedded within the prompt. The model's capacity to adhere to these instructions is a direct result of the training it received during the instruction tuning phase.

The common attributes of model behavior that can be controlled through instructions are outlined as follows:

- **Task**: This part gives clear instructions about what operation the model is expected to perform. The tasks correlate with the model capabilities discussed in *Chapter 3, GenAI in Industry*. The following list outlines some examples of tasks:
  - o Translate
  - o Summarize
  - o Rephrase
  - o Classify
- **Constraints**: This part specifies the limits that the model should adhere to. Consider the following examples:
  - o Length (`200 words, four or five lines`)
  - o Number of items (`provide three options`)
  - o Allowances (`do not answer if you do not have the information`)
- **Style**: Style can include various aspects of the generated output to make the output suitable for the intended purpose. A few examples of instructions pertaining to the style are as follows:
  - o Writing or drawing style (`in the style of Charles Dickens`)
  - o Level (`suitable for a 5-year-old`)

  - o Tone (**`assume a conversation tone`**)
  - o Language (**`use a language appropriate for a legal document`**)
- **Format**: Instructions can specify a particular way in which the output is expected from the model, such as:
  - o List or table (**`present as a table`**)
  - o Structure (**`give the output as key-value pairs`**)

The following is an example of a prompt using the instruction aspect:

```
import openai
# Set OpenAI API key
openai.api_key = "YOUR_OPENAI_API_KEY"
prompt = "Write a short story (8-10 lines) for high school students about a
teenager who discovers a hidden talent that changes their life. The story
should be engaging, inspiring, and have a positive message about self-
discovery and perseverance."

response = openai.chat.completions.create(
    model="gpt-4o-mini",
    messages=[
    {"role": "user", "content": prompt},
    ],
    temperature=0.7,
    max_tokens=300,
    n=1,
)

reply = response.choices[0].message
print("Response: ", reply.content)
```

The following instruction aspects were used in the preceding prompt:

- **Task**: **`Write a story`**
- **Constraints**: **`8-10 lines`**
- **Style**: **`for high-school students`**

You can run the code and see if the model produces the right kind of story.

Context

The prompt plays a crucial role in providing context to the model. Due to the attention mechanism, the model's output is heavily influenced by the context. Context can be incorporated into the prompt through various methods, some of which are detailed as follows:

- **Role:** The prompt tells the model to assume a certain role. The role can also include the responsibilities of that role, such as the following:
    - `You are a financial expert who advises the users on investment options`
    - `You are an expert graphic designer`
    - `You are a mathematician and tutor`
- **Background**: A prompt can provide contextual background for the problem that the model is tasked with solving. This can involve explaining terms used within the instructions. For instance, the following prompt provides context for extracting specific information from a cash flow statement:

```
"The cashflow statement is a financial statement that provides the detailed information on the company's cash inflows and outflows over a period of time. We are especially interested in the operational activities reported in the cash flow statement."
```

- **Scenario**: This part of the prompt centers on a detailed description of the problem to be addressed. As an example, consider the following scenario outlined in the prompt designed to generate a personalized poster for an HR event:

```
"The HR department hosts an event every month to felicitate employees who have done well in the previous month. This event serves to encourage the employees and boost their morale. As part of the event, a personalized poster is created for every employee. The poster matches with the kind of accomplishments they have achieved."
```

Context can be incorporated effectively into the prompt by utilizing the `role` parameter provided by model APIs. Although the OpenAI API is used in the example provided, most model APIs offer a mechanism for specifying roles within the prompt structure. Typically, contextual information is added to the **system** role. A code example is given as follows:

```
import openai
# Set OpenAI API key
openai.api_key = "YOUR_OPENAI_API_KEY"
```

```
system_prompt = "You are a financial investment expert and advisor. The client
is a 50 year old man in a senior position. His income is between 100-120K USD
per year. He has a family of four, including his wife and children aged 10 and
14."
user_prompt = "Suggest suitable investment for tax saving as well as capital
growth"

# Call the OpenAI GPT-4o-mini model
response = openai.chat.completions.create(
    model="gpt-4o-mini",
    messages=[
    {"role": "system", "content": system_prompt},
    {"role": "user", "content": user_prompt},
    ],
    temperature=0.7,
    max_tokens=400,
    n=1,
)

reply = response.choices[0].message

print("Response: ", reply.content)
```

The output is as follows:

```
Response: "Given your profile as a 50-year-old man with a family of four and an
annual income between $100,000 and $120,000, it's crucial to strike a balance
between tax efficiency and …(truncated)"
```

Prompt parameters

Beyond the instructions and context provided within the prompt, the output of GenAI models is also influenced by external parameters. These parameters, passed directly to the model during output generation, allow users to control aspects such as randomness, diversity, and response style.

Of these parameters, those that directly influence the next token generation process are particularly important. As discussed in *Chapter 1, Introduction to Transformer Models*, the final vector is processed by a classifier, which yields probabilities for various tokens. The selection of a single token as the next predicted token constitutes a decision-making task, which is governed by two key factors:

- **The number of tokens considered for selection (top-k)**: This parameter determines the quantity of probable tokens evaluated during the decision-making process. A lower top-k value restricts the selection to a smaller subset of highly probable tokens.
- **The method of token selection**: The most common approach involves selecting the token with the highest probability, resulting in a more deterministic and less creative output. This strategy favors predictable words and phrases. However, selecting lower-probability tokens introduces greater variability and creativity. The degree to which lower-probability tokens are selected is controlled by a parameter called **temperature**. A higher temperature value increases the likelihood of selecting lower-probability tokens.

From the preceding discussion, it is evident that higher values for top-k (20-40) and temperature (0.8-1.2) are appropriate for creative tasks such as storytelling or problem-solving. Conversely, lower values for these parameters (top-k: 3-5, temperature: 0.1-0.3) are more suitable for fact-based queries and summarization tasks.

Two additional parameters influence the model's output generation. The first, **frequency penalty**, aims to minimize the repetition of words. For instance, if the token *discuss* has already appeared in the generated text, subsequent occurrences of the same token within the list of probable tokens will be penalized, reducing their likelihood of selection. This parameter typically ranges from 0 to 2, with 0 indicating no penalty and 2 representing a severe penalty. The second parameter, **presence penalty**, encourages the model to introduce novel concepts rather than reiterating previously used ideas in a similar manner.

The **Max Tokens** parameter, as its name implies, limits the total number of tokens generated by the model. It is essential to ensure that excessively restrictive values do not truncate critical portions of the output. This parameter primarily serves to manage computational cost and response generation time.

The following table summarizes the usage of some of the parameters and their effects:

Parameter	Value	Effect	Suitable for
Temperature	0.1-0.3	More deterministic output.	Customer support chatbots, formal reports
Temperature	>0.8	More creative output	Content generation, problem solving
Top-k	5-10	More predictable and focused output	Financial queries, code generation
Top-k	40-100	More diverse, explanatory	Brainstorming, casual conversations
Frequency penalty	0.0-0.5	More repetitions of words	Technical writing
Frequency penalty	1.0-2.0	Less repetitions of words	Poetry, marketing content

***Table 4.1**: Summary of model parameter usage*

Note: The actual names and details of model parameters vary from model to model. For actual usage, you should check the model documentation.

In-context learning

Supervised fine-tuning (**SFT**), a phase in GenAI model training, involves presenting the model with prompt-response examples. During SFT, model parameters are adjusted to enhance the model's ability to generate appropriate responses to prompts, a learning paradigm familiar to many.

However, GenAI models also exhibit a distinct learning phenomenon during inference, termed **in-context learning** (**ICL**). First observed during the development of GPT-2, ICL occurs when prompt-response examples are included within the prompt itself. Remarkably, the model adapts its behavior without altering underlying parameters. This phenomenon, which emerges as models and training datasets surpass a critical size, is attributed to the model's enhanced pattern recognition capabilities, allowing it to discern patterns within the input itself.

ICL can be effectively employed as a prompt engineering technique. As previously mentioned, ICL entails providing the model with examples of prompts and their corresponding responses. The following code snippet demonstrates this approach:

Note: For brevity, subsequent code examples will illustrate the prompt and API call, excluding the API key setup.

```
prompt = "Analyze the sentiment of the following text and classify it as
Positive, Negative, or Neutral. Example: Text: I love this movie! Sentiment:
Positive"

# Call the OpenAI GPT-4o-mini model
response = openai.chat.completions.create(
            model-"gpt-4o-mini",
            messages=[
            {"role": "user", "content": prompt},
            {"role": "user", "content": "I absolutely love this product"}
            ],
            max_tokens=10,
        )

reply = response.choices[0].message
print(reply.content)
```

The output is as follows:

```
Sentiment: Positive
```

The example in the preceding prompt provides an example of how the output should be formatted.

Using in-context learning prompts

ICL prompts can incorporate either a single example (one-shot learning) or multiple examples (few-shot learning). From a prompt engineering perspective, the distinction between these two types of ICL is minimal. A practical guideline is to utilize an optimal number of examples. Insufficient examples may not provide adequate information for the model, while excessive examples can lengthen the prompt, thereby increasing computational cost and processing time.

Prompt engineers should consider examples as a form of instruction. While explicit instructions directly specify the desired model behavior, examples provide an indirect means of guiding the model. Consequently, the effects achieved through instructions, such as defining tasks, imposing constraints, specifying formats, and influencing style, can also be realized through the strategic selection of appropriate examples.

As an illustration, see the following code snippet:

```
prompt = "Your task is to extract information from given text. The information depends on the type of text provided" \
          "Example 1:" \
          "Text: Michael and Sarah traveled from San Francisco to New York" \
          "People: Michael, Sarah" \
          "Places: San Franscisco, New York" \
          "Example 2" \
          "Text: I recently bought the MegaGadget Pro for $99.50, and its display is outstanding." \
          "Product: MegaGadget Pro" \
          "Price: $99.50" \
          "Features: Outstanding display"

user_text = "My new xPhone Plus costed me $250. It has a great camera."

# Call the OpenAI GPT-4o-mini model
response = openai.chat.completions.create(
            model=”gpt-4o-mini”,
            messages=[
```

```
        {"role": "user", "content": prompt},
        {"role": "user", "content": user_text}
        ],
        temperature=0.3,
        max_tokens=50,
    )

reply = response.choices[0].message

print(reply.content)
```

The output is as follows:

```
Product: xPhone Plus
Price: $250
Features: Great camera
```

In the preceding code snippet, the prompt uses an explicit instruction to specify the task (**"Your task is to extract information"**), while the format and expected information is specified through the examples. Consider the following, closely related code example:

```
prompt = "Example 1:" \
        "Text: Michael and Sarah traveled from San Francisco to New York" \
        "People: Michael, Sarah" \
        "Places: San Franscisco, New York" \
        "Example 2" \
"Text: I recently bought the MegaGadget Pro for $99.50, and its display is outstanding.\
        "Product: MegaGadget Pro" \
        "Price: $99.50" \
        "Features: Outstanding display"

user_text =  "Bain and Phil recently went to Paris to attend an exhibition"

# Call the OpenAI GPT-4o-mini model
response = openai.chat.completions.create(
        model="gpt-4o-mini",
        messages=[
        {"role": "user", "content": prompt},
        {"role": "user", "content": user_text}
```

```
        ],
        temperature=0.3,
        max_tokens=50,
    )

reply = response.choices[0].message

print(reply.content)
```

The output is as follows:

```
Text: Bain and Phil recently went to Paris to attend an exhibition
People: Bain, Phil
Places: Paris
Event: Exhibition
```

The key modification in this example is the prompt, which omits any explicit task instruction. The model has inferred the task from the provided examples. Notably, the model also extracted an `Event` data point, which was not included in the example set. To prevent such unintended extractions, the inclusion of explicit instructions becomes necessary.

Providing implicit instructions through examples is particularly advantageous when specifying a desired output format or stylistic presentation. These aspects are often more effectively conveyed through demonstrative examples than through explicit textual instructions.

Applications of in-context learning

ICL can be useful in GenAI solutions in two different ways, which are as follows:

- **Alternative to model fine-tuning**: ICL offers a more efficient and accessible alternative to model fine-tuning, which is often a complex and resource-intensive process.
- **Enhanced instructions**: ICL provides a more adaptable method for instructing models. When direct instructions within a prompt fail to yield satisfactory results due to ambiguity, inconsistency, or inherent limitations, illustrative examples can be used to augment the instructions and improve the overall output.

Refer to the following examples for some applications where ICL plays a key role:

- **Translation of low-resource languages**: For low-resource languages, where training data may be limited, ICL can be employed to improve translation accuracy. Even if the model has limited exposure to a language's vocabulary, providing examples of translated sentences within the prompt can guide the model toward correct sentence formation. This approach offers a potential solution to translation challenges posed by languages with insufficient training corpora.

- **Personalization of generated content**: Specifying precise stylistic nuances can be challenging using explicit instructions alone. ICL facilitates this by enabling the provision of example texts that adhere to the desired style, ensuring the generated content aligns with specific requirements.
- **Code generation**: Generated code needs to adhere to certain standards of naming, indentation, and commenting. ICL provides a convenient method for conveying these requirements to the model through illustrative code examples.

Limitations of in-context learning

Despite its utility and suitability for specific problem domains, ICL presents certain limitations. The following is a list of the major limitations encountered when employing ICL:

- While we often think of the examples in ICL simply as instructions, they also provide the model with context. Due to this, the content in the examples affects the model in multiple ways. This can lead to bias and overfitting, especially if the examples are all from one field or industry. For example, if the model is only given healthcare examples, it might have trouble with questions about manufacturing.
- The incorporation of examples within prompts extends their overall length, presenting several practical considerations. Given the varying context window limitations of different models, extended prompts may prove incompatible with certain models. Furthermore, the increased computational cost and processing time associated with longer prompts are significant factors to consider.
- Even though examples can effectively inform what *should be* done to the model, they cannot inform what *should not be* done. This can result in some undesired output.
- It has been shown that examples cannot explain the logic to be followed in the model. While ICL can be used for solving simple reasoning problems, it fails to achieve good results in complex reasoning problems.

Chain-of-thought prompting

Chapter 3, GenAI in Industry, explored the reasoning capabilities of GenAI models, emphasizing their reliance on logic. The ability to apply logic becomes particularly valuable when combined with other functions such as information extraction or comprehension. As a result, logical instructions are often integrated into prompts. The following is a simple example featuring a partial prompt:

```
If the given material does not include the answer to the given question, answer
as 'The answer is not found in the given material'.
```

Notice that a prompt containing the **`If … then`** condition will require logical abilities on the part of the model. While most models can handle such logical tasks, they often struggle with more complex reasoning. Consider the following example:

```
If the sum of odd numbers in the given list is more than 36, say 'Yes': 2, 7,
5, 4, 13, 16, 11
```

Performing this task requires three logical steps, which are as follows:

- Deciding if the number is odd
- Adding all the odd numbers
- Setting the output to **Yes** if the sum is greater than 36

There is a good chance that the model will fail at tasks that require multi-step reasoning. Using ICL in the prompt does not help, as the model is not able to learn the expected logic from examples.

It was observed that if we can instruct the model to reason step by step, it can learn the logic. The prompt in the previous prompt can be modified as follows:

```
Is the total of odd numbers in the list more than 36?
Numbers: 2, 7, 5, 4, 13, 16, 11
Logic:
The odd numbers are: 7, 5, 13, 11
The total of odd numbers is 36.
36 is not greater than 36. Thus the answer is No.
Answer: No

Numbers: 22, 5, 11, 56, 12, 17, 7
Logic:
Answer:
```

ICL is used in the preceding prompt in a particular way. It trains the model to reason out loud. This type of prompting, called **chain-of-thought** (**CoT**), has proved very effective in improving logical and reasoning tasks.

The effectiveness of CoT reasoning lies in how LLMs generate output. The decoder of a transformer employs the following two types of attention when predicting the next token:

- **Cross-attention**: Determines the context of the input tokens.
- **Self-attention**: Considers the context of the tokens generated so far.

CoT leverages the decoder's self-attention mechanism by guiding the model to articulate its reasoning step-by-step. Each explanation provides context for the next step, improving the model's understanding and accuracy. For instance, in the previous problem involving odd numbers, the identification serves as context for the subsequent step, namely, summing them. By maintaining relevant context throughout the process, CoT enhances the precision of the final output.

Using chain-of-thought prompts

CoT prompting can be approached in two ways. The first method uses ICL by providing examples that demonstrate the reasoning process for a given problem. The second one leaves the reasoning to the model and merely instructs it to think aloud. Let us consider an example that demonstrates the first approach.

The example prompt finds out the *revenue per employee* of the given public company. This number is not usually available directly. However, it can be obtained using a simple calculation. Refer to the following code snippet:

```
prompt = "Your task is to calculate revenue per employee of the given
company." \
         "The user will provide the company name. Use step by step approach
         as given in the example." \
         "Example 1:" \
         "Company: Microsoft" \
         "Annual revenue for FY 2024: $245 billion" \
         "Number of employees in 2024: 228,000" \
         "Revenue per employee = Total revenue / Number of employees" \
         "Revenue per employee of Microsoft = $1,075,000"

user_input = "Company: Apple"

# Call the OpenAI GPT-4o-mini model
response = openai.chat.completions.create(
            model="gpt-4o-mini",
            messages=[
            {"role": "user", "content": prompt},
            {"role": "user", "content": user_input}
            ],
            temperature=0.3,
            max_tokens=250,
        )

reply = response.choices[0].message
print(reply.content)
```

The output is as follows:

```
To calculate the revenue per employee for Apple, we will follow the step-by-step approach:

1. **Identify the Annual Revenue for FY 2024**:
   - As of my last update, Apple's annual revenue for FY 2024 is estimated to be around $400 billion (please verify with the latest data).

2. **Identify the Number of Employees in 2024**:
   - As of 2024, Apple has approximately 164,000 employees (please verify with the latest data).

3. **Calculate Revenue per Employee**:
   - Revenue per employee = Total revenue / Number of employees
   - Revenue per employee = $400 billion / 164,000

4. **Perform the Calculation**:
   - Revenue per employee = $400,000,000,000 / 164,000
   - Revenue per employee ≈ $2,439,024.39

5. **Conclusion**:
   - Revenue per employee of Apple ≈ $2,439,024.39

Please verify the figures for the most accurate calculation.
```

The second approach involves instructing the model to generate a **reasoning trace**, i.e., a step-by-step record of its thought process as it works through the problem. This method is known as **zero-shot CoT**. In the following code example, we apply zero-shot CoT to solve the same problem of calculating revenue per employee:

```
prompt = "You are a financial analyst who understands various financial parameters" \
         "of companies. Your task is to calculate the revenue " \
         "per employee of the given company in 2024." \
         "The user will provide the company name." \
         "Use a step-by-step approach and provide the reasoning at every step"

user_input = "Company name: Apple"
```

```
# Call the OpenAI GPT-4o-mini model
response = openai.chat.completions.create(
            model="gpt-4o-mini",
            messages=[
            {"role": "user", "content": prompt},
            {"role": "user", "content": user_input}
            ],
            temperature=0.3,
            max_tokens=500,
        )

reply = response.choices[0].message
print(reply.content)
```

The output is as follows:

```
To calculate the revenue per employee for Apple in 2024, we will follow a step-by-step approach. Here's how we can do it:

### Step 1: Gather Revenue Data
First, we need to find the projected or estimated revenue for Apple in 2024. This information can typically be found in financial reports, earnings forecasts, or analyst estimates.
- **Assumption**: Let's say Apple is projected to generate $400 billion in revenue for the year 2024.
### Step 2: Gather Employee Data
Next, we need to find the number of employees working at Apple in 2024. This information can be found in the company's annual report, SEC filings, or through credible financial news sources.
- **Assumption**: Let's assume Apple has approximately 160,000 employees in 2024.
### Step 3: Calculate Revenue Per Employee
Now that we have both the revenue and the number of employees, we can calculate the revenue per employee using the following formula:
\[
\text{Revenue per Employee} = \frac{\text{Total Revenue}}{\text{Number of Employees}}
\]
### Step 4: Plug in the Values
```

```
Using our assumed values:
- Total Revenue = $400 billion
- Number of Employees = 160,000
Now we can perform the calculation:
\[
\text{Revenue per Employee} = \frac{400,000,000,000}{160,000}
\]

### Step 5: Perform the Calculation
Calculating the above expression:
\[
\text{Revenue per Employee} = 2,500,000
\]
```

It can be observed that CoT generates a lot of tokens during its working, which increases the cost and time of the processing.

Applications of chain-of-thought

CoT prompting is a powerful technique that can yield effective results in cases where basic or few-shot prompting falls short. It is particularly useful for tasks that demand a structured, logical approach. Some examples of such tasks include:

- **Financial analysis**: Analyzing large volumes of financial data, including statements, tables, and charts, requires completing multiple sub-tasks accurately. This process involves data extraction, computations, and conditional reasoning. CoT prompting provides an effective approach for managing these complexities.
- **Problem solving**: Addressing mathematical, scientific, or technical problems requires a structured and logical approach. While a GenAI model may not be capable of solving every problem, the step-by-step reasoning listed by CoT prompting can assist human problem solvers by guiding their focus toward the most relevant aspects.
- **Decision making**: Complex decision-making problems require analyzing multiple parameters and evaluating their impact. CoT prompting not only facilitates this process but also provides a step-by-step explanation, making it a valuable tool for those making critical decisions.
- **Code generation**: Writing code is a fundamentally logical task, making CoT prompting a natural fit for enhancing both code generation and debugging. This approach proves beneficial across various programming paradigms, including procedural languages, like Java and Python, declarative languages, such as SQL and HTML, and configuration-based scripting.

Limitations of chain-of-thought

While highly effective, CoT prompting has certain limitations that GenAI solution designers should consider. Refer to the following list for some of these challenges:

- **Increased cost and time**: CoT prompting requires the model to *think aloud* as it processes a task, generating a large number of tokens. While this enhances reasoning effectiveness, it also leads to higher computational costs, as most providers charge based on the number of tokens processed and generated. Therefore, CoT should be used judiciously in systems where cost efficiency is a priority.
- **Model dependency**: CoT prompting, while powerful, exhibits a heightened reliance on underlying model capabilities. Effective CoT necessitates models with advanced reasoning and comprehension. This constraint directly impacts system architecture, limiting the range of viable model choices. Furthermore, CoT prompts often demonstrate model-specific dependencies. Porting applications to alternative models may require significant prompt rewriting, introducing additional development overhead.
- **Propagation of errors**: Due to the sequential nature of CoT reasoning, any inaccuracy introduced at an early stage will propagate through subsequent steps. This cascading effect can amplify initial errors, leading to significantly compromised final outputs.
- **Complex reasoning**: While CoT prompting enhances logical reasoning, its effectiveness diminishes when faced with problems involving extensive branching or numerous potential solutions. The next section explores techniques to mitigate this limitation.

Tree-of-thought prompting

Tasks such as strategy formulation, decision-making, troubleshooting, and diagnosis often require selecting the best approach from multiple possible solutions. This process benefits from a structured reasoning method that leads to an optimal outcome. **Tree-of-thought (ToT)** is a prompting technique that builds upon CoT to explore different solution paths and identify the most effective one.

ToT involves generating multiple execution paths to solve a given problem, with each path acting as an independent *expert* working on the task. These experts employ CoT prompting to produce step-by-step solutions. At each stage, the solutions are evaluated, and only a selected number of experts proceed further. In the final step, one or more solutions are identified as the optimal outcome.

Consider the following example of a simple ToT prompt that uses self-evaluation by experts:

```
Solve the given question by using the following approach:

1. the problem will be solved in multiple steps

2. a maximum of 5 experts will work on the problem at any step
```

```
3. each expert will use step-step thinking to solve the problem.
4. At each step, the expert will self-evaluate its work and leave if the solution is not acceptable
5. At the final step, if more than one solution is remaining, a Judge will declare the winning solution
The question is:
How can the world avoid the potential harm to climate because of the increase in electricity demand due to growth of AI?
```

You can run the prompt using the code structure given in earlier sections. The results will provide you with a good insight into the way ToT works.

Applications of Tree-of-thought

The application areas of ToT largely overlap with those of CoT. However, ToT is particularly useful for problems that require exploring multiple solution approaches to arrive at a satisfactory outcome. The following are some example applications:

- **Business strategy**: Developing and evaluating multiple strategic approaches for optimal decision-making.
- **Project management**: Identifying various pathways to achieve project goals efficiently.
- **Script writing**: Generating and refining multiple narrative structures or creative directions.
- **Drug discovery**: Exploring different molecular formulations and their potential effects.
- **Automation of processes**: Designing efficient workflows by considering multiple automation strategies.
- **Public policy design**: Evaluating diverse policy options to determine the most effective solution.

Limitations of Tree-of-thought

ToT prompting also comes with certain challenges, including high computational cost, error propagation, and model dependency. Additionally, ToT prompts can become complex and difficult to manage. One notable issue is **thought divergence**, where irrelevant thoughts deviate from the main line of reasoning, leading the execution off track. Given these challenges, ToT should be employed carefully by system developers, particularly for problems that are otherwise difficult or impossible to solve using simpler approaches.

Development of the Marketing Assistant

The marketing department plays a crucial role in acquiring new customers, shaping the company's brand image, and providing valuable insights for product development. This section focuses on developing a GenAI-based **Marketing Assistant** (**MA**) to improve the efficiency of these tasks. By improving marketing productivity, MA can significantly impact both the company's revenue and its brand perception. The features offered by MA are described in the following section.

Features of the MA

GenAI-based techniques offer significant advantages to the marketing team, as outlined in *Chapter 3, GenAI in Industry*. During the development of MA, specific use cases are chosen to illustrate the application of prompt engineering methods. The key features are as follows:

- **Content creation**: The marketing team is responsible for generating content for various purposes, including outreach to potential customers and brand development. The success of these initiatives heavily depends on the effectiveness of the content, which must be relevant, appropriate, and aligned with its intended purpose.

  A major challenge in content creation is the need for personalization. Every piece of communication must be tailored based on factors such as the target audience, timing, and specific objectives. Meeting these customization demands manually is impractical for the marketing team. The MA is designed to address this challenge by providing an efficient and automated solution to personalization.

- **Campaign planning**: Marketing campaigns are designed to generate sales leads and can take various forms, such as advertisements or email campaigns. For a campaign to be effective, it must be carefully structured to reach the right audience and create the intended impact. The marketing team plays a crucial role in planning different aspects of a campaign during its initial phase.

  While major campaigns are typically planned by experienced marketing professionals, smaller and routine campaigns also require careful planning. However, due to the team's focus on larger initiatives, these smaller campaigns often receive insufficient attention, leading to inefficiencies. The MA addresses this challenge by offering dedicated campaign planning features.

- **Product strategy**: To remain competitive, organizations must continuously introduce new products and services while refining existing offerings. Well-managed companies typically have a dedicated product management team responsible for enhancing current products and developing new ones. The marketing team plays a supporting role by providing valuable insights and feedback to guide this process.

Although product strategy is critical to an organization's long-term success, it is not a primary focus of the marketing team. As a result, the necessary attention it requires is often lacking. This can hinder the organization's ability to adapt and innovate effectively, potentially impacting its market position. The MA can solve this problem by offering an easy-to-use product strategy feature to the marketing team.

Description of the solution

The MA will be accessible to marketing team members as a web application, allowing them to use it directly through a browser. It will feature an intuitive interface designed for ease of use, enabling seamless access to its functionalities.

Features

The features are divided into three main areas:

- Content
- Campaign
- Product

Each main feature will include multiple actions that users can perform. For instance, the **write an email** action will be part of the **content creation** feature. The following is the complete list of features and their corresponding actions:

- Content
  - Write an email
  - Create a social media post
- Campaign
  - Design the **Ideal Customer Profile** (**ICP**)
- Product
  - Suggest product improvement

Performing an action will require the user to provide specific input parameters. Once the input is submitted, the MA will process the request and generate an output. The output can be in the form of text, images, or markup. Users will have the option to copy or download the output for use as needed.

Users

Understanding user profiles is a crucial aspect of system design. As outlined earlier, the users of the MA consist of marketing team members. They are knowledge workers with proficiency in digital tools across desktop and mobile platforms. Skilled in handling text and image files, they are also adept at navigating web applications efficiently.

User stories

The following is an example of a typical user story:

Alice, a marketing executive, is responsible for communicating with prospective clients. Upon checking the CRM, she finds that she needs to send emails to three prospects today. These prospects come from different industries and have varying levels of prior engagement with the company. For instance, Prospect A has had an in-person meeting with the team, whereas Prospect B has only received a single email so far.

To craft personalized and relevant messages, Alice accesses the "write an email" feature in the MA. The system generates suitable email content tailored to each prospect's background and engagement history. She then uses her mailing program to send the emails and updates the CRM with the necessary details.

Similar user stories can be created for other features by outlining the user's role, their task, how they interact with the MA, and the final outcome.

Architecture

MA is a web application that utilizes the capabilities of GenAI models. It is built using multiple modules, each serving a specific function. The list of modules is as follows:

- **User interface (UI)**: The UI module enables users to access the functionalities of the MA as described in the previous section. It is developed using the **Streamlit** library in Python, which facilitates rapid application development without requiring knowledge of HTML or CSS. Streamlit also integrates seamlessly with Python's Data Science libraries, making it an ideal choice for building simple AI-driven applications.
- **Prompting functions (PF)**: This module contains the code responsible for generating prompts for the GenAI model. The functions are implemented in **Python**. These functions utilize various prompting techniques discussed earlier in this chapter to ensure effective interaction with the model.
- **GenAI models**: The MA leverages an LLM and an image-generation model for text and image generation. Both models are accessed via external APIs that are called from the PF module. The LLM used is **GPT-4o-mini** from OpenAI, while the image-generation model is **DALL-E 3**. These models enable the MA to generate high-quality text and images tailored to user requirements.
- **Configurations (Config)**: The Config module stores all essential configurations required to provide flexibility within the application. It is implemented as a global class and is accessed by the PF module to manage settings dynamically. This module ensures that key parameters, such as API keys, model preferences, and user-specific settings, can be easily modified without altering the core application logic.

Architectural considerations

The chosen architecture is designed for rapid application development, ensuring flexibility and ease of expansion. Its modular structure allows for the seamless addition of new features while maintaining scalability and enabling quick updates.

The code is organized into distinct layers, promoting maintainability and efficient development. The key technologies used, Python and Streamlit, are selected for their simplicity, ease of learning, and strong community support. Additionally, important parameters are centralized within the Config module, making customization straightforward.

System development

The development of the MA system will be done in the following sequence:

1. Development of the PF module, which includes the development of the Config module.
2. Development of the UI module.

Development of the PF module

The PF module consists of a collection of Python functions, each responsible for handling a specific action, such as writing an email. The core component of each function is the prompt, which determines the quality and relevance of the generated output.

Each prompt is designed with customizable parameters, which can be sourced from:

- User input provided through the UI.
- Configuration settings stored in the Config module.

The first action to be developed within this module is *writing an email,* which falls under the content feature.

Writing an email

An email serves as a means of communication with potential customers. To ensure effectiveness, certain factors related to the recipient must be taken into account, which are outlined as follows:

- **Buying stage**: A buyer progresses through different phases when purchasing a product or service. Common stages include *Awareness, Consideration, Decision,* and *Purchase.* Communication should align with the buyer's current stage. The MA system associates an **email type** with each phase, which the user selects accordingly.
- **Industry**: The content of the email should be customized based on the buyer's industry.
- **Role**: The message should be structured according to the recipient's role, whether they are a decision-maker, influencer, or evaluator.

- **Previous communication**: Any prior interaction with the recipient should be considered when drafting the email.

The following prompt will be used for generating the email:

```
You are an expert email marketer tasked with writing a persuasive and tailored email. The user will provide the following inputs. The email must be crafted based on these inputs:
1. **Buying Phase**
2. **Industry**
3. **Role** (this will be one of: decision maker, influencer, or evaluator)
4. **Previous Communication**
Using these inputs, please generate an email that meets the following criteria:
- **Personalization:** Address the recipient appropriately, referencing their industry and role.
- **Relevance to Buying Phase:** Tailor the tone and content of the email based on the buying phase (for example, introductory information for early stages, or detailed product benefits for later stages).
- **Context of Previous Communication:** Integrate any key points or context from the previous communication to ensure continuity and relevance.
- **Clear Call-to-Action:** Provide a clear next step or call-to-action that is aligned with the recipient's current position in the buying journey.
- **Professional Tone:** Maintain a tone that is both professional and engaging, reflecting the norms of the industry.

Also use the following information:
**Sender’s company name**:
**Product promoted**:
**Challenge addressed**:
**Information link**:

Compose the email ensuring that it seamlessly weaves all these inputs together into a coherent, compelling message.
```

Notice the use of instruction and context in this prompt. The prompting function is left with the responsibility of providing the missing values, sending the prompt to the mode, and using the output.

The missing values will be supplied from the following two sources:

- From the UI
- From Config

The user input will be passed to the function through the API. The Config module will be described first before moving to the actual prompting function.

Config module is made up of a Singleton Python class. Being Singleton, only one instance of this class exists. During initialization, all necessary configurations are stored in the class. The class code is as follows:

```
class MAConfig:
    _instance = None  # Singleton instance
    _config = {}  # Dictionary to store configurations

    def __new__(cls):
        if cls._instance is None:
            cls._instance = super(MAConfig, cls).__new__(cls)
          #Set the configurations
            cls._instance.setConfig()

        return cls._instance

    def setConfig(cls):
        #Set initial configurations
        cls.set("OurCompany","Visi Labs")
        cls.set("Product", "Congnivo")
        cls.set("Challenge Addressed", "Long TAT for insurance payments")

    def set(cls, key, value):
        #Set a configuration value
        cls._config[key] = value

    def get(cls, key, default=None):
        #Get a configuration value, return default if not found.
        return cls._config.get(key, default)

    def getAllConfig(cls):
        #Return all configurations as a dictionary
        return cls._config.copy()
```

Using the **MAConfig** class, the prompt parameters are retrieved.

The **Config** module is used in the prompting functions. Refer to the following code for the prompting function for the **writing an email** action:

```
def MA_Content_WriteEmail(phase, industry, role, previous_communication):

    config = MAConfig()

    prompt = "You are an expert email marketer tasked with writing a
persuasive and tailored email. " \
    "The user will provide the following inputs. The email must be crafted
    based on these inputs:" \
    "1. **Buying Phase** "\
    "2. **Industry** "\
    "3. **Role** (this will be one of: decision maker, influencer, or
evaluator)"\
    "4. **Previous Communication** " \
    "Using these inputs, please generate an email that meets the following
criteria: " \
    "- **Personalization:** Address the recipient appropriately, referencing
their industry and role. " \
    "- **Relevance to Buying Phase:** Tailor the tone and content of the email
based on the buying phase " \
    "(for example, introductory information for early stages, or detailed
product benefits for later stages)." \
    "- **Context of Previous Communication:** " \
    "Integrate any key points or context from the previous communication to
ensure continuity and relevance." \
    "- **Clear Call-to-Action:** Provide a clear next step or call-to-action
that is aligned with " \
    "the recipient's current position in the buying journey." \
    "- **Professional Tone:** Maintain a tone that is both professional and
engaging, reflecting the norms of the industry."\
    "Also use the following information given by the user:" \
    " **Sender’s company name**: " \
    "**Product promoted**: " \
    "**Challenge addressed**: " \
    "**Information link**: "\
"Compose the email ensuring that it seamlessly weaves all these inputs
```

```
together into a coherent, compelling message."

    user_input = "1. **Buying Phase** : " + phase + "\n" \
    "2. **Industry** :" + industry + "\n" \
    "3. **Role** : " + role + "\n" \
    "4. **Previous Communication** :  " + previous_communication + "\n" \
    " **Sender's company name**: " + config.get("OurCompany") + "\n"\
    "**Product promoted**: " + config.get("Product") + "\n"\
    "**Challenge addressed**: " + config.get("Challenge Addressed") + "\n" \
    "**Information link**: " + config.get("Information Link") + "\n"

    # Call the OpenAI GPT-4o-mini model
    response = openai.chat.completions.create(
             model="gpt-4o-mini",
             messages=[
             {"role": "user", "content": prompt},
             {"role": "user", "content": user_input}
             ],
             temperature=0.4,
             max_tokens=500,
        )

    reply = response.choices[0].message
    return reply.content
```

To test the preceding function, write the following temporary code in a Colab code cell:

```
email_text = MA_Content_WriteEmail("Awareness", "Healthcare", "Decision
Maker", "None")
print(email_text)
```

The generated email will be well-structured and tailored to the recipient based on the provided parameters. The actual parameters will be supplied by the user through the UI, which will be discussed at a later stage.

Create a post

The second action in the content feature is creating a social media post. Social media posts are created for various reasons, such as product launches, greetings for special days, industry awareness, and important updates. They serve the purpose of sending the right message to the users.

The **create a post** action takes a simplified approach to generating social media posts. It accepts a number of parameters from the user, such as the following:

- Purpose of the post.
- Social media targeted.
- Special mentions, such as news about the company or a special day.
- Whether an image is to be generated.
- Whether text should be generated.

The prompt for generating the text is given as follows:

```
You are an expert social media marketer tasked with creating an engaging and platform-appropriate social media post. The post must be crafted based on the following user inputs:

1. **Purpose:** (general, special day, news, launch)
2. **Social Media Platform:** (LinkedIn, Facebook)
3. **Special Mention:** (News details, special day name, or relevant context)
Using these inputs, generate a post that meets the following criteria:
- **Tone & Style:** Align with the platform's best practices (e.g., professional and insightful for LinkedIn, engaging and conversational for Facebook).
- **Relevance to Purpose:** Ensure the post reflects the user's intent—informative for news, celebratory for special days, exciting for a launch, etc.
- **Incorporation of Special Mention:** Seamlessly integrate the special mention (e.g., highlight a special day, announce a news update, or introduce a product launch).
- **Call to Action (if needed):** Encourage engagement such as comments, shares, sign-ups, or visits to a website.
- **Brevity & Readability:** Keep it concise while maintaining impact, ensuring clarity and engagement.
Compose the post in a way that is engaging, well-structured, and relevant to the intended audience.
```

The code is divided into two levels:

- The function `MA_CreatePost` checks whether text, image, or both should be generated.
- The functions `Generate_Post_Text` and `Generate_Post_Image` perform the actual generation.

The first function is as follows:

```
def MA_CreatePost(purpose, media, mention, generate_text, generate_image):

    if generate_text:
        post_text = Generate_Post_Text()

    if generate_image:
        post_image = Generate_Post_Image()

    return post_text, post_image
```

The function **Generate_Post_Text** is very similar to **MA_WriteEmail**. You should attempt this yourself using the prompt given in the preceding code. The following code is for **GeneratePostImage:**

```
import requests

def Generate_Post_Image(purpose, media, mention):

  config = MAConfig()

  prompt = "You are an expert visual designer tasked with creating an " \
  "eye-catching image for a social media post. The image must be designed " \
  "based on the following user inputs:" \

  "1. **Purpose:** (general, special day, news, launch)" \
  "2. **Social Media Platform:** (LinkedIn, Facebook, Instagram) " \
  "3. **Special Mention:** (News details, special day name)" \
  "Follow the following design-requirements" \
  "- **Platform-Specific Dimensions:**" \
  "Ensure the image follows the optimal size for the selected platform:" \
  "- **LinkedIn:** 1200 x 627 pixels" \
  "- **Facebook:** 1200 x 630 pixels" \
  "- **Instagram:** 1080x1080 pixels (square) or 1080x1350 pixels (portrait)"
\
  "- **Visual Style:** Align with the post's purpose—corporate " \
  " and professional for LinkedIn, engaging and social for Facebook, " \
  "visually appealing and aesthetic for Instagram. " \
```

```
"- **Integration of Special Mention:** " \
"If it's a special day, include relevant themes "\
"(e.g., a ribbon for World Cancer Day). "\
"If it's news or a launch, ensure the image conveys key details." \

"Create a visually engaging image that is optimized for the given platform " 
\
"and effectively communicates the intended message."

user_input = "1. **Purpose** : " + purpose + "\n" \
  "2. **Social Media Platform** :" +  media +"\n" \
  "3. **Special Mention** : " + mention + "\n" \

prompt = prompt + user_input

# Call the OpenAI API to generate the image
response = openai.images.generate(
    model='dall-e-3',
    prompt=prompt,
    n=1,
)

# Extract the image URL from the API response
image_url = response.data[0].url

# Download the image
image_response = requests.get(image_url)

file_name = config.get("Image_File_Path") + "generated_image.png"

with open(file_name, "wb") as file:
    file.write(image_response.content)

return file_name
```

The **campaign** feature is developed next. The action illustrated here is to **generate ICP**, which helps the marketing team in generating the ideal customer profile. Since the boilerplate code is very similar to the **write an email** action, only the prompt is explained in this section.

The ICP is decided based on many factors, which are as follows:

- Industry
- Company size
- Geographic region
- Buyer persona
- Buying behavior

The `Generate_ICP` action takes these parameters from the user through the UI. The prompt for generating ICP uses the CoT technique. Given the parameters, it forces the model to think step-by-step till it generates a clear and usable ICP. The prompt is as follows:

```
You are a skilled marketing strategist tasked with developing a detailed **Ideal Customer Profile (ICP)**. Use a **Chain of Thought (CoT)** approach to logically analyze and break down the inputs provided by the user.

The user will provide the following parameters:
1. **Industry**: (E-commerce, Healthcare, Finance)
2. **Company Size**: (Startup, SMB, Enterprises)
3. **Geographic Region**: (North America, Europe, APAC)
4. **Buyer Persona**: (C-level, Manager, Director, Specialist)
5. **Pain Points**:
6. **Budget & Spending Capacity**: (Low, Medium, High)
7. **Technology Stack **:
8. **Buying Behavior**: (Price-sensitive, Brand-loyal, Evidence-based)
9. **Decision-Making Process**: (Committee-based, Fast-moving, RFP)
10. **Competitors **:

### **Step-by-Step CoT Breakdown**:
- **Step 1: Industry & Market Context** - Analyze how this industry operates, common trends, and competitive landscape.
- **Step 2: Company Size & Regional Influence** - Identify how the company's size and region impact its decision-making process.
- **Step 3: Buyer Persona Analysis** - Evaluate the decision-maker's role, responsibilities, and pain points.
```

```
- **Step 4: Financial Capacity & Purchasing Trends** - Assess the budget constraints and spending behavior.
- **Step 5: Technology & Integration Needs** - Determine the tech stack they use and compatibility with our solutions.
- **Step 6: Buying Behavior & Decision Process** - Define how they evaluate vendors, key motivators, and barriers to purchase.
- **Step 7: Competitive Landscape** - Examine their current vendor relationships and potential opportunities for disruption.

### **Final Output:**
Generate a well-structured **Ideal Customer Profile (ICP)** that includes:
- **Customer Overview** (Industry, Company Size, Region)
- **Key Decision Makers** (Roles, Responsibilities)
- **Core Pain Points & Challenges**
- **Budget & Spending Behavior**
- **Tech Preferences & Constraints**
- **Purchase Behavior & Decision-Making Process**
- **Competitor Analysis & Market Positioning**

Ensure that the ICP is **data-driven, practical, and aligned with marketing and sales objectives**. The goal is to help the marketing team refine targeting strategies, optimize messaging, and improve conversion rates.
```

The task to complete the code to generate ICP using the preceding prompt is left to the reader.

Finally, the **suggest product improvements** action is developed. As before, only the prompt is discussed as follows:

Suggesting improvements for products is the ideal problem for ToT prompting, as it involves choosing a few options from many possible improvements. The approach discussed in the *tree-of-thought prompting* section can be utilized for this purpose. Following the practice set in the previous actions, key parameters are collected from the user and are added to the problem statement. The complete prompt is as follows:

```
You are part of a marketing team that is responsible for **suggesting new product improvement** to the product management team. The following method should be used to solve the problem:
1. the problem will be solved in multiple steps
2. 3 experts will work on the problem at any step.
3. Each expert will consider the following key parameters provided by the user:
```

```
**Product Category**:
**Target Audience**:
**Current User Pain Points**:
**Key Business Goals**:
**Competitor Features & Strengths**:
**Technology Stack & Limitations**:
**User Feedback & Reviews**:
**Market Trends & Innovations**:
4. each expert will use step-step thinking to come up with 4-6 product improvement suggestion.
4. the expert will self-evaluate its work and keep the top 2 suggestions.
5. At the final step, a judge will choose the top suggestion. The judge will provide the following for each suggestion: Why it matters, How it can be implemented, Priority level.
```

Development of UI module

The UI module is developed using the **Streamlit** library. Streamlit is a Python library that allows developers to build web applications rapidly. Streamlit development is usually done using a desktop development environment. Since we are using it through Google Colab, which is an online tool, we will need to follow a particular method. The steps involved are outlined as follows:

1. The entire code for the application will be added to a Python file called **`MA_App.py`**. Individual module codes will be tested in the Colab environment, as demonstrated in the previous sections. The codes will then be added to the **`MA_App.py`** file using an editor, such as notepad. This file will then be uploaded to Colab.
2. The Streamlit app will be run with the **`MA_App.py`** as the source. To make this application available over a public URL, another tool called **ngrok** will be used. This tool will make it possible to access the MA application using a browser.

The following is the code in the **`MA_App.py`** file:

Note: Only the UI code has been added. You will have to add the PF module code before uploading to Colab.

```
Import streamlit as st
st.set_page_config(page_title="Marketing Assistant", layout="wide")
st.sidebar.title("Features")
menu_main = st.sidebar.radio("Select Feature", ["Content", "Campaign",
"Product"])
```

```
submenu = None
if menu_main == "Content":
    submenu = st.sidebar.radio("Select Action", ["Write an Email", "Create a
Post"])
elif menu_main == "Campaign":
    submenu = st.sidebar.radio("Select Action", ["Generate an ICP"])
elif menu_main == "Product":
    submenu = st.sidebar.radio("Select Action", ["Suggest a product
improvement"])
st.title("Welcome to the Application")
if submenu:
    st.subheader(f"{submenu} Section")
    st.write(f"This is the {submenu.lower()} section.")
    if submenu == "Write an Email":
        industry = st.text_input("Industry")
        buying_stage = st.text_input("Buying stage")
        role = st.text_input("Role")
        previous_communication = st.text_area("Previous communication")

        if st.button("Write"):
            st.write("Generating email...")

            email_text = MA_Content_WriteEmail( buying_stage, industry, role,
            previous_communication )

            st.write("Here is a draft email:")
            st.write(email_text)
```

To use ngrok, complete the following steps:

1. Go to **ngrok.com** and register your account. After registration, create a Tunnel Auth Token.
2. In Colab, run the following code:

   ```
   !ngrok config add-authtoken YOUR_NGROK_AUTHTOKEN
   ```

Finally, use Streamlit and ngrok to run your web application, shown as follows:

```
import streamlit as st
from pyngrok import ngrok
import os
import threading
import time

# Function to run Streamlit
def run_streamlit():
    os.system("streamlit run MA_App.py")

# Start Streamlit in a separate thread
thread = threading.Thread(target=run_streamlit)
thread.daemon = True
thread.start()

# Wait for Streamlit to initialize
time.sleep(3)

# Open a public URL via ngrok
url = ngrok.connect(8501).public_url
print(f"Streamlit app is running at: {url}")
```

Using the MA

Clicking on the public URL given by ngrok will open the MA web application. The features and actions can be accessed from the menus on the left side of the screen. For example, clicking on **Write an Email** will show the following page:

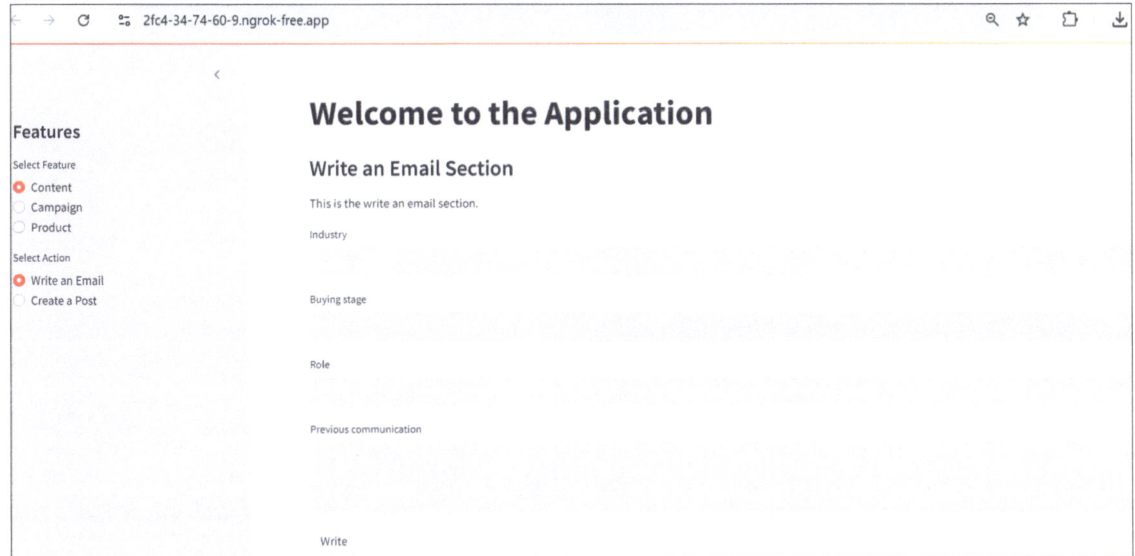

Figure 4.1: User interface for the write an email action

Enter the parameter values and click on **Write**. You will see the email draft generated by the model. The draft can be copied and used for sending the communication.

Conclusion

This chapter covered various prompting techniques, highlighting prompt engineering as a crucial skill for a GenAI solution developer. It introduced methods such as few-shot, CoT, and ToT, along with their applications and limitations. The final section focused on developing the Marketing Assistant, a GenAI application designed to support the marketing team in enhancing their work. In addition to demonstrating prompting techniques, the development of the MA also introduced Streamlit, a valuable tool for UI development.

Although prompting is a powerful technique for leveraging GenAI models, some industrial applications require models to follow specific behaviors. In such cases, fine-tuning offers a more effective approach than providing detailed instructions in every prompt. The next chapter will explore the fine-tuning of GenAI models.

CHAPTER 5
Fine-tuning Generative Models

Introduction

Generative AI (**GenAI**) models owe their popularity and quick adoption to pre-training, which allows models to perform a variety of tasks out-of-the-box. As described in the previous chapter, GenAI models are capable of responding to prompts in diverse ways to produce specific outputs. They are also able to learn from examples included within the prompts.

In some cases, the pre-trained capabilities of the GenAI models may prove insufficient for the intended application. For instance, a large language model used to build a legal advice chatbot may give inaccurate responses, despite well-crafted prompts, indicating insufficient domain-specific training.

The solution involves retraining the model with a targeted dataset specific to the desired domain. Though smaller than the original pre-training data, it is highly relevant and improves the model's suitability for the task, a process known as **fine-tuning**.

This chapter explores various techniques employed for fine-tuning GenAI models. It also presents several examples that illustrate this process. These examples mark a shift from earlier chapters. While previous code samples used model APIs, this chapter focuses on local model deployment. This chapter also introduces the use of **graphic processing units** (**GPUs**), a critical component that GenAI developers need to understand and consider in their work.

Fine-tuning is used in various scenarios where a model needs to be customized for a specific purpose. This chapter will cover several such applications and detail the development of the HR Assistant, a GenAI application leveraging the fine-tuning techniques discussed earlier.

Structure

This chapter covers the following topics:

- Basics of fine-tuning
- Parameter efficient fine-tuning
- Low Rank Adaptation
- Using GPU on Colab
- Development of the HR Assistant

Objectives

By the end of this chapter, you will gain a solid understanding of the importance of fine-tuning in generative AI models. You will learn the fundamentals of fine-tuning and how to apply techniques such as **Low Rank Adaptation** (**LoRA**) and **Quantized LoRA** (**Q-LoRA**), selecting the appropriate method based on the specific requirements of a given problem. These techniques allow you to efficiently adapt a **large language model** (**LLM**) to new tasks while reducing the computational cost typically associated with full model retraining. In addition, you will explore the step-by-step development of the HR Assistant, a practical GenAI application that demonstrates the real-world impact of fine-tuning. The HR Assistant leverages the power of a fine-tuned LLM to perform domain-specific tasks with improved accuracy and relevance. Through this example, you will gain hands-on insights into designing, training, and deploying fine-tuned models, equipping you to create specialized AI solutions in your own projects.

Basics of fine-tuning

The most crucial step in deploying a GenAI model for an industrial application is ensuring that it is appropriately adapted to the specific task. *Chapter 4, Prompt Engineering,* illustrated how prompting techniques can influence and adjust model behavior. *Chapter 6, Introduction to Retrieval-augmented Generation,* will introduce **retrieval-augmented generation** (**RAG**), another approach used to guide models toward task-specific outputs. However, both methods have inherent limitations. Fine-tuning offers a more robust and effective strategy for aligning pre-trained models with the intended application.

Need for fine-tuning

Pre-trained models require additional training because their performance may fall short when applied to a specific task. This underperformance can generally be attributed to the following two main factors:

- **Insufficient task capability**: GenAI models are generally pre-trained on basic tasks such as sentence completion or identifying hidden words. While this forms a strong foundation, it may not sufficiently equip the model to meet the specific demands of a particular application. The following are some examples where the model's capabilities may prove inadequate:
    - o **Classification**: Certain tasks involve categorizing input data, such as text, images, or audio, into predefined classes. Pre-trained models often struggle with classification when the data is domain-specific. For example, a model that has not been trained on manufacturing data may be unable to accurately classify images of products to detect defects.

  - **Reasoning**: Numerous reasoning tasks involve the application of domain-specific logic and rules. Pre-trained models generally lack familiarity with such customized reasoning frameworks and may therefore produce inaccurate or inconsistent results in these scenarios.
  - **Instructions**: As discussed in *Chapter 3, GenAI in Industry*, GenAI models are capable of following instructions. However, when the instructions become highly specific to a particular application, pre-trained models often struggle to comply accurately. For instance, instructions to modify generated code in a precise manner may not be properly executed by the model without further adaptation.

- **Domain knowledge**: GenAI applications often rely on the model's ability to access and apply relevant knowledge. In addition to general knowledge, these applications typically require domain-specific information. Consider, for example, a chatbot designed to assist customers with inquiries about a company's products. For such an application to function effectively, the underlying model must have comprehensive knowledge of the product offerings.

  There are two main reasons why pre-trained models may not possess the necessary knowledge for a specific application:

  - **Incomplete coverage in training datasets**: Pre-trained models are developed using publicly available datasets. These datasets do not, and should not, include proprietary or internal information from organizations. Furthermore, even within public data sources, the distribution of knowledge is often uneven. For instance, a model may have sufficient data on legal cases from the United States but limited or no information on cases from a smaller African nation.
  - **Knowledge cutoff in training data**: Even when certain information is included in the training data, it is limited to a specific point in time. This means there is always a cutoff date beyond which the model has no awareness of new developments. Continuing with the legal example, the model may have access to all cases up to a particular date but will lack knowledge of any cases decided afterward.

Concept of fine-tuning

Fine-tuning involves applying additional training to a pre-trained model in order to address the limitations outlined previously. This process differs from the original training phases the model undergoes prior to release. As explained in *Chapter 1, Introduction to Transformer Models*, GenAI models typically go through three main stages of training, which are as follows:

- **Base training**: Conducted on a massive dataset using self-supervised learning, this phase helps the model develop foundational capabilities and general knowledge.
- **Supervised fine-tuning (SFT)**: Performed on a smaller, curated dataset, this stage enhances the model's ability to follow instructions more accurately.

- **Reinforcement learning with human feedback (RLHF)**: This phase refines the model's outputs by aligning them more closely with human preferences, ensuring that responses are more appropriate and useful in real-world interactions.

The combined outcome of these training phases is the adjustment of the model's parameters, that is, the weights of its neural networks, enhancing its capabilities and expanding its knowledge.

Fine-tuning is carried out after the model has been released, with the primary goal of enhancing specific capabilities and knowledge required for a particular application. To achieve this, the training dataset is selected with care, ensuring it contains sufficient examples for the model to learn the relevant aspects effectively. The training process typically follows a supervised learning approach, similar to the SFT phase used during the model's initial development.

As with any form of training, fine-tuning modifies the model's parameters. As a result, the fine-tuned model becomes a derivative of the original and must be maintained as a separate version to preserve its distinct configuration and purpose.

Process of fine-tuning

The effectiveness of fine-tuning largely depends on the quality of the training data and the efficiency of the training process itself. Both aspects involve several critical factors that must be carefully managed to ensure successful outcomes.

Creating a training dataset

The training dataset is compiled from data gathered from a variety of sources, both internal and external to the organization. As it is used for supervised training, the dataset is structured into two distinct components, which are as follows:

- **Input**: The data submitted to the model during training.
- **Output**: The corresponding response that the model is expected to generate.

In the context of GenAI models, the input is referred to as the **prompt**, and the output as the **response**. Accordingly, the training dataset consists of a collection of prompt–response pairs. It must be kept in mind that both the input and output can contain various types of data such as text, images and audio.

The most important characteristic of a fine-tuning dataset is its alignment with the specific objective of the training. The samples included must directly support the intended improvement in the model's performance. For example, when fine-tuning a model for text classification, the dataset should meet the following criteria:

- The response in each sample should clearly represent the classification of the input text.

- All target classes should be adequately and evenly represented to avoid bias.
- The input texts should be drawn from a wide range of contexts and scenarios to ensure generalizability.
- The prompts should reflect diverse user instructions and preferences.

Training the model

The supervised training method used in fine-tuning adjusts the model's parameters to match the examples provided in the training dataset. This process is executed using software libraries that offer robust model training capabilities. The following aspects are critical to the effectiveness of the fine-tuning process:

- **Parameter strategy**: The model can be fine-tuned either fully or partially. Training all parameters of the model is computationally intensive and costly and is therefore seldom practiced. Instead, fine-tuning is often limited to smaller, specific parts of the model. These approaches, known as parameter-efficient fine-tuning methods, aim to reduce resource usage while still achieving meaningful improvements in performance.
- **Loss function used**: The loss function is central to guiding the model's learning during fine-tuning. It must be carefully chosen to reflect the specific task the model is expected to master. For instance, while cross-entropy loss is well-suited for classification tasks, tasks such as translation may benefit more from a loss function like cosine similarity.
- **Optimization method**: The loss computed by the loss function is used to update the model parameters through an optimization method. Optimization is the process of identifying the parameter values that minimize the loss across the training dataset. Most modern optimization techniques are variations of the gradient descent algorithm. Choosing an appropriate optimization method is crucial, as it directly influences the efficiency of the training process and how quickly it converges to a solution.
- **Learning parameters**: Training algorithms include several hyperparameters, such as learning rate, regularization strength, and weight decay, that can be tuned to enhance the efficiency and effectiveness of the training process.
- **Overfitting**: Fine-tuning often involves small, task specific datasets and large models, which increases the risk of overfitting. To mitigate this risk, it is important to closely monitor the model's performance on a validation set after each training cycle.

Challenges in fine-tuning

Fine-tuning pre-trained models introduces a set of challenges that require careful attention from a GenAI developer. The following are some of the key challenges:

- **Catastrophic forgetting**: One of the challenges associated with fine-tuning is the risk of the model losing some of its original capabilities, a phenomenon known as catastrophic forgetting. This occurs when the model becomes overly specialized in the new task at the expense of its general-purpose knowledge. To mitigate this issue, fine-tuning is often conducted in multiple phases, with only a subset of parameters being updated in each phase. Additionally, careful adjustment of training parameters, such as the learning rate, can help preserve the model's foundational abilities while still allowing it to learn the new task effectively.

- **Computational cost**: Although fine-tuning uses significantly smaller datasets compared to the original pre-training process, it still demands substantial computational resources. Parameter-efficient fine-tuning techniques can help reduce this cost by limiting the number of parameters that are updated.
- **Frequent updates**: To ensure the model remains aligned with the latest knowledge and evolving requirements, fine-tuned models often need to be updated regularly. This creates an ongoing maintenance activity within the organization, requiring dedicated processes and infrastructure to support continuous improvement.

Parameter efficient fine-tuning

As discussed in the previous section, fine-tuning can involve modifying all parameters of the model. However, this full-parameter approach introduces several challenges, which are as follows:

- **Overfitting**: When a large neural network is trained on a small dataset, there is a risk that it will simply memorize the specific examples rather than learn the underlying patterns. This phenomenon, known as overfitting, leads to poor generalization, meaning that the model performs well on the training data but fails to deliver accurate results on new, unseen inputs.
- **Computational cost and training time**: Fine-tuning relies on supervised learning, where the model's parameters are updated based on the loss computed over batches of training samples. This process is repeated over many iterations, known as steps. The total number of computations involved in fine-tuning can be estimated using the following formula:

  $$Calculations = Number\ of\ parameters \times Number\ of\ batches \times Number\ of\ steps$$

  The performance of a computing device is typically measured in **floating point operations per second** (**FLOPS**). For example, the NVIDIA A100 GPU is capable of performing up to 80 teraflops, or 80 trillion floating point operations per second. Each parameter update involves a certain number of floating point operations, and the total computational workload can be divided by the GPU's capacity to estimate the number of GPU hours required.

  As the number of model parameters increases, the required GPU time grows significantly. For very large models, those exceeding 40 billion parameters, fine-tuning may demand weeks or even months of GPU time, depending on the scale of the dataset and the training setup.

- **Catastrophic forgetting**: During fine-tuning, model parameters are updated based on a new dataset that is typically narrower in scope. In the process of optimizing for these new samples, the training algorithm may inadvertently overwrite earlier optimizations made during pre-training. This disruption of the original network layers can lead to a significant decline in the model's performance on general or previously well-handled tasks.

For the aforementioned reasons, GenAI researchers began to prefer approaches that do not involve modifying the entire model. Techniques that avoid training all parameters came to be known as **parameter-efficient fine-tuning** (**PEFT**).

The following are the common approaches that fall under PEFT:

- **Adding parameters**: Instead of altering the existing parameters, which can result in the issues previously described, this approach introduces additional parameters to the model. These new parameters are trained using the fine-tuning dataset. Two well-known techniques that follow this approach are as follows:
    - o **Adapter** modules, which insert a small network between two layers of the transformer.
    - o **Low Rank Adaptation** (**LoRA**), which adds parameters to the **Query** (**Q**), **Key** (**K**), and **Value** (**V**) matrices.
- **Learning embeddings**: Before being processed by the model, the input prompt is converted into embeddings. A category of fine-tuning techniques focuses on modifying these embeddings. Such modifications help the model perform more effectively on specific tasks. Several techniques fall into this category. Two examples are as follows:
    - o **Prompt tuning**: This involves learning a set of embeddings that are appended to the prompt. This prefix guides the model's behavior in the intended direction.
    - o **Prefix tuning**: The model learns specific vectors that influence the attention mechanism. These prefix vectors modify the key and value vectors involved in attention calculations. In this regard, the technique resembles LoRA, although the modification occurs in the vectors rather than in the model parameters.

Low Rank Adaptation

LoRA is an example of the parameter-adding approach within the PEFT framework. Instead of modifying the original model parameters, LoRA introduces a small set of trainable parameters into each transformer layer. These added parameters are specifically trained using the fine-tuning dataset and are designed to influence the model's attention mechanism.

As outlined in *Chapter 1, Introduction to Transformer Models,* the attention mechanism within transformer architectures relies on three matrices, i.e., **K**, **Q**, and **V**. These matrices interact with the input tokens to compute contextual representations, which are then passed from one transformer layer to the next. Each transformer layer maintains its own distinct set of K, Q, and V matrices, and their values are learned during the pre-training phase.

The dimensions of a matrix, defined by its number of rows and columns, are commonly referred to as its **rank**. In the context of transformer models, the K, Q, and V matrices tend to be high-rank, meaning they consist of a large number of parameters.

LoRA technique explained

Consider the following example:

```
Dimensions of K: 768 x 768
Parameters in K: 0.6 million (approx.)
Parameters in one layer, which contains KQV: 3 x 0.6 = 1.8 million
Assume 6 layers in the transformer. Total parameters: 6 x 1.8: 10.8 million
```

As previously discussed, retraining such a large number of parameters poses significant challenges.

While using the LoRA technique, one or more of the KQV matrices are added to two new low-rank matrices. Imagine that for the K matrix described previously, the following new matrices are created:

Matrix A with rank: 768 x 8

Matrix B with rank: 8 x 768

Observe that if we multiply A and B, we will get a matrix with rank 768 x 768. The number of parameters in A and B is as follows:

```
Parameters in A: 768 x 8 = 6144
Parameters in B: 8 x 768 = 6144
Total parameters: 12,288
```

Thus, we can create a 768 x 768 matrix by multiplying two low-rank matrices, with only 12,288 parameters as compared to the original 0.6 million.

The new matrices are combined with the K matrix at the time of attention calculation in the following way:

```
K-new = K + Alpha x AB
```

As the matrix AB has rank 768 x 768, the addition will work. The factor **`Alpha`** determines the extent of effect that the new parameters will have on the attention calculations.

This is the intuition behind how LoRA fine-tuning works. The following is an example of fine-tuning the Llama 2 7B model with r = 8 and Alpha = 16:

Specification	Value
Target matrices	Q, V
Dimensions of Q, V	4096 x 4096
LoRA rank (r)	8
Alpha	16
Transformer layers	32
Total model parameters	6.74 billion
LoRA parameters	4.19 million
Percentage of LoRA parameters to total	0.062%

Table 5.1: *Details of fine-tuning Llama 2 7B using LoRA*

Using LoRA to fine-tune DistilBERT

DistilBERT is a compact language model developed by Hugging Face. Its relatively small size allows it to fit within the memory constraints of most standard computing devices, making it a practical choice for example implementations. In the following example, the **distilbert-base-uncased** variant is used, which contains approximately 67 million parameters. This variant offers a good balance between performance and resource efficiency.

Google Colab is used as the coding environment. The first part of the following code sets up the configuration required for fine-tuning, ensuring that the model and associated components are properly initialized before training begins:

```
!pip install transformers
!pip install peft
from transformers import AutoModelForSequenceClassification, AutoTokenizer
from peft import get_peft_model, LoraConfig, TaskType

# Load the distilbert-base-uncased model
model_name = "distilbert-base-uncased"
model = AutoModelForSequenceClassification.from_pretrained(model_name,  num_
labels=2)

# Define LoRA configuration
lora_config = LoraConfig(
    task_type=TaskType.SEQ_CLS,
```

```
    r=8,                                    # Low-rank dimension
    lora_alpha=16,                          # Scaling factor
    lora_dropout=0.05,                      # Dropout before LoRA layers
    target_modules=["q_lin", "v_lin"],      # target matrices
    inference_mode=False
)
# Apply LoRA
model = get_peft_model(model, lora_config)
# Show number of trainable parameters
model.print_trainable_parameters()
```

The output is as follows:

```
trainable params: 739,586 || all params: 67,694,596 || trainable%: 1.0925
```

Only about 1% of the total model parameters are being trained. It must be remembered that these parameters will be added to the model, but since the percentage is quite small, it does not increase the model size appreciably.

The next section of the code demonstrates the actual fine-tuning process. The initial step involves loading an appropriate dataset. In this example, the widely recognized **AG News** dataset is used. It comprises 120,000 samples of news articles, with each sample categorized into one of four predefined classes:

Class name	Class label
World	1
Sport	2
Business	3
Sci/Tech	4

Table 5.2: *Classes in the agnews dataset*

The following code loads the dataset:

```
# Load dataset (AG News - 4 class text classification)
dataset = load_dataset("ag_news")

# Preprocess data
tokenizer = AutoTokenizer.from_pretrained(model_name)

def tokenize(example):
      return tokenizer(example["text"], truncation=True, padding="max_length",
      max_length=128)
```

```
encoded_dataset = dataset.map(tokenize, batched=True)
encoded_dataset = encoded_dataset.rename_column("label", "labels")
encoded_dataset.set_format("torch", columns=["input_ids", "attention_mask",
"labels"])
```

The preceding code performs several important steps to prepare the AG News dataset for fine-tuning. It begins by loading the dataset from Hugging Face and then applies tokenization. Tokenization is the process of converting raw text into embeddings, numerical representations that the model can understand and process.

In addition, the code handles formatting tasks required by the training function. These include preparing the dataset structure, organizing the input and output fields, and ensuring compatibility with the model and training utilities.

Following this preparation, the training configuration is defined. One of the first configurations is setting up the accuracy metric, which serves as a measure of how well the model is performing during and after training, shown as follows:

```
# Define metrics
accuracy = evaluate.load("accuracy")
def compute_metrics(eval_pred):
    logits, labels = eval_pred
    predictions = torch.argmax(torch.tensor(logits), dim=-1)
    return accuracy.compute(predictions=predictions, references=labels)
```

The **compute_metrics** function is responsible for evaluating the model's performance by comparing its predictions with the true labels provided in the dataset. It receives the predicted class labels from the model and matches them against the ground truth to calculate performance metrics. Specifically, the **accuracy.compute** function is used to determine how many predictions are correct relative to the total number of predictions made, thus yielding the accuracy score.

After defining this evaluation logic, the actual training configuration is established as follows:

```
# Training args
training_args = TrainingArguments(
    output_dir="./lora-distilbert-classifynews",
    per_device_train_batch_size=16,
    per_device_eval_batch_size=16,
    eval_strategy="epoch",
    save_strategy="epoch",
    num_train_epochs=3,
```

```
    learning_rate=2e-4,
    logging_dir="./logs",
    load_best_model_at_end=True,
    report_to="none"
)

# Trainer
trainer = Trainer(
    model=model,
    args=training_args,
    train_dataset=encoded_dataset["train"].shuffle(seed=42).
select(range(20000)),  # only a part of the dataset
    eval_dataset=encoded_dataset["test"].select(range(2000)),
    compute_metrics=compute_metrics,
)
```

The first line sets the various training parameters. The discussion of parameters is very important for understanding the training of models. The following are the most important ones:

- **Batch**: A set of training examples that is given to the model at one time. The GPU should have the capacity to hold the samples.
- **Epoch**: Once all the training examples are processed, an epoch is said to be completed. The parameter calculation is done at the end of each epoch.
- **Learning rate**: This parameter is used by the optimizer in calculating the model parameters. It has to be carefully decided to get the best training results.

Based on the aforementioned parameters, the LoRA training configuration done in the code can be described as follows:

- 3 epoch, with a batch size of 16 samples for training as well as evaluation.
- Evaluation and saving strategy is to be performed after each epoch.
- A learning rate of 0.0002, which is a typical learning rate for LoRA.
- Additional parameters to instruct the training function to save the best model at the end and not use any external logging tool.

Finally, the code invokes the training and the saving of the model as follows:

```
# Train
trainer.train()

# Save model
model.save_pretrained("./lora-distilbert-classifynews")
```

The training should take a few hours on the standard Colab runtime and should reach an accuracy of around 90%.

Using GPU on Colab

The development work described in this chapter is carried out on Google Colab. This includes both the fine-tuning process and the execution of a large language model, tasks that require GPU support.

Google Colab provides different service tiers. The free tier includes access to a GPU with 16 GB of RAM, which is adequate for training and running smaller models (up to approximately 4 billion parameters). However, larger models demand greater GPU memory, which is available through Colab's paid plans that offer more powerful GPUs, such as the NVIDIA A100.

Note: **All examples presented in this chapter are selected to be compatible with the free tier of Colab. Readers interested in experimenting with larger models can do so by making appropriate modifications to the code and utilizing one of the paid tiers.**

Development of the HR Assistant

The **human resources** (**HR**) department is essential for attracting top talent, fostering employee engagement, and ensuring smooth organizational operations. This section introduces a GenAI-based **HR Assistant** (**HRA**) designed to enhance the efficiency and effectiveness of these functions. By streamlining HR processes, HRA can contribute to improved employee satisfaction, better talent management, and operational agility. The features offered by HRA are described in the following section.

Features of the HRA

A GenAI-based solution can offer significant support to the HR team across a variety of functions. While the primary focus of this chapter is on the fine-tuning technique, outlining the potential use cases helps establish the broader relevance of the approach. The following sections will then illustrate how fine-tuning can be applied to tailor a model for a particular application within the HR domain.

Talent acquisition

Finding and recruiting the right people is a key responsibility of the HR team. Since people are the most valuable assets of any organization, effective talent acquisition directly supports the success of all other departments. This process involves understanding team requirements, drafting accurate job descriptions, sourcing potential candidates, and selecting the most suitable ones.

A major challenge in talent acquisition lies in accurately matching candidate skills with job requirements. While factors like experience and qualifications can be objectively compared, skills are often described in varied and inconsistent ways, making them harder to assess. The HRA addresses this challenge by processing both resumes and job descriptions to identify and align relevant skills more effectively.

Performance management

Managing employee performance is a vital function of the HR team, as it directly influences individual growth, team productivity, and organizational success. Performance management involves setting clear expectations, tracking progress, giving feedback, and facilitating employee development.

One of the main challenges in performance management is ensuring consistency and objectivity across roles and teams. Feedback can often be subjective, and it may be difficult to track goals or identify patterns over time. The HRA supports this process by analyzing performance data, summarizing feedback, and helping managers provide constructive and balanced evaluations. This leads to more transparent, data-driven performance assessments and supports continuous improvement.

Learning and development

Most organizations have specific processes that require specialized skills. Employees need to be trained in these areas to perform their roles effectively. For example, a machine operator must be trained on the exact machines used on the company's shopfloor. Training can cover a wide range of topics, including domain knowledge, internal processes, equipment handling, product features, and more. While **learning and development** (**L&D**) is a distinct function, it typically operates within the HR team.

Creating and maintaining high-quality training material is a major challenge for HR. The content must be regularly updated to stay aligned with current processes and technologies. The HRA supports the team by automatically generating training material from existing documents, manuals, or guidelines. It can also create assessments to evaluate the understanding of course content, making the training process more efficient and scalable.

Description of the solution

The HRA is a web-based application accessible through a standard browser. It provides an intuitive user interface that enables the HR team to access and utilize its various capabilities with ease. The main features of HRA are divided into usable functions.

The features are as follows:

- Talent acquisition
- Performance measurement
- Learning and development

The important functions in each feature are as follows:

- Talent acquisition:
  - o Write job description
  - o Match skills
- Performance management:
  - o Summarise feedback
- Learning and development:
  - o Create training course

The desired function will be accessed by the user through a suitable interface. Upon providing the required input, the system will generate an appropriate output in text format. This output can then be copied and utilized for further processing or integrated into other workflows as needed.

Users

As outlined earlier, the users of the HRA consist of members of the HR team. They are knowledge workers with experience in managing employee-related information and processes. Proficient in using digital tools on both desktop and mobile platforms, they are familiar with handling documents, spreadsheets, and internal portals. HR professionals are also comfortable working with web applications and navigating systems that support recruitment, performance management, and employee development.

User story

The following discussion focuses exclusively on a user story that illustrates the application of fine-tuning in GenAI, specifically, matching resumes with job descriptions.

Bob, a member of the HR team, receives a job description (JD) from the software development department. He downloads a set of resumes that appear to align with the required experience and qualifications. To identify the most suitable candidates, Bob uses the Match Skills function within the HRA application. He submits both the JD and each resume as input. The HRA analyzes the content and returns a list of matching skills, along with the skills mentioned in the JD that are not found in the resume. Bob repeats this process for all shortlisted resumes and selects the ones with the highest number of relevant skill matches.

Architecture

The HRA system consists of the following four main components, each playing a distinct role in enabling skill-based resume matching using fine-tuned GenAI:

- **GenAI model**: At the core of the HRA is a GenAI model fine-tuned specifically to extract relevant skills from both resumes and JDs. A wide range of open-source models can be adapted for this purpose. For practical reasons, such as the ability to fine-tune and run within a Google Colab environment, the instruction-tuned variant of the T5 model, Flan-T5, is selected. The fine-tuning technique used is **Quantized Low Rank Adaptation** (**Q-LoRA**), which enables efficient training with reduced memory requirements.
- **Prompting function (PF) module**: This module contains the logic for prompting the model to extract skills. It is implemented as a set of Python functions that interact with the model. Additionally, this module handles the comparison between the skill sets extracted from the resume and the JD to identify matches and gaps.
- **Configurations**: This component is inherited from *Chapter 4, Prompt Engineering*. It contains reusable configurations related to model prompts, API parameters, and environment setup. Since it remains unchanged, its implementation is not repeated in this chapter.
- **User interface (UI)**: The user interface is built upon the UI design introduced in *Chapter 4, Prompt Engineering,* with necessary modifications to accommodate the new Match Skills function. These changes are relatively minor and will be outlined briefly.

Development

The development will happen in two phases.

1. Fine-tuning the model.
2. Development of PF and UI modules. The configuration module used is from *Chapter 4, Prompt Engineering*.

Fine-tuning the model

The **Match Skills** function relies on a model capable of identifying skills mentioned in both the resume and the JD. Although a pre-trained model can accomplish this task, the extracted skills may lack consistency in terminology. Skills are often described in various ways, which can lead to instances where the same skill appears in both documents but is recognized under different names. To address this issue, an LLM trained on a carefully curated dataset is employed to ensure accurate and standardized skill extraction.

As noted previously, the Flan-T5-large model is utilized for this task. Flan-T5 models are part of the T5 family developed by *Google* and are based on the transformer architecture, incorporating both an encoder and a decoder. This design makes them well-suited for text generation tasks. The prefix *Flan* signifies that these models have been fine-tuned to follow instructions effectively. The large variant comprises approximately 770 million parameters and can be efficiently run on the GPU provided in the free tier of Google Colab.

The method used for fine-tuning is a variant of LoRA called Q-LoRA.

About Q-LoRA

Q-LoRA combines two techniques to enhance the efficiency of training and deploying large language models:

- **Quantization**, which reduces the computational resources required for training and hosting by compressing the model's parameters.
- **LoRA**, which enables fine-tuning by adjusting only a limited number of additional parameters.

To illustrate this approach, consider the Llama 2 7B model discussed earlier in the chapter. In its default configuration, the model uses FP16 precision, where each parameter occupies 2 bytes. Based on this, the model requires approximately 13 GB of storage. Through quantization, each parameter is reduced to 4 bits, lowering the storage requirement to around 3.5 GB. It should be noted that the actual size of 4-bit quantized models is slightly larger due to the inclusion of additional metadata generated during the quantization process.

When LoRA is applied to a quantized model, the original parameters remain in their 4-bit format and are not modified during fine-tuning. Instead, LoRA introduces a small number of additional parameters, which are stored at 16-bit precision. As shown in *Table 5.1*, there are only 4.2 million LoRA parameters, making the additional memory footprint minimal.

The primary benefit of Q-LoRA lies in its reduced GPU memory requirements during fine-tuning, which is particularly advantageous when using platforms such as the free tier of Google Colab.

The HRA utilizes the Flan-T5-large model, which contains 770 million parameters at full precision. Compared to the Llama 2 7B model, this represents a significantly smaller scale. When quantized to 4-bit precision, the model's size is expected to be approximately 0.5 GB. This compact size not only facilitates faster fine-tuning but also makes it more efficient to host, particularly in resource-constrained environments.

The dataset

Preparing the training dataset is a crucial step prior to fine-tuning. For the skill matching task, the dataset should consist of the following two key components:

- Text extracted from resumes or job descriptions
- The corresponding standardized skill

This dataset can be created either manually or with the assistance of another model. In the manual approach, a data engineer extracts relevant segments of text from existing resumes and job descriptions, then assigns the appropriate skill label to each segment. It is essential that the skills are standardized, meaning each skill must be represented by a consistent, unique name, even if it appears in different forms across various documents.

An example dataset entry (in json format) will look like the following:

```
{
  "input": "Extract the skills from this resume:\n\nDesigned and deployed scalable backend systems, optimized database queries, and ensured data consistency across services.",
  "output": "SQL, Data Engineering"
}
```

The dataset created for this demonstration includes approximately 200 entries. In a real-world scenario, however, the dataset should include at least one example for each skill to ensure comprehensive coverage. Such a dataset would typically consist of several thousand rows.

The actual Q-LoRA fine-tuning utilizes the **transformer**, **peft**, and **bitsandbytes** packages from Hugging Face. The first part of the code imports the necessary packages and loads the model in 4-bit quantization mode, shown as follows:

```
from transformers import AutoTokenizer, AutoModelForSeq2SeqLM,
TrainingArguments, Trainer, DataCollatorForSeq2Seq, BitsAndBytesConfig
from datasets import Dataset
from peft import get_peft_config, get_peft_model, LoraConfig, TaskType
import torch
import bitsandbytes as bnb


# Load tokenizer and quantized model
model_name = "google/flan-t5-large"
tokenizer = AutoTokenizer.from_pretrained(model_name)


bnb_config = BitsAndBytesConfig(
```

```
    load_in_4bit=True,
    bnb_4bit_use_double_quant=True,
    bnb_4bit_quant_type="nf4",
    bnb_4bit_compute_dtype=torch.bfloat16
)
model = AutoModelForSeq2SeqLM.from_pretrained(
    model_name,
    device_map="auto",
    quantization_config=bnb_config
)
```

The next part of the code deals with setting up the LoRA training configuration, demonstrated as follows:

```
# LoRA config
lora_config = LoraConfig(
    r=8,
    lora_alpha=32,
    target_modules=["q", "v"],
    lora_dropout=0.1,
    bias="none",
    task_type=TaskType.SEQ_2_SEQ_LM
)
model = get_peft_model(model, lora_config)
```

The dataset is then loaded and preprocessed to make it suitable for the trainer function. The code assumes that the dataset is in JSON format with **text** and **skills** as the dictionary keys. In case the dataset is a csv, appropriate changes need to be made, shown as follows:

```
#Load the dataset. The file path is stored in config
dataset = Dataset.from_dict(config.get("SkillsDatset"))

# Preprocess
def preprocess(example):
    input_text = example["text"]
    target_text = example["skills"]
    model_input = tokenizer(input_text, truncation=True, padding="max_length",
max_length=256)
```

```
    with tokenizer.as_target_tokenizer():
        labels = tokenizer(target_text, truncation=True, padding="max_length",
max_length=64)
    model_input["labels"] = labels["input_ids"]
    return model_input

tokenized_dataset = dataset.map(preprocess)
```

Once the tokenized dataset is available, the training parameters are set. Here, the batch size is set as 2 to keep the memory requirements under control. Note the parameter **`fp16=True`**, which indicates that the LoRA parameters are kept in 16 bits, unlike the model parameters, shown as follows:

```
# Training Parameters
training_args = TrainingArguments(
    output_dir="./q_lora-flan-t5-extract-skills",
    per_device_train_batch_size=2,
    num_train_epochs=3,
    learning_rate=2e-4,
    logging_dir="./logs",
    evaluation_strategy="epoch",
    save_strategy="epoch",
    report_to="none",
    fp16=True
)

data_collator = DataCollatorForSeq2Seq(tokenizer, model=model)

trainer = Trainer(
    model=model,
    args=training_args,
    train_dataset=tokenized_dataset,
    tokenizer=tokenizer,
    data_collator=data_collator
)
```

The final part is the actual training, which is demonstrated as follows:

```
# Train
trainer.train()
```

To evaluate the model, a mechanism similar to the one described in the section on **LoRA** can be used. This is left as an exercise to the reader.

Once the training is over, the fine-tuned model for the HRA is available. The PF module prompts this module to extract skills.

Development of the PF module

The PF module is designed to utilize the fine-tuned model to extract skills from resumes and job descriptions. In the current demonstration project, this module accepts a block of text as input and returns a list of skills identified within that text. The user interface enables users to submit text and view the extracted skills.

In a more advanced version of the system, the PF module could be extended to accept both the resume and the job description, subsequently identifying and presenting the matched and unmatched skills. Implementing this enhancement is suggested as an exercise for the reader.

The following code demonstrates how the fine-tuned model can be employed to extract skills from a given input. The initial section of the code loads the model from a specified path, which is obtained from the configuration settings, shown as follows:

```
import torch
import bitsandbytes
from transformers import AutoTokenizer, AutoModelForSeq2SeqLM

# Load fine-tuned model from config
model_name = Config.get("HRA_Model")
tokenizer = AutoTokenizer.from_pretrained(model_name)

model = AutoModelForSeq2SeqLM.from_pretrained(
    model_name,
    device_map="auto",
    quantization_config={
        "load_in_4bit": True,
        "bnb_4bit_quant_type": "nf4",
        "bnb_4bit_use_double_quant": True,
        "bnb_4bit_compute_dtype": torch.bfloat16
    }
)
```

The subsequent section defines the function that will be used by the UI module to extract skills from the provided text. Notably, the prompt includes the instruction *Extract skills*, which the model is able to interpret effectively as a result of the fine-tuning process. This clear instruction ensures that the model focuses on identifying and returning relevant skills from the input text, shown as follows:

```
# Function to extract skills
def HRA_Extract_Skills(text: str):
    prompt = f"Extract skills: {text}"
    inputs = tokenizer(prompt, return_tensors="pt", truncation=True,
padding=True).to(model.device)

    with torch.no_grad():
        output = model.generate(
            input_ids=inputs["input_ids"],
            attention_mask=inputs["attention_mask"],
            max_new_tokens=64,
            do_sample=False
        )
    return tokenizer.decode(output[0], skip_special_tokens=True)
```

Development of the UI module

The use of Streamlit for user interaction was outlined in *Chapter 4, Prompt Engineering*. The process involved the following three steps:

1. Creating a Python application file and uploading it to Colab.
2. Running Streamlit on Colab using the application file as the source.
3. Using ngrok to expose the web application through a public URL.

For the HRA application, the second and third steps remain unchanged. The modification lies in the Python application file, which has been updated to incorporate features specific to the HRA module. The following code presents the contents of the `HRA_App.py` file, which delivers the **Match Skills** functionality as part of the Talent Acquisition feature:

```
import streamlit as st


st.set_page_config(page_title="HR Assistant", layout="wide")
st.sidebar.title("Features")
menu_main = st.sidebar.radio("Select Feature", ["Talent"])
submenu = None
```

```
if menu_main == "Talent":
    submenu = st.sidebar.radio("Select Action", ["Match Skills"])
st.title("Welcome to the Application")
if submenu:
    st.subheader(f"{submenu} Section")
    st.write(f"This is the {submenu.lower()} section.")
    if submenu == "Match Skills":
        resume_text = st.text_input("Resume")
        jd_text = st.text_input("JD")

        if st.button("Get Skills"):
            st.write("Extracting skills...")

            resume_skills = HRA_Talent_Extract_Skills(resume_text)
            jd_skills = HRA_Talent_Extract_Skills(jd_text)

            st.write("Skills mentioned in the resume")
            st.write(resume_skills)

            st.write("Skills mentioned in the JD")
            st.write(jd_skills)
```

Using the HRA

The HR team accesses the HRA by navigating to the **Talent | Match Skills** menu. They input the text copied from the resume and the job description, then click the **Get Skills** button. After a short processing period, the standardized skills extracted from both sources are displayed. This enables the team to assess the candidate's alignment with the job requirements. The user interface closely resembles the one illustrated in *Chapter 4, Prompt Engineering*, during the discussion of the MA.

Conclusion

Pre-trained GenAI models must be adapted to meet the specific requirements of individual use cases. One of the most effective methods for achieving this adaptation is fine-tuning. This process involves training the pre-trained model using carefully selected data. Rather than re-training the entire model, which may compromise its original capabilities, it is often more effective to fine-tune only specific parts. Common techniques for fine-tuning include adapters, LoRA, and prompt fine-tuning.

Fine-tuning is particularly useful for aligning a model with organization-specific data. In the development of the HRA, this approach was used to standardize skill extraction by fine-tuning the Flan-T5-large model with a curated skills dataset.

However, in scenarios where the source data changes frequently, fine-tuning becomes less practical. In such cases, a method known as RAG offers a more suitable alternative. The next chapter provides a detailed exploration of RAG.

CHAPTER 6
Enhancing GenAI with RAG

Introduction

When generative AI models are used in complex, real-world applications, they often need adaptation to perform effectively. *Chapter 5, Fine-tuning GenAI Models*, showed how fine-tuning helps align models with specific use cases. This process becomes necessary when a model struggles to follow instructions or lacks domain expertise. Fine-tuning enhances instruction-following and can, to a limited degree, extend a model's knowledge, evident in the case of the HR Assistant. However, while it is a valuable tool for improving performance, fine-tuning has its limitations, especially when it comes to significantly updating or expanding a model's underlying knowledge base.

Knowledge is inherently dynamic and subject to frequent changes. Continuously fine-tuning a model to keep its knowledge current is often impractical. A more efficient method for enriching a model's access to updated information is **retrieval-augmented generation** (**RAG**).

RAG may be considered an advancement of prompt engineering, as it facilitates the integration of relevant information directly into the prompt. This approach minimizes the model's dependence on its pre-existing internal knowledge.

RAG supports the application of an organization's internal data in a wide range of tasks involving generative AI. Its adaptability has led to widespread adoption in enterprise environments, with implementation observed across various industries such as manufacturing, logistics, chemicals, consulting, and law.

This chapter introduces the foundational concepts of RAG before examining its operational details. Langchain, a widely used framework for implementing RAG-based solutions, is also discussed. To demonstrate the practical potential of RAG, a contract intelligence system is developed in the chapter.

Structure

This chapter covers the following topics:

- Basics of RAG
- Components in detail

- Introduction to LangChain
- Applications of RAG
- Development of contract intelligence

Objectives

By the end of this chapter, you will have a solid understanding of the RAG technique for building GenAI applications. You will learn about the architecture of a typical RAG system and gain insight into its core components. You will also become familiar with LangChain, one of the most widely used frameworks for implementing RAG. Finally, you will explore the development of the **contract intelligence** (**CI**) system, an application that demonstrates the practical power of RAG in a real-world context.

Basics of RAG

The need for RAG arises from the limitation that models do not always possess the necessary knowledge to complete a given task. Consider the following question:

```
Who won yesterday's Arsenal-Livingpool match?
```

It is not possible for the model to answer this question accurately, as the training dataset could not have included information about a match that occurred only the day before. Some reasons for the lack of model knowledge are:

- **Training cut-off**: As illustrated in the previous example, model training data typically includes information only up to a specific date. In practice, this cut-off is often set well before the model is released, due to the time required for testing and deployment.
- **Private data**: Another limitation arises from the inaccessibility of private data. Organizational data, such as internal documents and databases, is often confidential and therefore cannot be included in the training datasets of generative AI models.
- **Data coverage**: When curating datasets for training, designers must make selective choices about which information to include. It is impractical to incorporate all publicly available data, particularly given the diversity of regions and languages worldwide. As a result, there is always a possibility that the model has not encountered the specific data needed for a particular task.

RAG tries to cover the knowledge limitation of GenAI models.

Intuition behind RAG

RAG leverages the ability of generative AI models to utilize context provided within the prompt. Consider the following prompt template:

```
Based on the information given in the ##Material section, answer the question
given in ##Query. Do not answer the question if the answer is not contained in
the material.

##Material:

##Query:
```

Most models are effective at following instructions embedded in the prompt. By inserting both the query and the relevant material into this template before submitting it to the model, the model can respond using the provided context rather than relying on its internal knowledge. This approach forms the core principle behind RAG.

Performing a task using the previously mentioned approach involves two clear steps:

1. Identifying the material required for the task.
2. Incorporating the material into the prompt.

While the second step is generally straightforward, the first step requires more detailed consideration.

Identifying the material

The concept of relevant material is most easily understood in the context of a **question-answer** (**QA**) task. In such cases, the challenge lies in locating the content that contains the answer to the given question. The following are a few examples that illustrate this scenario:

- **Question**: *The machine is giving an error 'Incorrect code'. What should I do?*

  Material. *Relevant pages from the machine manual that describe the mentioned error and its resolution.*

- **Question**: *What are the documents required for applying for a personal loan?*

  Material: *Documentation of the personal loan product of the bank.*

To identify the appropriate material, the underlying knowledge must be well organized and supported by an indexing mechanism that can guide the system. Additionally, there must be a method to assess whether a particular piece of information contains the answer to the given question. Identifying the right material thus involves two key activities:

1. Organizing knowledge in a systematic manner
2. Determining whether a specific segment of the knowledge contains the answer to the question

These activities will be examined in greater detail later in the chapter.

Incorporating the material in the prompt

A typical RAG prompt will have at least three sections:

- Instructions
- Material
- Query

Once the material is retrieved, it is copied into the material section. Incorporating the material into the prompt thus looks straightforward. However, certain considerations must be addressed carefully.

Generative AI models have a defined context length, which indicates the maximum number of tokens they can accept as input. It is important to ensure that the selected material does not cause the prompt to exceed this limit. Since different models have different context lengths, the prompt may need to be adjusted accordingly if a different model is used.

RAG architecture

The preceding sections outlined the two main components of the RAG architecture:

- A **retriever** component that identifies and retrieves relevant material from a knowledge store.
- A **prompt generator** that constructs the final prompt using the query and the retrieved material.

In addition to these, a complete RAG system also includes the generative AI model responsible for performing the task and the underlying knowledge store. The full schematic of this architecture is presented as follows:

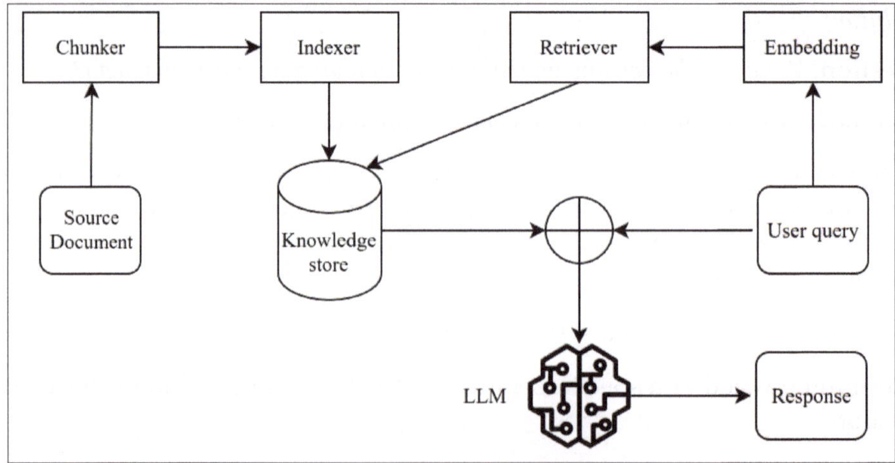

Figure 6.1: Architecture of the RAG system

The components of the RAG system are explained in detail in the following section.

Components in detail

The retriever is the most critical component of a RAG system. However, its effectiveness depends on the presence of a well-structured knowledge store. The next two sections examine these components in detail, along with the interaction between them.

Knowledge store

The knowledge store contains all the information that will contain the answers to the user queries. It also makes it possible for the retriever to match and retrieve the right information. This indicates that there are two types of objects in the knowledge store:

- **Data objects**: The data objects contain all the information. Examples of data objects are documents, presentations, spreadsheets, websites, images, and audio. The data store will be holding some objects physically, while some, such as websites, might be only linked to it.
- **Indexes**: The knowledge store includes various types of indexes that make it easy to search the store of objects.

Storing data objects

It is important to recognize that the primary role of data objects within an RAG system is to supply material for prompt construction. Therefore, these data objects must be suitable for that purpose. To ensure usability, different types of data objects require specific forms of processing before being stored:

- **Text files**: These include documents with primarily textual content, such as Microsoft Word files, web pages, and PDF documents. While the text in these files can be directly inserted into prompts, their size may exceed the context limits of generative AI models. Despite the increasing context lengths available, including large volumes of material in a prompt can lead to slower response times and diminished output quality. To address this, such files are divided into smaller units known as **chunks**. Various chunking strategies will be discussed in the following section.
- **Scanned text documents**: These resemble text files but consist of images containing embedded text, such as scanned legal contracts or invoices. These files must first undergo image-to-text conversion, commonly referred to as **Optical Character Recognition** (**OCR**), before chunking can be performed.
- **Data records**: Files such as Microsoft Excel spreadsheets and database tables contain structured rows of data. In addition to the data itself, the schema plays a vital role. These records must be transformed into a textual format that is suitable for processing by a generative AI model.

- **Hybrid content**: Documents such as Microsoft PowerPoint presentations often include a combination of text, images, diagrams, and other relevant content. These files require specialized parsing techniques to ensure that all meaningful context is captured and converted into usable chunks.
- **Audio and video**: Since prompts in RAG systems must be text-based, audio and video files must be transcribed using speech-to-text techniques, as outlined in *Chapter 2, The SOTA GenAI Models*. The resulting transcriptions can then be chunked and stored accordingly.

Chunking

As described in the previous section, chunking plays a crucial role in the object storage process within an RAG system. The choice of chunking strategy directly affects the quality of the retrieved material and, consequently, the overall effectiveness of the system. Several chunking strategies are commonly employed, each with its own strengths and limitations:

- **Fixed-length chunking**: In this approach, all chunks contain text of uniform length, measured in tokens or characters. For example, a strategy might involve dividing the text into chunks of 1,000 characters each. Although this method is simple to implement, it often separates related content across multiple chunks, potentially leading to incomplete information retrieval. This approach is typically used in demonstrations and prototype systems.
- **Sliding window chunking**: This strategy builds upon fixed-length chunking by allowing the chunks to overlap. Each chunk shares some content with the preceding and following chunks, thereby reducing the likelihood of breaking important contextual connections. While this improves continuity, it requires additional storage. It is particularly well-suited for conversational applications such as chatbots.
- **Sentence-level chunking**: In this method, each sentence is treated as an individual chunk. This strategy is effective in applications requiring precise citation, where the system must reference the exact source of the retrieved information. Document-based information retrieval tasks often benefit from this approach.
- **Semantic chunking**: This technique groups content based on meaning rather than structure or size. Chunks in this case may correspond to coherent sections of a document or logically related information. Although this method is more complex to implement and must be tailored to the document type, it is especially useful in applications involving comparison, such as analyzing different versions of a document.

Each of these strategies has its place within different RAG use cases, and selecting the appropriate method depends on the specific requirements of the application.

Indexing

After a data object has been chunked, the next step is indexing. Indexing enables the retriever to locate the most relevant material for a given user query. The overall effectiveness of an RAG system is closely tied to the quality of its indexing. Various indexing methods are employed in RAG implementations, each with distinct characteristics. The principal approaches include:

- **Vector indexing**: This is the most widely used method. Each chunk is transformed into a high-dimensional vector and stored in a vector database. When a query is received, it is similarly converted into a vector, and a comparison is made with the stored vectors. This approach captures the semantic similarity between the query and the chunks. However, the results of vector-based retrieval are generally opaque and difficult to interpret. Vector indexing is also referred to as **dense indexing**.

- **Keyword indexing**: This traditional method involves extracting specific keywords from each chunk and storing them as the index. A commonly used technique for keyword extraction is **Term Frequency-Inverse Document Frequency** (**TF-IDF**). The retriever matches keywords from the user query with those in the index, using either exact or fuzzy comparison. While this approach is fast and its results are easily interpretable, it may fail to retrieve relevant content when the query uses different words that are semantically similar. Keyword indexing is also known as **sparse indexing**.

- **Hybrid indexing**: In this approach, both dense and sparse indexes are created for each chunk. During retrieval, scores from both indexes are considered to rank the search results. This method offers improved reliability across a broader range of queries but is more complex to implement and manage compared to single-index systems.

- **Hierarchical indexing**: This technique involves creating multiple levels of related indexes. For instance, individual chunk indexes may be linked to a higher-level index representing the entire document. The retriever first identifies the most relevant document, then narrows the search to specific chunks within that document. This approach yields more meaningful results, particularly when working with lengthy or structured documents, though it introduces additional complexity in both development and execution.

Each of these indexing strategies has specific use cases and trade-offs, and the selection of an appropriate method depends on the requirements of the RAG application. Indexing is used by the most important component in the RAG system, the retriever, described in the following section.

Retriever

The retriever serves as the central component of an RAG system, responsible for locating the most relevant chunks from the knowledge store in response to a user query. As outlined in the previous section, the knowledge store is organized and indexed to facilitate efficient retrieval. The retriever operates by interacting with this index and performs its task through the following four steps:

1. Accept the user query.
2. Transform the query into a format appropriate for the type of index. For instance, if the knowledge store uses dense indexing, the query is converted into a vector. In the case of sparse indexing, it is transformed into a set of keywords.
3. Conduct a search over the indexed chunks using the appropriate retrieval mechanism.
4. Return the top-k chunks, those with the highest relevance scores, to be used in prompt construction.

The following section explains the working of the retriever for dense indexing.

Retriever using dense index

Dense indexing involves converting text chunks into embeddings and storing them in a vector database such as **FAISS** or **Pinecone**. Each chunk is embedded using a consistent embedding model and a fixed embedding size. For example, a knowledge store might use 768-dimensional embeddings generated by a BERT-based model. The embedding and storage process can be represented using the following pseudocode:

```
For each Chunk in the store:
    EmbeddedChunk = EmbeddingModel.Embedd(Chunk)
    VectorDatabase.Store(EmbeddedChunk)
```

To retrieve relevant chunks, the retriever converts the user query into an embedding using the same model:

```
SearchEmbedding = EmbeddingModel.Embedd(UserQuery)
```

The retriever then uses the vector database's search functionality to find the most relevant chunks. While the specifics vary across databases, the generalized process can be represented as:

```
Top-k_Chunks = VectorDatabase.Search(SearchEmbedding, k)
```

Here, the `Search` method takes the query embedding and the number of chunks to retrieve (`k`). Vector databases rely on optimized search algorithms to implement this method. These algorithms may include:

- Vector similarity measures such as cosine similarity, dot product, or Euclidean distance.
- Exact nearest neighbor search.
- **Approximate nearest neighbor** (**ANN**) search techniques, which trade off some accuracy for faster performance and scalability.

Prompt generator

The prompt generator component is responsible for assembling the prompt that is submitted to the model once the most relevant chunks have been retrieved. Its role is to construct the prompt in a manner that enables the model to produce accurate and contextually relevant responses to the user query.

The final prompt typically consists of the following elements:

- **Instructions**: These guide the model on how to process the input. Basic instructions direct the model to answer the query using the provided context. More advanced instructions may define the model's role, specify rules to follow, set the desired output format, and incorporate other considerations as outlined in *Chapter 4, Prompt Engineering*.
- **Material**: This section contains the contextual chunks retrieved by the retriever.
- **User query**: This is the original question or request submitted by the user, which the model must address using the information in the material.

The following pseudocode shows the working of a basic prompt generator:

```
Instructions = "Using the context specified by ##MATERIAL##, answer the
##QUERY"

Material = CombineChunks( top-k_Chunks)

prompt = Instructions + "##MATERIAL##" + Material + "##QUERY##" + UserQuery
```

The **CombineChunks** method processes the list of retrieved chunks to generate the material text. This is typically done by concatenating the chunks in a coherent and structured manner. The most important consideration is the context length of the model. If the material exceeds the context length, only a part of the list can be accommodated.

As outlined in this section, the RAG pipeline comprises several components that must be assembled thoughtfully, with appropriate choices at each stage. This can present challenges for solution developers. To simplify the process, various frameworks offer foundational structures to support the implementation. Among these, LangChain stands out as one of the most widely adopted frameworks for building RAG solutions. The following section examines LangChain in greater detail.

Introduction to LangChain

LangChain is an open-source framework developed in Python and JavaScript, designed to simplify the development of applications using **large language models** (**LLMs**). It is widely utilized for creating prototypes and **proof-of-concept** (**POC**) solutions in RAG and other generative AI applications.

Its effectiveness in supporting RAG implementations stems from three core strengths: built-in functionality, pre-integrated tools, and the ability to construct flexible, modular pipelines.

Built-in functionality

Building an RAG application involves the development of various pieces of functionality. LangChain removes the need for development by offering built-in functionality. The following are the main ready functionalities offered by LangChain that are important for RAG development:

- Chunking
- Indexing
- Retrieving

Chunking

LangChain provides classes that facilitate the division of documents into meaningful chunks. At the core is the `TextSplitter` base class, from which various specialized chunking classes are derived. The most commonly used implementations include:

- **Character-based chunking**: This method splits the document into segments containing a fixed number of characters. It is implemented by the `CharacterTextSplitter` class.
- **Hierarchical chunking**: The `RecursiveCharacterTextSplitter` class creates a hierarchy of chunks based on the structure of the text, such as paragraphs and sentences.
- **Structured content chunking**: Suitable for documents with predefined structure, such as Markdown, this method is handled by the `MarkdownHeaderTextSplitter` class.

Indexing

Indexing consists of two primary steps: embedding the chunks and storing them in a vector database, particularly in the case of dense indexing. LangChain provides built-in functionality to handle both steps and enables them to be executed as a single operation. The steps are as follows:

1. **Embedding**: LangChain supports multiple embedding models sourced from providers such as OpenAI and Hugging Face. These are accessible through the `langchain.embeddings` package, which offers a variety of embedding options.
2. **Vector store**: LangChain includes built-in integrations with widely used vector databases such as FAISS and Weaviate. These integrations are available through the `langchain.vectorstore` package. The corresponding classes offer methods that can perform chunking, embedding, and storing of entire documents in a single step.

Retrieving

The retriever component in an RAG system is tasked with fetching the most relevant chunks from the knowledge store. LangChain provides a built-in abstraction for the retriever through the base class **`BaseRetriever`**. Retrievers are typically instantiated by the **`vectorstore`** objects, ensuring consistency in the search methodology between storage and retrieval of chunks.

Prompt generation

The prompt generator in an RAG system creates the final prompt by combining the retrieved text chunks with the user query. LangChain offers the **`PromptTemplate`** base class, which enables the insertion of these variables into a predefined prompt format. For greater flexibility, the **`ChatPromptTemplate`** class allows enhanced control over the interaction by incorporating both system prompts and user prompts.

Pre-integrated tools

LangChain includes a range of pre-integrated tools that streamline RAG development. The primary categories of these tools are:

- Document loaders
- Embedding models
- Vector databases
- LLMs

Embeddings and vector databases were discussed in the previous section. This section focuses on document loaders and LLMs.

Document loaders

Extracting text from documents and other sources serves as the initial step in the RAG pipeline. LangChain offers integration with a range of sources, and the output from these integrations is standardized using the **`Document`** class. Key integrations include:

- **File loaders**: These are capable of extracting text from various file formats, including plain text, **comma separated values** (**CSV**), JSON, HTML, and others.
- **Web loaders**: These are designed to retrieve information from websites, encompassing content from web pages, sitemaps, and recursively linked pages.
- **Database loaders**: These support connections with multiple types of databases, including SQL, NoSQL, and graph databases.

The following table lists several examples of document loader classes available in LangChain:

Loader type	Source type	Class
Document	Text	`TextLoader`
Document	PDF	`PyPDFLoader`
Document	JSON	`JSONLoader`
Web	Sitemap	`SitemapLoader`
Web	Web page	`BeautifulSoupLoader`
Web	Web page (recursive)	`RecursiveUrlLoader`
Database	SQL	`SqlLoader`

***Table 6.1**: Examples of loaders in LangChain*

Large language models

LangChain enables connectivity with a wide range of popular LLM APIs for delivering the final prompt. Examples of integrated models include those from OpenAI, Google, Anthropic, and Cohere. Additionally, open-source models can be incorporated through dedicated pipelines offered by providers such as Hugging Face and Ollama.

Flexible pipeline

As outlined in this chapter, an RAG system comprises multiple components that are intricately connected to function cohesively. It involves two distinct processes:

- The **ingestion** process, responsible for creating and updating the knowledge store.
- The **querying** process, which handles user queries.

These processes are interconnected through a shared indexing mechanism. LangChain facilitates the construction of both processes in a modular and flexible manner. The following characteristics define the process pipelines offered by LangChain:

- **Modularity**: LangChain includes a wide range of built-in functionalities and integrated tools, each of which can be modified independently. For instance, consider a pipeline that ingests text documents, indexes them using OpenAI embeddings, and stores the results in a FAISS vector database. If a developer chooses to add a database loader to this setup, the indexing and storage components remain unaffected. This modularity enables agile development and seamless updates.
- **Custom workflows**: LangChain accommodates various RAG workflows, such as:
  - o **Simple chains**: Used for sending prompts directly to the language model.
  - o **RetrievalQA chains**: Designed for classic RAG scenarios, combining retrievers with the language model.

- o **Custom chains**: Tailored for complex applications, these workflows support advanced RAG use cases that are discussed in *Chapter 7, Advanced RAG in Action*.

The flexible pipelines offered by LangChain facilitate extensive experimentation and enable rapid modifications. This adaptability is particularly valuable given that LangChain is primarily employed for developing prototypes of generative AI applications, where iterative changes are often essential.

Example RAG code with LangChain

The preceding sections have outlined the built-in capabilities, tools, and pipelines that LangChain offers for rapidly developing RAG applications. This section presents a practical example demonstrating how these components can be implemented. The example illustrates both the ingestion and query pipelines.

The ingestion pipeline consists of the following steps:

1. Loading the provided text.
2. Dividing the text into chunks using a fixed character length with overlap.
3. Indexing the chunks with OpenAI embeddings.
4. Storing the indexed data in a FAISS vector database.

The query pipeline involves:

1. Embedding the user query.
2. Retrieving the most relevant text chunks.
3. Constructing the final prompt.
4. Generating a response to the query using an OpenAI language model.

The following code is for the ingestion pipeline, to be run inside a Google Colab note:

```
#install the necessary packages
!pip install langchain openai faiss-cpu
!pip install langchain_community

#Set the OpenAI key
import os
os.environ["OPENAI_API_KEY"] = YOUR_OPENAI_API_KEY
#Import required packages
from langchain.text_splitter import CharacterTextSplitter
from langchain.embeddings import OpenAIEmbeddings
```

```
from langchain.vectorstores import FAISS
from langchain.docstore.document import Document

#This text will be stored in the knowledge store
text = """
Recent advancements in generative artificial intelligence (AI) are
revolutionizing the field of drug discovery, offering unprecedented potential
to accelerate the development of new therapeutics. Traditionally, drug
discovery is a lengthy, expensive, and often unpredictable process. However,
generative AI models can now design novel molecular structures with desired
properties, predict their binding affinities to target proteins, and even
simulate their interactions within biological systems. This capability
significantly streamlines the initial phases of drug development, reducing the
need for extensive wet-lab experimentation. By leveraging vast datasets of
chemical compounds and biological interactions, AI can explore a far wider
chemical space than human researchers alone, identifying promising candidates
that might otherwise be overlooked. This shift promises to bring life-saving
medications to patients faster and more efficiently.
"""

#Wrap the text in a Document object
docs = [Document(page_content=text)]

#Using fixed-character, overlapped chunking
splitter = CharacterTextSplitter(chunk_size=200, chunk_overlap=50)
chunks = splitter.split_documents(docs)

#Index using OpenAI embeddings
embedding_model = OpenAIEmbeddings()

#Store the embeddings in FAISS
vectorstore = FAISS.from_documents(chunks, embedding_model)

print("Text has been chunked, indexed, and stored in FAISS.")
```

The code is straightforward and utilizes several pre-built tools to carry out the required steps:

- The **`Document`** class is employed to load the text.
- The **`CharacterTextSplitter`** is used to divide the text into chunks of 200 characters each, with an overlap of 50 characters on both sides.

- The **OpenAIEmbeddings** class indexes the chunks using an OpenAI embedding model.
- The **FAISS** class offers a pipeline to index each chunk with the embedding model and insert it into the vector store. Notably, both operations are performed through a single call to the **FromDocuments** method.

The following code demonstrates the query pipeline.

```
from langchain.chains import RetrievalQA
from langchain.llms import OpenAI

#Create a retriever
retriever = vectorstore.as_retriever(search_type="similarity", k=3)

#Initialize the LLM
llm = OpenAI(temperature=0)

#Create the RetrievalQA chain
qa_chain = RetrievalQA.from_chain_type(
    llm=llm,
    retriever=retriever,
    return_source_documents=True
)

#The user query
query = "How is generative AI transforming the early stages of drug
discovery?"
result = qa_chain({"query": query})

print("\nAnswer:")
print(result["result"])
```

The output is as follows:

```
Answer:
Generative AI is transforming the early stages of drug discovery by designing novel molecular structures, predicting their binding affinities, and simulating their interactions within biological systems. This streamlines the initial phases of drug development and allows for exploration of a wider chemical space, potentially identifying promising candidates that may have been overlooked by human researchers.
```

The code demonstrates the following operations:

- The `as_retriever` method generates a `RetrievalQA` object from the vector store, ensuring that the retrieval process is consistent with the method used during the store's creation.
- The QA pipeline is constructed using the `from_chain_type` method of `RetrievalQA`, which links the vector store with the `OpenAI` LLM instantiated from the llms package.
- The pipeline is executed to carry out three tasks in sequence:
    1. Retrieve the top three matching chunks from the vector store.
    2. Construct a prompt for the LLM.
    3. Submit the prompt and generate a response from the model.

    The prompt is generated implicitly by the QA chain, making this approach suitable for most straightforward use cases.

This example demonstrates how a basic RAG application can be constructed using LangChain with minimal code. The LangChain classes offer a range of advanced options and parameters that allow for further customization and fine-tuning of the process. Several of these features will be explored in the project developed at the end of this chapter.

Applications of RAG

RAG is arguably the most widely adopted form of generative AI application. It is utilized in a broad spectrum of industry and everyday life applications. Some key areas where RAG applications are employed include:

- **Learning**: RAG facilitates access to extensive knowledge bases, enabling the creation of personalized educational content.
- **Research**: It assists researchers by simplifying the navigation of large volumes of literature and by providing summaries and compilations.
- **Automation**: Tasks involving the processing of large datasets can be automated through RAG, leading to streamlined workflows and reduced manual effort.
- **Generation**: By leveraging existing information, RAG enables language models to produce content that is both relevant and factually accurate.
- **Recommendation**: RAG supports the generation of precise recommendations by referencing sources such as manuals, data sheets, and product information.
- **Quality check**: Content can be evaluated against established guidelines and standards using RAG, ensuring consistent quality.

- **Decision support**: RAG retrieves pertinent data to aid decision-makers in basing their conclusions on reliable and comprehensive information.

RAG applications can be broadly categorized into two groups: those designed for consumers and those developed for businesses. The following sections explore each of these categories in detail.

RAG applications for consumers

RAG can be employed to develop applications that serve everyday needs for a wide range of individuals, including students, learners, and researchers. Some examples include:

- **Personalized learning**: Students can benefit from intelligent tutoring systems that utilize resources such as textbooks, question papers, and academic journals to design personalized learning plans. By applying RAG, these systems can generate authentic educational and assessment content tailored to individual learners. As students often have distinct learning preferences, such as visual explanations or narrative-based formats, the same topic can be presented in different ways to suit each student's learning style.

- **Research assistance**: Researchers often need to review extensive reading material, including journal papers, articles, and datasheets. RAG simplifies this process by incorporating the content into a knowledge store and enabling question-answering and summarization capabilities. This approach significantly reduces the time spent on reading and information retrieval, allowing researchers to concentrate more on analysis and problem-solving.

- **Virtual assistants and chatbots**: Customized chatbots that address specific informational needs, such as those related to tax, health, or investment, can be developed using the RAG approach. These systems can also support professionals such as chartered accountants, consultants, and lawyers by providing quick access to relevant knowledge. An emerging trend includes chatbots built around significant books, which have proven beneficial to a broad audience.

RAG applications for business

Businesses possess substantial volumes of internal data and are increasingly leveraging RAG to transform this data into actionable insights. RAG applications offer value across nearly all enterprise functions. Examples include:

- **Human resources (HR) chatbot**: An RAG-enabled chatbot can address employee queries related to company policies, documentation, payroll procedures, and other HR data sources. This reduces the workload on HR staff and enhances employee satisfaction.

- **Assistant for design team**: RAG can support design teams by referencing manuals, industry standards, research documents, and past designs. This allows designers to quickly access technical specifications, receive suggestions based on historical data, and make informed design decisions more efficiently.
- **Assistant for legal teams**: RAG-based applications can assist legal departments in managing contracts, litigation, and compliance tasks. By accessing repositories containing laws, regulations, notifications, existing contracts, and case records, such systems can reduce the time spent on legal research and negotiations while enhancing regulatory compliance.
- **Learning and development (L&D)**: Organizations often struggle to disseminate internal knowledge effectively. RAG systems can generate personalized training content from organizational data, helping employees acquire relevant skills and knowledge that contribute to operational efficiency.
- **Customer service assistants**: These applications utilize service records, technical manuals, product documentation, and customer interaction histories to support service agents. This enables better understanding of customer queries, creation of effective responses, and faster issue resolution, resulting in shorter call durations, reduced employee stress, and higher customer satisfaction.
- **Sales enablement**: RAG tools provide sales teams with easy access to accurate product information sourced from brochures, manuals, case studies, and **customer relationship management** (**CRM**) systems. This helps sales personnel address customer queries effectively, accelerate sales cycles, and onboard new hires more efficiently.
- **Automatic proposal creation**: One widely used application of RAG is the generation of proposals based on previous submissions, pricing data, and product documentation. This capability enables proposal teams to produce more proposals in less time, thereby boosting sales and revenue.

The final section of this chapter will concentrate on the development of a business-oriented RAG application, namely, *contract intelligence*.

Development of contract intelligence

The legal department plays a vital role in safeguarding the company's interests, ensuring compliance, and supporting business operations through sound legal advice. This section introduces a GenAI-powered CI application designed to streamline contract analysis, review, and drafting. By enhancing the efficiency and accuracy of legal workflows, CI can significantly reduce risk and accelerate deal cycles. The capabilities of CI are outlined in the following section.

Features of the CI

GenAI-based techniques offer significant advantages to legal teams, as outlined in *Chapter 3, GenAI Models in Industry,* and discussed earlier in this chapter. In developing CI, carefully chosen use cases illustrate how RAG can be integrated into legal workflows. The primary capabilities of CI include:

- **Question answering on contracts**: Legal teams frequently require timely and accurate responses to specific inquiries about contract terms, whether for internal decisions, negotiations, or compliance checks. The value of these responses lies in their relevance, clarity, and alignment with the surrounding legal context.

  One of the main challenges is the need to sift through lengthy and complex legal documents to extract the required information. Manual review for each query is inefficient and time-consuming. The CI application is designed to overcome this limitation by providing an automated and intelligent question-answering system that delivers contextually accurate information drawn directly from the contract content.

- **Summarization of contracts**: Legal documents are often lengthy and densely structured, containing crucial information spread across various sections. For effective decision-making and collaboration, stakeholders, including those outside the legal team, need rapid access to key terms and obligations without reading the full document. The utility of a summary hinges on its accuracy, completeness, and relevance to the user's role.

  Different departments, such as finance or legal, focus on different elements of a contract. Preparing customized summaries manually is both time-intensive and susceptible to errors. The CI application addresses this by offering automated, context-sensitive summarization that adapts to the specific needs of different stakeholders.

- **Identification of risky clauses**: Contracts may include clauses that introduce legal, financial, or operational risks. Identifying such clauses, covering aspects like indemnity, liability caps, or termination, is vital to mitigating risks before finalizing an agreement. The effectiveness of this task depends on the system's ability to detect non-standard or unfavorable language in accordance with legal best practices and internal policies.

  One of the key challenges is that risky language may be subtle, context-specific, and vary by jurisdiction or contract type. Manual review alone is insufficient, as it increases the risk of oversight and slows the contract review process. The CI application addresses this by automatically flagging potentially risky clauses through retrieval-augmented techniques that compare contract language with internal playbooks, regulatory guidelines, and historical data.

The development of CI in this section focuses on the first two capabilities, question answering and summarization, while the third, clause risk identification, is suggested as an extension for further exploration.

Description of the solution

The CI application will be accessible to legal team members as a web-based tool, allowing them to interact with it directly through a browser. It will offer a user-friendly interface designed for simplicity and efficiency, enabling seamless access to its core functionalities.

Features

CI will provide users with two core features:

- Question answering on contracts
- Customized contract summaries

The customized summary feature will include two tailored formats: one designed for the finance team and another for the operations team.

To access the available features, legal team members must begin by uploading a contract. The question answering and summarization functionalities will operate on the uploaded document. The CI application will include three main menu options, with the **Summarize** menu containing two sub-menus:

- Upload Contract
- QA
- Summarize
    - o Summary for Finance
    - o Summary for Operations

Users

Understanding user profiles is a key consideration in system design. As outlined earlier, the primary users of the CI application are members of the legal team. They are knowledgeable professionals with expertise in handling complex legal documents and are proficient in using digital tools on both desktop and mobile platforms. Experienced in working with text-heavy content, they are also comfortable navigating web-based applications efficiently.

User stories

Here is a typical user story:

Raj, a legal associate, is reviewing several contracts as part of a due diligence process for a new partnership. Each contract is lengthy and covers different aspects such as service terms, liabilities, and intellectual property. Since the stakeholders involved, such as the finance and compliance teams, require only the key highlights, Raj needs to generate concise summaries for each contract.

To streamline this task, he uses the Summarize feature in the CI application. The system automatically produces tailored summaries that highlight the most relevant clauses based on the intended audience. Raj then shares the summaries with the respective teams and archives the documents for future reference.

A similar user story can be created for the QA feature by describing the user's role, the task they need to complete, how they interact with the CI system, and the resulting outcome.

Architecture

The architecture of the CI system mirrors the solutions introduced earlier in this book. It is organized into four primary components, each dedicated to a distinct function that enables question answering and summarization using RAG techniques:

- **GenAI models**: The CI application employs an LLM for summarization and comprehension tasks. These models are accessed through external APIs and invoked within the RAG module. The model used is GPT-4o-mini from OpenAI, which allows CI to deliver high-quality legal insights and responses tailored to user queries.
- **RAG module**: This module houses the core RAG functionalities that enable contract analysis. It is implemented as a set of Python functions responsible for indexing, retrieval, and prompt generation. The LangChain library discussed earlier is used for constructing these components.
- **Configurations**: Adapted from *Chapter 4, Prompt Engineering,* this component includes reusable configurations such as API credentials and environment variables. Since the implementation remains unchanged, it is not detailed again here.
- **User interface (UI)**: The interface builds on the design from *Chapter 4, Prompt Engineering,* with specific enhancements to support CI's features, such as question answering and summarization. A key addition is the Upload Contract feature, which involves supplementary coding to enable document ingestion.

System development

The system development will include developing the RAG and UI module. The Configuration module is used as it is from previous projects.

Development of the RAG module

The **RAG module** in the CI application consists of a collection of Python functions, responsible for implementing parts of the RAG pipeline. The following functionalities are supported by the RAG module:

- Ingest the given contract file
- Ask a question based on the contract

- Summarize the contract for the finance team
- Summarize the contract for the operations team

An important part of the RAG module is the vector database, which is saved on the disc in a location given in the config.

The first function to be developed within this module is **Ingest File**, which takes the file uploaded by the user and stores it in the vector store. Here is the code:

```
import os
from langchain.vectorstores import FAISS
from langchain.embeddings import OpenAIEmbeddings
from langchain.document_loaders import PyPDFLoader
from langchain.text_splitter import RecursiveCharacterTextSplitter

def CI_Ingest_File(pdf_path: str):
    # Set OpenAI API Key
    os.environ["OPENAI_API_KEY"] = config.get("OPEN")

    # Load the PDF document
    loader = PyPDFLoader(pdf_path)
    documents = loader.load()

    # Split the documents into manageable chunks
    text_splitter = RecursiveCharacterTextSplitter(chunk_size=1000, chunk_
overlap=100)
    docs = text_splitter.split_documents(documents)

    # Initialize embeddings
    embeddings = OpenAIEmbeddings()

    faiss_index_path = config.get("VectorDBPath")

    # Load existing FAISS index or create a new one
    if os.path.exists(faiss_index_path):
        print("Loading existing FAISS index...")
        vectorstore = FAISS.load_local(faiss_index_path, embeddings)
    else:
        print("Creating new FAISS index...")
```

```
        vectorstore = FAISS.from_documents(docs, embeddings)

    # Save the updated FAISS index
    vectorstore.save_local(faiss_index_path)

    print(f"PDF added to FAISS index and saved at {faiss_index_path}")
```

The code closely resembles the example provided in the *Introduction to LangChain* section, with two key distinctions:

- Instead of using plain text, LangChain is now configured to load content from a file. The file path is provided as an argument, and a different loader, PyPDFLoader, is employed for this purpose.
- The vector store is saved to a local file (in Google Colab) at the end of the process. This file will later be accessed by other functions for retrieving the vector store.

The next function described is responsible for answering user queries. It utilizes the LangChain retriever and QA chain to retrieve relevant information and generate responses. The implementation is provided as follows:

```
import os
from langchain.vectorstores import FAISS
from langchain.embeddings import OpenAIEmbeddings
from langchain.chat_models import ChatOpenAI
from langchain.prompts import PromptTemplate
from langchain.chains import RetrievalQA

def CI_Answer_Query(query: str) -> str:
    # Set OpenAI API Key
    #os.environ["OPENAI_API_KEY"] = YOUR_OPENAI_API_KEY

    faiss_index_path = config.get("VectorDBPath")

    #Load embeddings and FAISS vector store
    embeddings = OpenAIEmbeddings()
    vectorstore = FAISS.load_local(faiss_index_path, embeddings, allow_
dangerous_deserialization=True)

    #Set up retriever and LLM
    retriever = vectorstore.as_retriever(search_type="similarity", search_
kwargs={"k": 5})
```

```
# Define a custom prompt template
prompt_template = """
    You are a legal expert that answers questions based on provided contract
    documents.

    Context:
    {context}

    Question:
    {question}

    Answer in a clear and concise manner, using only the information in the
    context. If the answer is not in the context, say "The information is
    not available in the provided documents."
    """

prompt = PromptTemplate(
    template=prompt_template,
    input_variables=["context", "question"]
)
```

In the next step, a retrieve type chain is created to perform the retrieval:

```
# Load LLM
llm = ChatOpenAI(model_name="gpt-4o-mini", temperature=0)

# Set up RetrievalQA with custom prompt
qa_chain = RetrievalQA.from_chain_type(
    llm=llm,
    chain_type="stuff",
    retriever=retriever,
    chain_type_kwargs={"prompt": prompt},
    return_source_documents=False
)
```

The final step is to run the chain to get the response:

```
# Run query through the chain
response = qa_chain.run(query)
return response
```

The code employs the **PromptTemplate** class to construct a custom prompt instead of relying on LangChain's built-in prompting functionality. The remainder of the implementation aligns with the QA chain example presented in the *Introduction to LangChain* section in this chapter.

The final implementation in the RAG module is that of the Summarization feature. The following code shows the summarization for the finance team. Code for the operations team will be similar and is left for the reader.

The first part of the code loads the vector database. The retriever is also set up:

```
import os
from langchain.vectorstores import FAISS
from langchain.embeddings import OpenAIEmbeddings
from langchain.chat models import ChatOpenAI
from langchain.prompts import PromptTemplate
from langchain.chains import RetrievalQA

def CI_Summarize_For_Finance() -> str:
    # Set OpenAI API Key
    #os.environ["OPENAI_API_KEY"] = openai_api_key

    #faiss_index_path = config.get("VectorDBPath")
    faiss_index_path = "VectorDB"

    # Load FAISS vector store
    embeddings = OpenAIEmbeddings()
    vectorstore = FAISS.load_local(faiss_index_path, embeddings, allow_
dangerous_deserialization=True)
    # Set up retriever
    retriever = vectorstore.as_retriever(search_type="similarity", search_
kwargs={"k": 10})
```

The next part of the code prepares the prompt to get the right material from the document:

```
    # Define custom summarization prompt for the finance team
    prompt_template = """
      You are a legal assistant summarizing a contract for the finance team of
      a company.

      Based on the context provided, generate a clear, concise summary that
      highlights:
      - Payment terms and schedules
      - Financial obligations or liabilities
```

```
    - Penalties for delays or breaches
    - Tax responsibilities
    - Any clauses with financial impact

    Context:
    {context}

    Write a short summary tailored for the finance team:
    """

prompt = PromptTemplate(
    input_variables=["context", "question"],
    template=prompt_template
)
```

Finally, the material and the prompt are used to create the summary:

```
# Load LLM
llm = ChatOpenAI(model_name="gpt-4o-mini", temperature=0)

# Create QA chain using custom prompt
qa_chain = RetrievalQA.from_chain_type(
    llm=llm,
    retriever=retriever,
    chain_type="stuff",
    chain_type_kwargs={"prompt": prompt},
    return_source_documents=False
)

# Run a dummy query to trigger summarization
summary = qa_chain.run("Summarize this contract for the finance team.")
return summary
```

The summarization feature involves a modified use of the QA chain. In this case, the user does not provide a question, so the prompt must include all necessary guidance for the retriever. Additionally, the number of retrieved chunks is increased to ten to ensure comprehensive coverage of relevant content for effective summarization. All other aspects of the implementation remain consistent with the QA function.

Development of UI module

For the development of the UI module, the three main steps will be used:

1. Creating a Python application file and uploading it to Colab.
2. Running Streamlit on Colab using the application file **CI_App.py** as the source.
3. Using ngrok to expose the web application through a public URL.

In the CI application, the second and third steps follow the same approach as described in earlier projects. Readers can consult *Chapter 4, Prompt Engineering,* for those details. The main difference lies in the **CI_App.py** application file, which has been adapted to include features unique to the CI module. This file integrates all previously developed functions along with the following Streamlit code:

```
import streamlit as st
st.set_page_config(page_title="Contract Intelligence", layout="wide")
st.sidebar.title("Features")

# Main Menu
menu_main = st.sidebar.radio("Select Feature", ["Upload Contract", "QA",
"Summarize"])
submenu = None

# Submenus if "Summarize" is selected
if menu_main == "Summarize":
    submenu = st.sidebar.radio("Select Summary Type", ["Summary for Finance",
"Summary for Operation"])

st.title("Contract Intelligence")

# Upload Contract Section
if menu_main == "Upload Contract":
    st.subheader("Upload Contract")
    uploaded_file = st.file_uploader("Choose a PDF contract file", type=["pdf"])
    if uploaded_file:
        st.success("Contract uploaded successfully.")
        # Placeholder for processing
        st.write("Processing and indexing the contract...")
        CI_Ingest_File(uploaded_file.name)
        st.success("Contract indexed successfully.")

# QA Section
elif menu_main == "QA":
    st.subheader("Ask a Question About the Contract")
```

```
    user_question = st.text_input("Enter your question")
    if st.button("Get Answer"):
        st.write("Searching for answer...")
        # Replace with your QA function
        response = CI_Answer_Query(user_question)
        st.write(response)

# Summarize Section
elif menu_main == "Summarize":
    st.subheader(f"{submenu}")
    if submenu == "Summary for Finance":
        if st.button("Generate Finance Summary"):
            st.write("Generating summary for the finance team...")
            summary = CI_Summarize_For_Finance()
            st.write(summary)
    elif submenu == "Summary for Operation":
        if st.button("Generate Operations Summary"):
            st.write("Generating summary for the operations team...")
            # Call summarize_contract_for_operations(...)
```

The **CI_App.py** file is available in the code repository of the book.

Conclusion

This chapter explored the RAG technique, which extends the memory of GenAI models by incorporating external knowledge sources. It began with an intuitive explanation of RAG and a breakdown of its typical system architecture. Key components, such as chunking, indexing, retrieval, and prompting, were discussed in detail to provide a comprehensive understanding of how RAG systems function.

The LangChain framework was introduced as a powerful tool that simplifies and accelerates the development of RAG applications. Its built-in functionalities, modular components, and flexible pipelines were highlighted as major advantages. The chapter also examined a wide range of RAG applications for both consumers and businesses, demonstrating its impact across domains such as learning, research, HR, and sales.

The chapter concluded with a hands-on example: the development of a CI application designed to assist corporate legal teams.

While this chapter covered the foundational techniques for building RAG pipelines, basic pipelines can be limited in complex, real-world scenarios. The next chapter explores advanced RAG techniques designed to overcome these limitations and enhance system performance.

CHAPTER 7
Advanced RAG in Action

Introduction

Large language models (**LLMs**) have achieved significant success across various industrial applications. Despite their capabilities, these models are constrained by limitations in their internal knowledge. To address these shortcomings, the **retrieval-augmented generation** (**RAG**) framework was introduced, as outlined in *Chapter 6, Enhancing GenAI with RAG*. The basic variant discussed in that chapter, often referred to as naïve RAG, possesses several inherent limitations.

The initial motivation behind RAG was to enhance the knowledge available to language models. However, as the use of RAG matured, the need to improve the factual accuracy of its outputs became increasingly evident. In response, a range of techniques has been developed to address the limitations of naïve RAG, resulting in an enhanced variant commonly referred to as **advanced RAG**.

The RAG pipeline comprises four key stages: indexing, retrieval, prompt preparation, and generation. Advancements have been made in each of these components, with the retrieval stage receiving the most focused attention.

This chapter begins by examining the limitations of naïve RAG and introduces key principles of advanced RAG. A focus is placed on knowledge graphs, highlighting their structure, role, and integration within the RAG pipeline. Advanced RAG encompasses a variety of methods tailored to specific contexts, several of which are discussed in detail. The chapter concludes with a case study on the Customer Service Navigator, an enterprise GenAI application that demonstrates the practical use of selected advanced RAG techniques in client support.

Structure

This chapter covers the following topics:

- Problems with simple RAG
- Basics of advanced RAG
- Basics of knowledge graph
- Advanced RAG with knowledge graph

- RAG with fine-tuning
- More techniques
- Development of Customer Service Navigator

Objectives

By the end of this chapter, you will have a comprehensive understanding of advanced RAG techniques and how they enhance the performance and reliability of GenAI applications. You will learn how to improve each stage of the RAG pipeline (indexing, retrieval, and post-retrieval) using methods such as hybrid retrieval, multi-hop retrieval, query reformulation, summary indexing, and reranking. You will also explore the role of knowledge graphs and fine-tuned models in enriching queries and optimizing information retrieval. Finally, you will examine the development of the **Customer Success Navigator** (**CSN**), a GenAI application built using these techniques, to see how advanced RAG can solve real-world challenges in customer service and knowledge management.

Problems with simple RAG

The principal problem with simple RAG systems is that of accuracy. As the range of tasks expected from an RAG system widens, the naïve method falls short of producing the desired outputs. The roots of the limitations can be traced to the functioning of the RAG method.

RAG enhances the knowledge capabilities of LLMs by incorporating external information into the generation process. Its functioning can be broadly divided into three phases:

- **Pre-retrieval**, which involves indexing knowledge sources and acquiring the user query
- **Retrieval**, where relevant knowledge chunks are selected
- **Post-retrieval**, where the retrieved content is used to generate the final response

Each phase introduces specific challenges that can affect overall system accuracy. In the pre-retrieval phase, limitations often stem from the embedding and chunking strategies used during indexing. An unsuitable chunking approach or embedding model may lead to poor representation of the source material, resulting in suboptimal retrieval.

Among the three stages of the RAG pipeline, the retrieval phase plays the most decisive role in determining the overall effectiveness and accuracy of the system. It acts as the central mechanism that connects the user's query with the external knowledge required for generating a meaningful and accurate response. However, this phase is also where the system encounters some of its most persistent and consequential challenges. These challenges can be broadly categorized into issues related to the user query, the matching process, and the ranking of retrieved results, described as follows:

- **Challenges related to the user query** arise primarily from the nature of human interaction with search-based systems. Most users tend to input brief, under-specified queries, often assuming that the system will infer their intent. This brevity, while convenient, can severely limit the system's ability to retrieve contextually relevant content. Since the retrieval process depends entirely on the query for selecting knowledge chunks, an imprecise or vague query can lead to a failure in identifying the most pertinent information. As a result, relevant knowledge may remain undiscovered, compromising the completeness and accuracy of the final output.
- **Matching-related issues** further compound the problem. Typically, the retrieval mechanism ranks and selects knowledge chunks based on similarity metrics such as cosine similarity, computed between the embedded representations of the query and the indexed content. While efficient, such metrics often fall short in capturing deeper semantic relationships, especially across diverse domains and query types. Consequently, the system may retrieve content that appears syntactically similar but is semantically irrelevant, leading to false positives. At the same time, truly relevant chunks may be missed if they do not exhibit a strong surface-level similarity, resulting in false negatives. This trade-off between precision and recall can significantly affect the reliability of the retrieved information.
- **Ranking challenges** present another layer of complexity. Even when the retrieval system successfully identifies a set of potentially useful chunks, it must assign relevance scores to prioritize what gets included in the final prompt. This ranking is critical because only a limited number of chunks can be passed to the generation model due to context length constraints. In practice, however, relevance scoring is prone to inaccuracies. More informative or contextually important chunks may receive lower scores than less relevant ones, leading to suboptimal inclusion. This mis-prioritization not only reduces the usefulness of the retrieved information but also introduces inconsistencies and omissions in the generated output.

The post-retrieval phase faces constraints related to context length. Since only a limited amount of content can be passed to the language model, selecting the most informative segments becomes essential. Inaccurate selection at this stage can significantly affect the quality of the generated response.

While generation-related issues such as hallucination and bias persist in RAG systems, these are broader challenges associated with language models in general and are not exclusive to the RAG framework.

Taken together, these issues underscore the fragility and importance of the retrieval phase within the RAG framework. They highlight why enhancements to retrieval mechanisms are central to the development of more accurate, robust, and context-aware RAG systems. The following sections in this chapter explore how advanced RAG techniques have been specifically designed to address these challenges.

Basics of advanced RAG

Advanced RAG incorporates a range of techniques aimed at addressing the limitations inherent in naïve RAG systems. In particular, it introduces pre-retrieval, retrieval, and post-retrieval strategies that enhance the quality and relevance of the responses generated in relation to the input query.

Pre-retrieval strategies

Pre-retrieval measures fall into two categories: improving the indexing and improving the query.

Improving the indexing

Chapter 6, Enhancing GenAI with RAG, presented foundational indexing techniques. Building on that discussion, more advanced indexing methods aim to structure the knowledge corpus to support more accurate and context-sensitive retrieval. A variety of strategies are employed to accomplish this, including the following:

- **Hybrid indexing**: A combination of sparse and dense indexing, known as hybrid retrieval, leverages the precision of keyword matching with the contextual understanding of dense representations. This approach increases the likelihood of retrieving both lexically relevant and semantically aligned documents.
- **Metadata enrichment**: Incorporating metadata such as document type, source reliability, temporal context, or domain-specific tags can significantly enhance retrieval quality. This enriched metadata allows for filtered or weighted retrieval, prioritizing more relevant or trusted documents.
- **Summary indexing**: In this approach, summaries are generated for each content chunk and indexed alongside or in place of the original text. These summaries capture the essence of the content, reducing noise and improving retrieval efficiency. Summary indexing is particularly useful in advanced retrieval strategies, where high-level relevance must be quickly assessed before deeper inspection.

Improvements to indexing serve as the foundation for more effective retrieval, rather than directly affecting the quality of responses.

Improving the query

In RAG systems, the user query plays a pivotal role in guiding retrieval. Since the quality of the retrieved content is directly dependent on the clarity and structure of the query, vague or incomplete queries can significantly impair downstream generation. Advanced RAG introduces several strategies, outlined as follows, to refine the query before retrieval, with the goal of better aligning it with the structure and semantics of the indexed knowledge:

- **Query rewriting and transformation**: This technique modifies the original query to better match the retrieval corpus. It includes restructuring incomplete or ambiguous questions into well-formed, answer-seeking formulations that align with how information is stored. In advanced RAG, this is often performed by an LLM or a fine-tuned **small language model** (**SLM**) trained on historical query-response pairs. These transformations can be tailored to domain-specific knowledge representations, especially when used in conjunction with structured knowledge such as graphs.
- **Query expansion**: To increase recall, advanced RAG systems enrich the query with related terms, concepts, or entities. This expansion is typically guided by semantic similarity measures derived from embedding models or external knowledge resources. Knowledge graphs can make expansion more precise. For example, a query about a specific medical condition can be expanded using graph-connected terms such as symptoms, treatments, or associated diseases.

Retrieval strategies

Retrieval strategies play a central role in determining which chunks from the knowledge store are selected for response generation. In advanced RAG systems, these strategies are designed to improve the relevance, diversity, and contextual fit of the retrieved information. They operate on top of the enhanced indexing techniques described earlier and often involve interaction between retrieval and generation components to guide the selection process. Three important retrieval strategies used in advanced RAG include hybrid retrieval, summary retrieval, and multi-pass retrieval, described as follows:

- **Hybrid retrieval**: Hybrid retrieval combines sparse retrieval methods, such as BM25 or TF-IDF, with dense retrieval based on semantic embeddings. Sparse retrievers are effective for exact keyword matching, while dense retrievers excel at capturing semantic similarity between queries and documents. By integrating both approaches, hybrid retrieval balances precision and recall, increasing the likelihood of retrieving content that is both lexically and semantically aligned with the query. In advanced RAG, this combination is particularly useful when queries include both specific terminology and abstract concepts.
- **Summary retrieval**: In this strategy, the system indexes and retrieves summaries of content chunks rather than the full text. Summaries are generated during the indexing phase and serve as compressed representations of the original material. Summary retrieval improves efficiency by reducing the amount of text evaluated during retrieval and enhances relevance by focusing on the key ideas within each chunk. This approach is particularly beneficial in multi-document contexts or when using limited retrieval budgets, as it prioritizes high-level relevance over volume. It also enables a preliminary filtering layer in multi-pass retrieval architectures.
- **Multi-pass retrieval**: Multi-pass retrieval involves multiple stages of retrieval and refinement. The first pass typically retrieves a broad set of candidate chunks using

lightweight or recall-oriented methods. In subsequent passes, more computationally intensive models, such as cross-encoders, rerankers, or generation-informed selectors, narrow down the selection to the most relevant documents. This iterative process improves the overall quality of the retrieved context by introducing progressive filtering and re-evaluation. Multi-pass retrieval is often used in systems that incorporate feedback loops, such as generation-aware reranking or user-guided query refinement.

Post-retrieval strategies

Once the knowledge chunks relevant to the user query have been retrieved, the next step in advanced RAG involves refining this material to retain only what is most useful. This refinement process not only improves the accuracy of the final response but also reduces the computational load, thereby improving generation efficiency. Several techniques are commonly employed to optimize this stage, such as the following:

- **Reranking**: Although the initial retrieval process identifies chunks related to the query, these chunks may not necessarily contain the specific information required to answer it. To address this, an additional evaluation step can be introduced using a model such as a cross-encoder. This model jointly considers both the query and each chunk, assigning relevance scores based on the likelihood that the chunk contains the correct answer. Chunks are then re-ordered according to these scores to improve the relevance of the final selection.
- **Diversity ranking**: In cases where the answer spans multiple documents, selecting chunks exclusively from a single source can lead to incomplete or biased responses. Diversity ranking mitigates this by ensuring that the selected chunks represent a broader range of sources, thus increasing the likelihood of covering different aspects of the query.
- **Chunk summarization**: When individual chunks are lengthy, much of the included content may be extraneous to the user query. To address this, summarization techniques are applied to condense the information. Extractive summarization involves selecting specific sentences or passages directly relevant to the query, while abstractive summarization generates a condensed version of the chunk that preserves the most pertinent information in a coherent form.

These post-retrieval strategies contribute significantly to improving the effectiveness of the RAG pipeline by ensuring that only the most relevant and concise content is passed to the language model for response generation.

The following sections present several key techniques that form the foundation of advanced RAG. As previously noted, knowledge graphs play a significant role in enhancing various aspects of these methods. The next section provides an introduction to knowledge graphs and their relevance within the RAG framework.

Basics of knowledge graph

A knowledge graph is a structured method of storing and representing knowledge. It captures entities or concepts and the relationships that connect them. A common way to visualize a knowledge graph is as a network of nodes, where each node represents a concept or entity, and the edges between nodes represent the relationships among them.

Knowledge graphs are particularly effective in representing complex, interconnected information, making them valuable in a wide range of applications. The following examples illustrate their practical use:

- A knowledge graph linking diseases, genes, and chemical compounds can support drug discovery by revealing previously unknown associations.
- A graph that maps account holders, corporate entities, and financial transactions can aid in identifying suspicious activity and detecting money laundering.
- A knowledge graph connecting legal clauses, concepts, and judicial precedents can be used to analyze contracts and identify potentially risky provisions.

These examples demonstrate how knowledge graphs enable richer, more context-aware retrieval of information, which is especially useful in enhancing RAG systems.

A comparison of knowledge graphs with two other prominent methods of knowledge storage, relational databases and language models, offers useful insights into their distinct roles and capabilities.

Relational databases are designed to store large volumes of data, particularly instances of entities. In contrast, knowledge graphs excel at representing the definitions and relationships of entities within a conceptual network, making them more suitable for modeling structured knowledge.

Language models, while also capable of storing extensive information, do so through statistical representations rather than symbolic structures. These models do not retrieve predefined knowledge; instead, they generate responses dynamically based on probabilistic patterns. In comparison, knowledge graphs store explicitly structured symbolic data, enabling precise and consistent retrieval.

Structure of knowledge graphs

The fundamental unit of a knowledge graph is the **triplet**, which consists of three components: **subject**, **predicate**, and **object**. Each triplet represents a factual statement in the form of a directed relationship. For instance, the statement *Aspirin treats Headache* can be represented as a triplet, where *Aspirin* serves as the subject, *treats* as the predicate, and *Headache* as the object. In this structure, the predicate defines the relationship linking the subject and the object.

Graphically, each triplet can be visualized as a directed edge connecting two nodes. When multiple triplets are combined, they form a more complex network. For example, adding the triplet *Aspirin is a Painkiller* to the previous example results in a connected graph with five nodes and two edges, illustrating how knowledge graphs grow by linking related triplets.

A knowledge graph is constructed by storing and interlinking a collection of such triplets. Two widely adopted standards for representing and storing triplets are **Resource Description Framework** (**RDF**) and **Web Ontology Language** (**OWL**).

RDF is a W3C standard designed to model the structure of knowledge graphs. It expresses information as a set of triples, where each element, such as the subject or object, is either a **Uniform Resource Identifier** (**URI**) or a literal value. RDF enables the unique identification of concepts and relationships, allowing consistent interpretation and reuse across different graphs. RDF data is typically maintained in specialized databases known as triplestores (e.g., Apache Jena, Virtuoso) and can be queried using SPARQL, a query language tailored for RDF data.

OWL builds on RDF by providing additional expressive power, including features such as class hierarchies, property restrictions, and logical axioms. These capabilities are essential for constructing ontologies, comprehensive knowledge graphs that define the entities and relationships within a specific domain. OWL-based ontologies are particularly valuable in domains requiring rigorous conceptual modeling, such as biomedical informatics.

Populating knowledge graphs

The construction of a knowledge graph involves the identification of entities and their interrelationships, followed by the representation of this information in the form of triplets. Source data for this process may include books, scholarly publications, web pages, structured databases, and various domain-specific repositories.

The typical workflow for populating a knowledge graph comprises the following steps:

1. **Entity extraction**: The process begins with the application of **named entity recognition** (**NER**) techniques to identify meaningful entities such as individuals, organizations, locations, chemical compounds, diseases, or events. These entities serve as the nodes within the graph. **Natural language processing** (**NLP**) models are commonly employed for this task, with the use of LLMs becoming increasingly prevalent.

2. **Entity linking**: Entities extracted from diverse sources often refer to the same underlying concept or real-world object. Entity linking addresses this by associating textual mentions with canonical identifiers. For example, mapping the *USA* and *United States* to a single node. This step may also involve introducing implicit or provisional edges between entities when a relationship is inferred but not explicitly defined.

3. **Relationship identification**: The identification of predicates, i.e., relationships that connect entities, is a crucial step in forming complete triplets. This task is typically

carried out using **rule-based systems**, **pattern-matching approaches**, or machine learning models trained on annotated data. The outcome is a semantically rich edge connecting two entities, such as in the triplet (*Aspirin, treats, Headache*).

4. **Duplicate removal**: To maintain consistency, duplicate entities and redundant relationships must be detected and consolidated. This requires the application of disambiguation and normalization techniques, which are particularly important when integrating data from multiple, heterogeneous sources.

5. **Graph storage**: Once entities and relationships have been extracted, the graph is stored using formal representations such as RDF or OWL. These formats are typically managed within specialized **graph databases** or triplestores, which support efficient querying, reasoning, and interoperability with other knowledge systems.

In the case of updating an existing graph, a similar pipeline is followed, with the inclusion of a verification step to check whether new triplets already exist in the graph. This prevents redundancy and helps preserve structural and semantic integrity. In high-stakes or domain-sensitive applications, a final step of **human curation** is often incorporated to validate the extracted knowledge, ensuring its accuracy, trustworthiness, and relevance.

Storing and managing knowledge graphs

Knowledge graphs can be stored using two principal approaches: by encoding triplets in RDF or OWL formats, or by employing graph databases optimized for representing and querying interconnected data. In either case, the storage solution must support comprehensive graph management functionalities, including updating, querying, validation, and reasoning over the stored knowledge.

The tools commonly used for storing and managing knowledge graphs can be categorized as follows:

- **Ontology management tools**: These tools are designed for the creation, editing, and validation of ontologies, particularly when OWL is used as the representation format. They enable the definition of classes, properties, relationships, and logical constraints within a domain model. Protégé, developed by Stanford University, is a widely used open-source ontology editor that supports both OWL and RDF and offers features for visualizing and verifying ontological structures.

- **RDF stores**: RDF stores are specialized databases intended for storing RDF-encoded triplets. They support SPARQL, the standard query language for RDF data, and often include additional features such as reasoning, inference mechanisms, and access control. Apache Jena Fuseki is a well-known example of such a triplestore, providing robust tools for RDF data storage and querying.

- **Graph databases**: Graph databases represent knowledge graphs as collections of nodes and edges, rather than as discrete triplets. This model supports efficient querying and traversal of large-scale graph-structured data. Many modern graph databases also offer compatibility with RDF serialization and limited support for SPARQL through integration plugins. Neo4j is among the most widely adopted graph databases; it uses the Cypher query language and supports RDF integration through various extensions.

Querying the knowledge graph

Querying refers to the process of retrieving information stored within a knowledge graph. Given that knowledge graphs consist of entities and the relationships between them, queries are typically designed to extract specific entities, relationships, or subgraphs that satisfy defined criteria.

In the context of advanced RAG, query patterns may include the following:

- Retrieving the object corresponding to a given subject-predicate pair, such as querying (Aspirin, treats) to obtain (Headache).
- Fetching all triplets in which a particular entity appears, regardless of its position in the triplet.
- Exploring deeper relationships by retrieving second-order or third-order connections involving an entity.

Knowledge graph platforms offer several methods for formulating and executing such queries. RDF and OWL-based systems commonly support SPARQL, a query language designed to specify complex patterns among triplets. In contrast, graph databases typically employ other query languages, such as **Cypher**, used by Neo4j, or **Gremlin**, supported by Apache TinkerPop. These languages are optimized for traversing and manipulating graph-structured data at scale.

The following is an example of a SPARQL query on a knowledge graph about medicines and diseases. The query finds all medicines that are used to treat *Headache*.

```
PREFIX ex: <http://example.org/>
SELECT ?medicine
WHERE {
  ?medicine ex:treats ex:Headache .
}
```

In the preceding example:

- `PREFIX ex:` defines a shorthand for the namespace `http://example.org/`, which helps simplify the query.
- `SELECT ?medicine` specifies that the variable `?medicine`, which represents medicines in the graph, is to be retrieved.

- The **WHERE** clause defines the pattern to match the triplets where the subject (**?medicine**) has a predicate (**ex:treats**) and the object (**ex:Headache**).

Suppose that the knowledge graph contains triplets like:

```
ex:Aspirin ex:treats ex:Headache
ex:Paracetamol ex:treats ex:Headache
```

The output will be:

```
medicine
---------
ex:Aspirin
ex:Paracetamol
```

Applications of knowledge graph

Knowledge graphs are foundational to many modern information systems, enabling better organization, retrieval, and reasoning over data. Some key applications include:

- **Search and recommendation**: Knowledge graphs enhance search relevance and personalization by understanding user intent and linking related entities, as seen in systems like Google Search or product recommendations.
- **Enterprise knowledge management**: Organizations use knowledge graphs to integrate and structure internal knowledge, documents, processes, and expertise, supporting decision-making and collaboration.
- **Master data management**: Knowledge graphs help unify data from different systems by resolving inconsistencies and establishing relationships among core entities like customers, products, or suppliers.
- **Finance**: In financial systems, knowledge graphs are used to detect fraud, assess risk, and map relationships between accounts, transactions, and entities across regulatory and operational contexts.
- **Drug discovery**: Biomedical knowledge graphs link genes, diseases, compounds, and clinical trials to uncover novel therapeutic targets and drug repurposing opportunities.
- **Chatbots**: By incorporating knowledge graphs, chatbots can provide more accurate, context-aware responses through entity grounding and structured reasoning.

The following section will explore the use of knowledge graphs in the advanced RAG techniques.

Advanced RAG with knowledge graph

Advanced RAG techniques make use of knowledge graphs in several ways. As noted in an earlier section, these techniques are applied across the indexing, pre-retrieval, retrieval, and post-retrieval stages. Knowledge graphs contribute to each of these stages, helping to enhance the quality of the ultimate response.

Knowledge graphs in indexing

Knowledge graphs can be used not only to store knowledge but also to index it in a structured and semantically meaningful way. Their graph-based structure, comprising entities, relationships, and attributes, makes them especially well-suited for organizing hierarchical or interconnected content, such as taxonomies, ontologies, or multi-level concepts within a domain.

In the context of indexing, knowledge graphs support several advanced capabilities:

- **Semantic tagging**: Nodes and edges in the graph can serve as semantic tags for unstructured text. For example, a paragraph discussing a medical condition can be tagged with related entities such as symptoms, treatments, and associated genes.
- **Conceptual indexing**: Rather than relying on surface-level keywords, knowledge graphs enable indexing based on abstract concepts and their relationships.
- **Hierarchical organization**: Graphs naturally support hierarchical indexing, where entities are arranged in parent-child or part-whole relationships.

Knowledge graphs in pre-retrieval

The pre-retrieval techniques in the advanced RAG center around improving the query, specifically in expanding the query. In cases where vector matching is used for retrieval, the more relevant concepts that are included in the query, the better the retrieval performance. Knowledge graphs are instrumental in this process, as they provide a structured way to identify and retrieve related concepts based on the entities and relationships present in the original query.

The method can be described as follows:

1. **Entity recognition**: The original query is analyzed to identify key entities using named entity recognition or linking techniques.

2. **Graph lookup**: These entities are then matched to nodes in a knowledge graph, and the surrounding nodes, such as related concepts, synonyms, associated categories, or hierarchical parents or children, are retrieved.

3. **Query expansion**: The related concepts are then appended to or embedded within the query representation, enriching it with semantically relevant terms.

An example of the query expansion technique is a biomedical question answering system that augments user queries with concepts derived from the **Unified Medical Language System (UMLS)** knowledge graph prior to executing dense retrieval. Similarly, some enterprise knowledge platforms leverage internal ontologies to augment queries with related business terms, improving retrieval coverage and accuracy in domain-specific contexts.

The following is a code snippet that uses the in-memory knowledge graph **networkx** to expand the given query:

```
def expand_query_with_kg(query_entity, graph, depth=1):
   neighbors = set()
    for i in range(depth):
        direct = set(graph.neighbors(query_entity))
        neighbors.update(direct)
        for node in direct:
            neighbors.update(graph.neighbors(node))
    return list(neighbors)
```

Knowledge graphs in retrieval

In the retrieval step, knowledge chunks relevant to the query are fetched from the knowledge store. This step is crucial in determining the quality and relevance of the generated response. Knowledge graphs enhance this phase by enabling retrieval that is structurally aware and semantically grounded. Several techniques are employed in advanced RAG systems to incorporate graph-based reasoning into retrieval:

- **Hybrid retrieval**: This technique combines dense vector retrieval with knowledge graph-based retrieval. For this to be effective, textual chunks must be linked to entities and represented as nodes or attributes within the knowledge graph. The user query is first converted into a set of keywords or entities, which are then matched against the nodes in the graph. Chunks connected to these mapped entities are retrieved. Simultaneously, the vector store performs retrieval using semantic similarity. The results from both retrieval paths are merged or re-ranked, reducing the chances of missing relevant content and offering a more balanced retrieval outcome.

- **Multi-hop retrieval**: This approach extends the hybrid method by incorporating iterative graph traversal. Initially, documents are retrieved using standard vector-based similarity. These documents are then scanned for entities, which serve as anchors for a second stage of retrieval through the knowledge graph. By following links from these entities, across one or more relationship *hops*, the system retrieves additional contextually relevant chunks that may not have been accessible through surface-level matching alone. This is particularly useful for complex queries requiring indirect evidence or reasoning across connected concepts.

These graph-informed strategies help advanced RAG systems retrieve more complete, accurate, and interconnected information, especially in domains where relationships between entities are critical for understanding context, such as biomedical, legal, and technical domains.

Knowledge graph in post-retrieval

The post-retrieval strategies in advanced RAG process the chunks obtained during retrieval. While the retrieval mechanism typically assigns relevance scores to each chunk, these scores may not fully reflect the semantic alignment with the original query. Post-retrieval re-ranking helps refine this ordering to ensure that the most contextually appropriate and factually aligned chunks are prioritized before generation.

Knowledge graphs assist in the re-ranking process by providing structured, relational insights that can be used to evaluate the relevance of retrieved content. The following are two common methods that illustrate the use of knowledge graphs in re-ranking:

- **Entity-relationship alignment**: In this approach, entities and their relationships extracted from the user query are compared with those found in each retrieved chunk. Chunks that contain entities directly referenced in the query, or those closely linked via meaningful relationships in the graph, are assigned higher relevance. This helps ensure that not just keyword overlap, but also conceptual consistency is preserved in the selected inputs.
- **Proximity scoring**: This method involves calculating the graph-based distance between query-related entities and the entities found in the retrieved chunks. The shorter the path or the stronger the semantic connection within the knowledge graph, the higher the chunk is ranked. This graph traversal-based technique is especially valuable when the connection between the query and supporting information is indirect or multi-hop in nature.

By incorporating these techniques based on knowledge graphs, advanced RAG systems can more effectively filter, refine, and rank retrieved information.

RAG with fine-tuning

RAG and fine-tuning are typically regarded as distinct methods for enriching a model's knowledge. Finetuning involves re-training the model using smaller, domain-specific datasets to internalize accurate information, while RAG introduces external knowledge at inference time by incorporating it into the model's input context without modifying the model itself.

Each method offers specific strengths and limitations. Finetuning often results in more precise responses but may still suffer from knowledge gaps and hallucinations. RAG, on the other hand, relies on the quality of its retrieval mechanisms and may face challenges in selecting the most relevant information. Recent developments have demonstrated that combining finetuning with the RAG framework can lead to improved outcomes. Finetuned models can enhance performance across the pre-retrieval, retrieval, and post-retrieval stages of the RAG pipeline.

Finetuned models in pre-retrieval

Finetuned models can be used to improve the user query before retrieval, increasing the likelihood of retrieving relevant and contextually appropriate information. In the pre-retrieval stage of advanced RAG, these models help address limitations such as vague phrasing, missing context, or domain-specific terminology. Several methods are employed to refine the query using fine-tuned models:

- **Query rewriting**: A language model fine-tuned on a dataset of paired user queries and their more effective reformulations is used to rewrite the query in a clearer, more retriever-friendly form. This helps reduce ambiguity and align the query more closely with the knowledge corpus vocabulary.
- **Query expansion**: Finetuned models can expand the original query by appending semantically related terms or entities. These additions are derived from domain-specific corpora or knowledge graphs. The model can be used directly, or the entities extracted can be used to retrieve the additional material from a knowledge graph.
- **Entity enrichment**: A fine-tuned entity recognition or linking model can identify key entities in the query and replace or supplement generic terms with canonical forms. This is particularly useful in technical domains like healthcare, where synonyms and abbreviations are common.
- **Query classification**: Finetuned classifier models can identify the user's intent more precisely and tailor the query accordingly. For instance, distinguishing between a query seeking a definition versus one asking for a procedure.

The following table shows some examples of finetuned models used in pre-retrieval:

Model name	Purpose	Fine-tuned on	Use in advanced RAG
QReCC-T5	Query rewriting	QReCC	Rewriting context-dependent queries
T5 (CQR models)	Query rewriting	CANARD, QReCC	Conversational query reformulation
DocT5Query	Query expansion	Synthetic queries on MSMARCO	Augmenting queries and documents for retrieval
PEGASUS	Query rewriting	News, **question-answering** (**QA**) rewriting datasets	Complex or verbose query reformulation
DistilBERT (fine-tuned)	Query classification	Custom intent datasets (e.g. **Frequently asked questions** (**FAQs**), retail, support)	Classifying queries into types or domains

Table 7.1: Finetuned models used in pre-retrieval

Finetuned models in retrieval

Finetuned models are used to improve the retrieval process in the RAG pipeline by increasing the relevance, accuracy, and domain alignment of the retrieved chunks. These models adapt standard retrievers to perform better in specific domains or tasks, going beyond general-purpose semantic similarity. Some methods are mentioned as follows:

- **Hybrid retriever finetuning**: Hybrid retrieval combines sparse and dense retrieval. Finetuned models are used to extract keywords or entities that are most likely to be part of the graph database. This method ensures balanced retrieval performance, especially when queries may rely on specific keywords, named entities, or domain-specific jargon.
- **Retrieval aware finetuning (RAFT)**: This technique trains an LLM to directly select the right documents from the user query. It can also produce reasoning about why a particular document is more relevant for the query. The RAFT technique is especially suitable for agentic systems that can use the reasoning further.
- **Multi-stage retrieval**: Fine-tuned retrievers can be chained, an initial coarse retriever followed by a refined model, each trained for different levels of granularity or query complexity. This staged approach enhances recall without sacrificing precision.

Models such as BERT and T5 have been finetuned on various datasets to support RAG applications in domains such as biomedical and scientific question answering, as well as news-related tasks. In the RAFT approach, researchers employed a Llama-2 7B model for retrieval finetuning, enabling its application across multiple use cases, including PubMed QA and Trivia QA.

Finetuned models in post-retrieval

Post-retrieval techniques in advanced RAG are designed to enhance the selection of relevant content by re-ranking the initially retrieved material. Although the base retriever generates a ranked list based on similarity scores, finetuned models can provide more nuanced evaluations to improve the quality of the final selection. Several approaches are commonly employed for re-ranking:

- **Cross-encoder re-ranking** involves models that are finetuned to jointly process the query and each retrieved chunk. These models generate relevance scores based on a combined representation of the input pair. Fine-tuning is typically performed using labeled datasets that include query–chunk pairs along with relevance scores.
- **Semantic matching models** are finetuned to evaluate the semantic alignment between a query and a retrieved passage. These models assess whether the retrieved content addresses the underlying intent of the query, rather than relying solely on surface-level similarity. They can be used to eliminate responses that are lexically similar but contextually irrelevant.

- **Graph-aware re-rankers** are employed in systems that incorporate knowledge graphs. These finetuned models consider the alignment of entities and relationships between the query and the retrieved content. They are trained to prioritize chunks that are linked to the same subgraph or share related semantic structures with the query.

An example of a finetuned re-ranking model is **Contextual Late Interaction Bert** (**ColBERT**), developed by the Stanford team using the BERT base model and the MS MARCO dataset. Domain-specific re-rankers have also been created, such as MonoT5-BioMed, which is finetuned from the T5 model for applications in the biomedical domain.

More techniques

The previous section examined the role of knowledge graphs and finetuned models in advanced RAG. Beyond these methods, a wide range of additional techniques is available to GenAI developers working to improve retrieval quality, strengthen the grounding of generated responses, and enhance overall system performance. This section outlines several commonly adopted techniques.

Hybrid retrieval

Hybrid retrieval combines the strengths of both sparse (lexical) and dense (semantic) retrieval methods to enhance the relevance and completeness of retrieved content. Sparse retrieval, typically based on keyword matching, is effective in retrieving documents that contain exact query terms. In contrast, dense retrieval employs vector representations to capture semantic similarity, enabling the retrieval of content even when different vocabularies are used.

The integration of both methods helps mitigate the limitations associated with each approach. Sparse retrieval contributes high precision, while dense retrieval improves recall, particularly for queries requiring contextual understanding or interpretation of paraphrased content. In practical implementations, hybrid retrieval systems often reconcile overlapping results through merging strategies that balance the contributions of both retrievers.

This approach is especially beneficial in domain-specific applications, such as legal, biomedical, or technical question answering, where terminology can vary significantly and information may be expressed in diverse forms. Within advanced RAG pipelines, hybrid retrieval helps prevent omissions of relevant context, thereby supporting the generation of more accurate and comprehensive responses.

A commonly used sparse retrieval method is **Best Matching 25** (**BM25**). BM25 scores documents by evaluating the frequency of query terms, incorporating term importance, and document length normalization. Building upon the **Term Frequency-Inverse Document Frequency** (**TF-IDF**) framework, BM25 introduces tuneable parameters to address issues such as term frequency saturation and document length bias. It is particularly effective in high-precision tasks, including legal and enterprise search. RAG developers use tools like **ElasticSearch** or the **rank_bm25** Python package to implement BM25.

Multi-hop retrieval

Multi-hop retrieval is a technique used when answering a query requires combining information from multiple sources or reasoning across several steps. Unlike single-hop retrieval, which fetches documents solely based on the initial query, multi-hop retrieval proceeds through a series of retrieval stages:

- In the **first hop**, an initial set of chunks is retrieved using dense or sparse methods.
- These chunks are then analyzed to extract key entities, terms, or concepts.
- A **second query** is constructed using the extracted information, and a second round of retrieval is performed to fetch additional chunks that are contextually related but may not be directly linked to the original query.

Multi-hop retrieval is often implemented in combination with knowledge graphs or fine-tuned retrievers to ensure better contextual alignment. It is particularly effective for answering complex questions that require reasoning across multiple facts.

For example, in a medical query about genetic treatments for breast cancer, the first hop may retrieve chunks about genetic mutations, and the second hop will retrieve information on treatments targeting those mutations. Similarly, a financial query about the impact of inflation on an industry may first retrieve inflation trends, followed by industry-specific performance data.

Summary indexing

Indexing summaries is a technique that enhances retrieval by creating and storing condensed representations of chunks alongside the full content. These summaries capture the core meaning of the original text in a more concise form, which improves the quality of retrieval.

Summaries can be generated using extractive or abstractive methods, and their index is linked to the original chunks. During retrieval, queries may be matched against summaries first, helping the retriever prioritize the most relevant content. Since summaries typically reduce noise in the information, they increase the chances of retrieving contextually aligned results, especially when dealing with long or verbose documents.

This method is particularly useful when combined with the **multi-hop strategy**, where the first hop can match the query against summaries. Overall, indexing summaries enables faster, more accurate retrieval and improves the quality of responses in advanced RAG pipelines.

As an example, in a system focused on **tax litigation**, past judgments can be stored along with structured summaries containing the legal issue, jurisdiction, relevant precedents, and court opinions. Such summaries align closely with the types of queries posed by lawyers seeking guidance on ongoing cases.

Query reformulation

Query reformulation is an advanced RAG technique designed to address issues arising from vague or broad user queries. In many cases, user queries may not directly align with the terminology used in source documents, resulting in suboptimal retrieval performance. Query reformulation improves retrieval quality through iterative refinement of the query. It can be considered a variant of the multi-hop retrieval technique, but with a focus on generating a revised query at each step.

The process typically involves three stages:

1. Initial retrieval is conducted using the original query.
2. Reformulation is carried out by analyzing the retrieved content to extract key terms, entities, or concepts, which are then used to generate a more specific and focused query.
3. Second-pass retrieval is performed using the reformulated query to obtain improved or complementary results.

This loop can be repeated multiple times until a satisfactory set of relevant chunks is retrieved.

The iterative process may be supported by finetuned models or knowledge graph–based methods. Query reformulation enhances both recall and precision, making it particularly valuable in complex domains, such as law, medicine, and scientific research, where user queries often require deeper interpretation. By aligning retrieval more closely with the user's intent, this technique significantly improves the generated responses.

Post-generation fact check

Even with high-quality retrieval, language models may produce fluent but incorrect or unsupported content, commonly referred to as hallucinations. Post generation fact checking addresses this issue by evaluating the factual consistency of the generated output against the retrieved documents used during inference.

This process generally involves assessing each factual statement in the generated response to determine whether it is supported by the retrieved content. Several techniques are employed in this context:

- **Claim verification**, where individual factual assertions are extracted from the output and systematically checked against the retrieved chunks for supporting evidence.
- **Verification models**, which use trained classifiers to evaluate whether the retrieved material logically entails the claims made in the generated text.
- **Retrieval-based validation**, where specific claims are re-queried independently to confirm their validity, regardless of the original context.

In some implementations, external fact-checking APIs or knowledge graphs are also used to cross-reference and verify factual claims. In high-stakes domains, such as medical guidance, financial reporting, and legal analysis, post-generation fact checking plays a critical role in ensuring trustworthiness and reliability.

Retrieval caches

While earlier techniques emphasized enhancing the quality of responses generated by the RAG system, optimizing system performance is equally critical, particularly in chatbot-like applications. **Retrieval caching** is a performance optimization method used in advanced RAG systems to store and reuse the results of prior retrieval operations. Given that retrieval can be computationally intensive, especially with dense vector searches, hybrid approaches, or multi-hop strategies, a cache helps eliminate redundant computations by preserving query–retrieval pairs. This enables repeated or similar queries to bypass the full retrieval process and return results more efficiently.

The cache generally includes the following elements:

- The original query
- Retrieved document identifiers or content chunks
- Associated metadata such as retrieval scores or timestamps

Some implementations employ **semantic caching**, which detects semantically equivalent queries using embeddings or clustering techniques, allowing for broader reuse of retrieval results beyond exact matches.

Retrieval caching is particularly useful in applications, such as chatbots, customer support systems, and educational assistants, where user queries often follow repetitive or closely related patterns. This technique enhances responsiveness, reduces backend computational load, and accelerates response generation without compromising output quality.

Development of Customer Success Navigator

Customer service plays a crucial role in shaping a company's reputation, customer loyalty, and long-term success. It serves as the primary touchpoint between a business and its customers, directly influencing how the brand is perceived. High-quality customer service can lead to increased customer satisfaction, repeat business, and positive word-of-mouth referrals, all of which are vital for revenue growth and market competitiveness.

In an increasingly competitive landscape, customers expect quick, personalized, and effective support. When companies meet or exceed these expectations, they build trust and emotional connection, turning one-time buyers into loyal advocates. On the other hand, poor service experiences can lead to negative reviews, customer churn, and long-term brand damage, often outweighing the cost of acquiring new customers.

Good customer service also provides valuable feedback that can inform product improvements, identify market trends, and highlight operational inefficiencies. It acts as a strategic advantage by helping businesses stay customer-centric and agile. In sectors where products are commoditized, service quality often becomes the key differentiator. Therefore, investing in robust, intelligent, and responsive customer service systems is not just a support function; it is a business imperative that drives growth, retention, and competitive resilience.

This section introduces the CSN, a GenAI-based application that uses advanced RAG techniques. Using CSN can improve the efficiency, accuracy, and responsiveness of customer service operations.

Features of the CSN

The **Customer Success** (**CS**) team faces a number of operational challenges that directly impact the quality and efficiency of support. Common issues include:

- Long resolution times, where agents struggle to quickly locate accurate information.
- Inconsistent answers, often resulting from varying levels of experience or incomplete access to institutional knowledge.
- Knowledge fragmentation, where critical information is scattered across multiple systems, documents, and communication channels.

These challenges not only reduce customer satisfaction but also increase agent workload and the risk of errors.

The CSN helps the CS team to overcome these challenges by serving as an intelligent assistant that supports team members in their daily activities. It enhances the efficiency and quality of customer interactions by delivering accurate, contextual, and timely information. Designed with advanced RAG techniques, CSN brings structure to unstructured knowledge, promotes consistency, and significantly reduces response time.

The main features offered by CSN are outlined in the following subsections.

Finding the right information

In a typical customer support environment, team members handle a wide range of queries, from billing issues to product troubleshooting. A major challenge they face is the time and effort required to locate the correct information to resolve a customer's issue. This information may be spread across internal documents, product manuals, training materials, or even previous tickets. As a result, agents often spend a significant portion of their time searching through disconnected sources, switching between tools, or asking colleagues for guidance. This not only delays resolution time but also impacts the overall customer experience.

CSN addresses this challenge by acting as a unified assistant that responds to queries in natural language. Instead of searching through multiple systems, agents can simply ask CSN a question and receive a clear, relevant, and context-aware response. Most importantly, CSN finds past tickets and solutions that are similar to the one being handled. By providing quick access to the right information, CSN reduces response time, helps agents feel more confident in their answers, and allows them to focus on engaging meaningfully with customers.

Ensuring consistent responses

Consistency in customer communication is critical to maintaining trust and professionalism. However, in large support teams, especially those spread across locations or shifts, it is common for different agents to interpret policies, product features, or service processes in slightly different ways. This variation can lead to customers receiving inconsistent answers to similar questions. Such inconsistency not only affects customer satisfaction but may also result in rework, follow-ups, or even escalations. It becomes particularly problematic when team members rely on memory or outdated resources, or when there is no easy way to verify the most current and correct guidance.

The CSN helps to standardize the information by delivering answers based on the most current and validated knowledge. It supports the team by drawing from the latest internal documentation, policy updates, and best practices, ensuring that all team members refer to a single, reliable source. With CSN, responses across the team are similar, which enhances customer trust, reduces confusion, and strengthens the company's professional image.

Working with scattered knowledge

Customer service environments often suffer from scattered information. Critical knowledge is distributed across documents, spreadsheets, archived emails, chat logs, and more. Over time, as processes evolve and updates are added in silos, it becomes difficult for agents to know where to look or which version of a document is reliable. This fragmentation leads to duplicated effort, missed information, and delays in issue resolution. It can also be demotivating for agents who spend more time searching for information than solving customer problems.

The CSN helps overcome this challenge by consolidating information from diverse sources into a single, cohesive interface. Rather than navigating multiple systems, agents interact with one assistant that synthesizes relevant content and presents it in a clear and actionable manner. By doing so, CSN significantly reduces the overhead of knowledge retrieval. Team members spend less time searching and more time resolving issues, resulting in improved productivity, better collaboration, and a smoother customer experience.

Description of the solution

The CSN is a web-based application accessible through a standard browser. It features an intuitive user interface designed to support customer service team members in performing their tasks efficiently. The capabilities of CSN are organized into distinct, easy-to-use functions that align with the key activities of a customer support operation.

The main features of CSN are:

- **Customer query resolution**: Support agents can submit customer questions to CSN in natural language. The system returns information that is relevant to resolving the issue, enabling faster and more informed responses.
- **Case documentation support**: CSN assists agents in composing responses or documenting case notes by generating coherent and context-aware drafts based on the query and related information.
- **Knowledge exploration and discovery**: Team members can use CSN to deepen their understanding of the supported systems, customer history, or operational procedures by querying the knowledge base directly.

The CSN application contains a knowledge store comprising various documents such as previous tickets, product manuals, and standard operating procedures. For demonstration purposes, a dataset of past tickets has been ingested into the system. In a real-world deployment, this store would be significantly larger and continuously updated with new content.

Users access each function through a simple, task-oriented interface. By entering a query or case-specific input, the system generates a relevant and well-structured text response. This output can be reviewed, copied, or directly used in support workflows.

The current implementation serves as a pilot version and supports only the **Customer Query Resolution** functionality. The other two features can be implemented by the reader as an exercise.

Architecture

The architecture of CSN closely follows the design of the **contract intelligence** (**CI**) system described in *Chapter 6, Enhancing GenAI with RAG*. It builds upon the same RAG foundation, with one key enhancement: the integration of a graph database. This addition enables the implementation of advanced RAG techniques such as query enrichment and hybrid retrieval, which are essential for resolving complex, multi-faceted customer queries.

The CSN system comprises the following modules:

- **GenAI module**: This module provides the language generation capability of the system. It uses the **OpenAI GPT-4o-mini model** via the OpenAI API to generate responses based on the retrieved context. The module is designed to work seamlessly with the RAG module and supports controlled generation aligned with CS guidelines.
- **RAG module**: The core logic of the system is implemented in this Python-based module. It handles all tasks related to query processing, document retrieval, and context assembly. It also includes components for:
    - o Query reformulation.
    - o Retrieval from a vector store.

- o Traversal and query of the graph database. The **networkx** graph database is used for this purpose. This choice is suitable for the pilot application. In a production-grade system, this would be replaced with a dedicated graph database such as Neo4j.

This module acts as the back-end service layer for the UI and supports the advanced capabilities of CSN.

- **UI module**: The user interface is implemented using **Streamlit**, offering a clean and interactive web-based front end. Through this interface, customer service agents can enter queries and view responses.
- **Configurations**: This module is adopted from the previous projects.

The modular nature of CSN makes it suitable for future expansion. While the current pilot implementation focuses on the **Customer Query Resolution** functionality, the same architecture can be extended to support additional features such as case documentation support and knowledge exploration with minimal changes.

Development

By this stage, the reader is familiar with the overall development pattern followed throughout the book. Accordingly, only the newly introduced aspects are revisited in this section. The focus of the RAG module development will be on the incorporation of advanced RAG techniques. The user interface module remains largely unchanged from the implementation presented in *Chapter 6, Enhancing GenAI with RAG,* and therefore, its code is not repeated here.

Development of the RAG module

The RAG module exposes a set of Python functions that are invoked by the UI module to support the application's core functionality. The primary functions include:

- **Ingest past tickets dataset**: This function processes a dataset of historical support tickets provided in CSV format. Each ticket is ingested into two components of the system:
  - o The **vector database**, where each ticket is stored as a text chunk for semantic retrieval.
  - o The **knowledge graph**, where relevant keywords and relationships extracted from the ticket data are added as nodes and edges.

  This dual storage approach enables both dense similarity search and graph-based reasoning during query resolution.
- **Customer query resolution**: This function takes as input a user-submitted query from a new support ticket. It retrieves the most relevant past tickets from the vector database and suggests a potential response based on the retrieved context.

The code for the **ingest past tickets** function is explained first. It begins with the necessary imports and configurations. Refer to the following:

```
import pandas as pd
import networkx as nx
from langchain.embeddings import OpenAIEmbeddings
from langchain.vectorstores import FAISS
from langchain.text_splitter import CharacterTextSplitter
from langchain.chat_models import ChatOpenAI
from langchain.chains import LLMChain
from langchain.prompts import PromptTemplate
import os

# Config
os.environ["OPENAI_API_KEY"] = "YOUR_OPENAI_API_KEY"
config.set("CSV_FILE") = "sample_data/2512_07_Ticket_Dataset.csv"
config.set("VECTOR_DB_PATH") = "csn_vector_index"
config.set("GRAPH_FILE") = "csn_graph.gml"
```

Next comes the definition of the function. First, the vector database is created, using a similar method as that used in CI development, shown as follows:

```
def CSN_Ingest_Dataset(ticket_dataset)
  # Load Ticket Data
  df = pd.read_csv(ticket_dataset)

  # Combine into single text chunk per ticket
  tickets = []
  for i, row in df.iterrows():
      text = f"Ticket ID: {i+1}\nTitle: {row['Title']}\nDescription:
{row['Description']}\nModule: {row['Module']}\nResolution:
{row['Resolution']}"
      tickets.append(text)

  #Add to Vector Store
  splitter = CharacterTextSplitter(chunk_size=500, chunk_overlap=0)
  texts = splitter.create_documents(tickets)

  embedding_model = OpenAIEmbeddings()
```

```
  vectorstore = FAISS.from_documents(texts, embedding_model)
  vectorstore.save_local(VECTOR_DB_PATH)
```

The next part of the function deals with populating the knowledge graph. The LLM is used to extract entities from the ticket text. Refer to the following code:

```
  # Extract Entities with LLM
  entity_prompt = PromptTemplate.from_template(
      "Extract the main issue, affected component, and suggested resolution
from the following ticket:\n\n{ticket}\n\nReturn as comma-separated values in
the format: Issue,Component,Resolution."
  )

  llm = ChatOpenAI(model="gpt-4o-mini", temperature=0)
  chain = LLMChain(llm=llm, prompt=entity_prompt)
```

Finally, the entities are added to the networkx knowledge graph, shown as follows:

```
  # Create Knowledge Graph
  G = nx.Graph()

  for i, text in enumerate(tickets):
      response = chain.run(ticket=text).strip()
      try:
          issue, component, resolution = [x.strip() for x in response.
split(",")]
          issue_node = f"Issue: {issue}"
          component_node = f"Component: {component}"
          resolution_node = f"Resolution: {resolution}"

          G.add_node(issue_node, type="Issue")
          G.add_node(component_node, type="Component")
          G.add_node(resolution_node, type="Resolution")

          G.add_edge(issue_node, component_node, relation="occurs_in")
          G.add_edge(issue_node, resolution_node, relation="resolved_by")
      except Exception as e:
          print(f"Failed to parse response for ticket {i+1}: {response}")

  #  Save Graph to Disk
  nx.write_gml(G, GRAPH_FILE)
```

Both the vector and graph databases are saved to disc for use in the query functions.

The **resolve customer query** function used both the vector and graph databases. The code for the function is given as follows. It begins with loading the vector store and graph database from disk.

```
def CSN_resolve_customer_query(user_query: str, k: int = 2):
    """Resolves a customer query using vector retrieval, graph enrichment, and 
LLM generation."""

    # Load vector store
    embedding_model = OpenAIEmbeddings()
    vectorstore = FAISS.load_local(VECTOR_DB_PATH, embedding_model, allow_
dangerous_deserialization=True)

    # Load graph
    G = nx.read_gml(GRAPH_FILE)
```

It then retrieves similar tickets using vector similarity from the FAISS database. The retrieved tickets are used to search for similar content in the graph database. Note that this is a simple method of searching in the knowledge graph, suitable for this demonstration. Refer to the following code:

```
    # Retrieve Similar Tickets
    docs = vectorstore.similarity_search(user_query, k=k)
    retrieved_texts = [doc.page_content for doc in docs]

    # Enrich with Graph Context
    enrichment_context = ""
    for node in G.nodes:
        if user_query.lower().find(node.lower().replace("Issue: ", "")) != -1:
            neighbors = list(G.neighbors(node))
            for n in neighbors:
                edge = G.edges[node, n].get("relation", "related_to")
                enrichment_context += f"{edge.title().replace('_', ' ')}: 
{n}\n"
```

We now use the LLM to generate the answer using a prompt enriched with the content from the graph as follows:

```
    # Enrich the prompt from the graph nodes
    prompt = PromptTemplate.from_template(
        """You are a customer support assistant.
```

```
Use the following retrieved tickets and enriched context to answer the
customer's question.
Customer Question: {query}

--- Retrieved Tickets ---
{tickets}

--- Enriched Context ---
{context}

Write a clear and helpful response."""
    )

    llm = ChatOpenAI(model="gpt-4o-mini", temperature=0)

    final_input = prompt.format(
        query=user_query,
        tickets="\n\n".join(retrieved_texts),
        context=enrichment_context or "None"
    )

    response = llm.predict(final_input)

    return retrieved_texts, response
```

Development of the UI module

The Streamlit-based UI module closely follows the UI module for CI outlined in *Chapter 6, Enhancing GenAI with RAG*. Readers are encouraged to adapt it for CSN by incorporating the following functions:

- Provide the menu Resolve Query.
- Accept the customer query from the user.
- Call the **`CSN_resolve_customer_query`** function.
- Display the similar tickets and generated response.

Conclusion

This chapter explored the evolution of RAG from its basic form to a more robust and capable framework known as advanced RAG. While naïve RAG enhances language models by retrieving external knowledge, it suffers from several limitations. Advanced RAG addresses these gaps through techniques such as indexing methods, query refinement, and hybrid and multi-hop retrieval. The integration of knowledge graphs plays a central role by adding semantic enrichment. The chapter also highlighted how fine-tuned models can be embedded into each phase of the RAG pipeline.

To ground these techniques in a real-world context, the chapter concluded with the development of the CSN: a GenAI application built on advanced RAG principles. CSN demonstrates how intelligent assistants can streamline customer service by providing fast, accurate, and consistent responses. It has a modular design, powered by vector search and a knowledge graph, that delivers a scalable, efficient, and context-aware enterprise solution.

The next chapter builds upon this foundation by exploring LLM agents, autonomous systems that can reason, plan, and act. These agents go beyond single-turn question answering to perform multi-step tasks, interact with tools, and adapt dynamically to goals.

Chapter 8
Agentic Workflows

Introduction

Generative AI models have been applied in various practical contexts. They are commonly used through prompting and can be further enhanced via finetuning or methods such as **retrieval-augmented generation** (**RAG**). Several such approaches have been explored earlier in this book. A shared characteristic of these applications is that the models are limited to generating content and do not initiate any actions; execution remains the user's responsibility. In this sense, the role of the GenAI system is advisory in nature.

Systems that leverage GenAI capabilities to perform actions belong to a distinct category known as **agents** or **agentic workflows**. The ability to take action significantly increases the practical value of these systems in industrial settings, where they can be used to automate routine and time-consuming tasks. This contributes to reducing manual effort, enhancing operational efficiency and accuracy, and ultimately improving organizational profitability.

This chapter examines the key components involved in constructing agentic workflows. It starts with an introduction to the fundamentals and progresses toward exploring the diverse architectures commonly employed in their implementation. Several frameworks have gained popularity among developers working on agentic systems. One such framework is used in this chapter to illustrate the development of a real-world agentic system designed to automate IT processes within an organization.

Despite their recent emergence, agentic workflow systems have seen rapid and widespread adoption across various industries. For developers working with GenAI, understanding how to build such systems is both highly practical and increasingly important.

Structure

This chapter covers the following topics:

- Basics of AI agents
- ReAct framework
- Reflexion framework
- Applications of agents

- Practical issues of debugging and optimization
- Introduction to LlamaIndex
- Development of the IT Ops Agent

Objectives

By the end of this chapter, you will have a clear understanding of agentic workflows and how they extend the capabilities of language models through reasoning, planning, and tool integration. You will learn the foundational concepts of AI agents, including their definition and the three core components: tools, memory, and orchestration. You will explore two widely used frameworks for building agents, namely, ReAct and Reflexion, and understand how they enable more intelligent, adaptive behavior. You will also examine real-world applications of AI agents across industries. Finally, you will study the development of ITOA, an AI agent implemented using the LlamaIndex framework, to see how such agents can help in automating IT operations.

Basics of AI agents

A variety of terms are commonly used in the industry to describe agentic workflows. These include AI agents, agentic AI, agentic workflows, LLM agents, and agents, often used interchangeably. In this chapter, the terms **agent** and **agentic workflow** are used with equivalent meaning.

There is also considerable ambiguity surrounding the definition of an agent. With numerous AI-based solutions in use, it is easy to misidentify any GenAI-powered system as an agent. The most effective way to clarify what constitutes an agent is through comparison with other types of systems that employ generative AI models, such as chatbots.

Defining an agent

There are two primary ways in which generative AI models are utilized by users:

- **Directly prompting the model**: In this mode, the user provides a prompt comprising text, images, or other modalities, and the model responds by generating a corresponding output. This interaction can be considered *conversational*, where the responsibility for crafting effective prompts and interpreting or using the output lies entirely with the user.

- **Building a system that uses the model**: In this approach, the model is embedded within a software system to perform specific tasks as part of a broader workflow. The user does not interact with the model directly and may not even be aware of its involvement. For instance, an accounts payable system might employ a large language model to compare invoices with purchase orders during payment processing.

An agent represents the second type of usage of generative AI models. However, not all systems that utilize models in this way qualify as agents. To be considered an agent, a system must meet the following three additional requirements:

- **The system should be aware of its environment**: The environment includes all parameters that influence the system's behavior. For example, in the case of a self-driving car, the environment would encompass the area surrounding the vehicle as well as the current status of internal components such as the engine and battery. This forms the sensing capability of the agent.
- **The system must perform some action**: The actions taken by the system are determined by both the input and the current state of the environment.
- **The system should be autonomous**: Autonomy implies that the system determines its own processing workflow using an AI model.

In summary, agents are systems that integrate AI models, are aware of their environment, and act in an autonomous manner.

Strictly speaking, agents are not necessarily AI systems. Autonomous systems, such as CD players that automatically switch disks, existed before the development of AI. However, this discussion focuses specifically on AI agents, those that utilize AI to perform actions and automate workflows.

Sensing the environment

Sensing the environment is a fundamental capability of an agent. The quality of the agent's performance depends largely on how effectively it can sense its surroundings. The environment can be viewed as an implicit input to the agent. Consider an agent designed to detect cyberattacks: it must access logs of all relevant activities, connect to every available data source, and collect this information on a regular schedule. The components that enable an agent to gather such information about its environment can be referred to as its sensors.

Performing action

GenAI models by themselves are limited to generating content, such as text, images, or code. They cannot directly interact with the external world or execute tasks. To enable action, these models must be augmented with tools and connected systems that allow them to trigger operations. For example, an agent may use APIs to update a database, send an email, or control enterprise software. The model decides what action is needed, while the tools execute it. This combination of reasoning from the model and execution through tools transforms a passive content generator into an active, task-performing agent.

Automating task workflow

While a single action performed by a model may be sufficient to complete simple tasks, real-world tasks are often more complex and require a structured workflow. A workflow consists of a series of steps, each responsible for carrying out a specific action. These steps are not always executed in a simple linear sequence; instead, they often involve branching logic, conditional sub-flows, and iterative loops to handle different scenarios. For example, an IT automation agent resolving an incident may first analyze logs, then decide whether to restart a service, escalate the issue, or collect additional diagnostic data.

By orchestrating such workflows dynamically, agents can handle tasks of varying complexity, adapt to changing conditions, and ensure that the right actions are performed in the correct order. This ability to automate multi-step workflows is what makes agentic systems highly valuable for industrial and enterprise applications.

Components of agents

The fundamental capabilities of an AI agent encompass three essential aspects: the ability to take actions, the capacity to sense and interpret its environment, and the competence to operate autonomously without constant human intervention. To realize these capabilities in practice, an agent must be built upon three core components: tools, orchestration, and memory. Tools enable the agent to interact with external systems and perform specific tasks. The following sections explore each of these components in detail, using the example of a travel booking agent to illustrate their role and significance.

Tools

Tools are external systems that give an agent the capability to interact with and gather information from the outside world. Common examples include:

- Searching on the web
- Performing mathematical calculations
- Accessing a database
- Making a payment

Most tools are software systems designed to be accessed by other programs, typically through an **application programming interface** (**API**). They play a vital role in enabling two essential functions of an agent: sensing the environment and taking actions within it.

For a travel booking agent, useful tools may include:

- Searching for hotels and flight bookings
- Currency conversion

- Weather services
- Payment gateways

Each tool serves a specific function. For example, a search tool can be used to identify suitable flights and hotels along with their prices. Choosing the right set of tools is critical for an agent's performance, as their effectiveness depends on their capabilities. Ideally, these tools should be general-purpose enough to handle a variety of similar tasks, ensuring the agent remains versatile and adaptable.

Orchestration

Orchestration forms the core of an AI agent and acts as the primary source of its intelligence. Its responsibilities include:

- Converting the user's goal into a series of actionable steps and planning the subtasks necessary to achieve that goal.
- Selecting the most suitable tools to perform each subtask.
- Managing the flow of operations so that tasks are executed in the correct order and interdependencies are handled effectively.
- Identifying inconsistencies, such as contradictory outputs from different tools or missing information, and deciding on appropriate resolutions.
- Deciding whether the user should be informed or consulted before proceeding, particularly when decisions or exceptions arise.

In contemporary AI agents, orchestration is often driven by a **large language model** (**LLM**) with reasoning capabilities, enabling it to decompose complex objectives into manageable parts and determine the best way forward. It may also make use of specialized models for targeted functions, such as price estimation or sentiment evaluation.

For a travel booking agent, orchestration might start with receiving a user's request, for example, arranging a trip between two cities within a specified budget. It would then plan the subtasks, finding flights, comparing hotel options, checking weather forecasts, and calculating the overall cost. Each of these subtasks would be delegated to the appropriate tool, and the gathered results would be consolidated into a unified, coherent output. Orchestration is therefore the decisive factor in ensuring the agent's overall effectiveness and in delivering a satisfactory user experience.

Memory

Memory is a crucial element of an AI agent, allowing it to store and organize task-related information so that the entire process remains coherent and consistent. It preserves context across all stages of execution, enabling the agent to operate with continuity and efficiency.

Without memory, each step would be disconnected, forcing repeated retrieval of the same data and increasing the risk of incomplete or conflicting results.

Orchestration makes extensive use of memory to retain:

- The user's initial request
- Intermediate results generated during execution
- Decisions taken at various stages
- Constraints and preferences that must be upheld throughout the task

This context enables the orchestrator to make informed choices, resolve conflicts, and maintain a smooth flow of operations.

Tools also rely on memory, especially when their outputs and inputs are interdependent. For example, a flight search tool may need previously chosen travel dates or preferred airlines, while a hotel booking tool may require the destination city identified earlier in the workflow.

Memory can be implemented in several forms, such as short-term memory for ongoing tasks and long-term memory for storing historical interaction data. It may be managed in structured databases, vector stores for semantic retrieval, or graph databases, such as those discussed in *Chapter 7, Advanced RAG in Action,* which are well-suited for representing interconnected information.

In a travel booking agent, memory might hold details such as the destination, budget, travel dates, and earlier search results. This allows the agent to refine recommendations, avoid redundant queries, and keep all subtasks aligned, ensuring accuracy, consistency, and a seamless user experience.

The following figure highlights the important components of an AI agent:

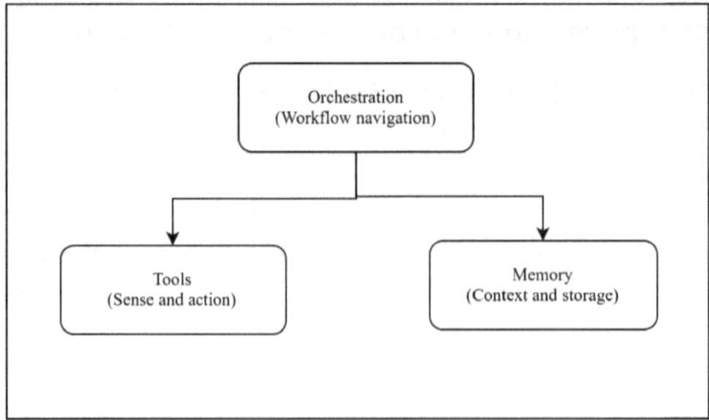

***Figure 8.1**: Components of an AI agent*

Building agentic workflows presents significant challenges, largely due to their autonomous nature, which requires coordination, decision-making, and adaptability without constant human oversight. To address these complexities, several frameworks have recently been developed to assist developers in designing and implementing such systems. This chapter will focus on two notable examples, ReAct and Reflection, examining how each framework structures the workflow, manages reasoning and action, and supports the development of effective AI agents.

ReAct framework

Using a framework as a guide simplifies the process of developing AI agents by providing a clear structure for their design. ReAct is not a programming framework but a conceptual approach that helps frame any problem statement in terms of an agent's reasoning and actions. Introduced in recent research, it combines reasoning steps with tool usage in a unified process, enabling agents to think, act, and learn iteratively. This makes it applicable across a wide range of problem domains.

Basics of ReAct

Out of the three core components of an AI agent, i.e., tools, orchestration, and memory, the ReAct framework is primarily concerned with implementing the orchestration function. It provides a structured way for an agent to plan and execute actions by combining reasoning and acting in a single process. ReAct relies on prompt engineering techniques, particularly the **chain-of-thought** (**CoT**) method, to guide the agent's decision-making. It can be recalled from *Chapter 4, Prompt Engineering*, that CoT involves asking the model to share its intermediate observations.

The framework operates in a loop that continues until the task is completed. This loop consists of four repeating steps:

1. **Thought**: In this step, the agent reflects on the current state of the problem, breaks it down into manageable parts, and decides the next course of action. The reasoning is explicitly represented in natural language, making the process transparent and easier to audit.

2. **Action**: The agent performs an operation based on its reasoning. This could involve invoking a tool such as querying a database, conducting a web search, or any other predefined task.

3. **Observation**: The result of the action is recorded. This may be raw data, retrieved information, or an error message. The observation provides the evidence that will inform the next reasoning step.

4. **Thought (repeat)**: The agent processes the observation, reassesses the situation, and determines the next action, continuing the loop until the overall goal is achieved.

By alternating between reasoning and acting, the ReAct framework enables agents to adapt dynamically to new information and maintain coherent progress toward their objectives.

ReAct framework makes use of the other two components of the agent. **Tools** are invoked during the **Action** step to perform specific operations, such as retrieving data or executing transactions. **Memory** supports both reasoning and decision-making by storing the user's request, thoughts, as well as the observations, ensuring that each loop iteration builds on prior steps. Together, tools and memory work alongside orchestration to maintain continuity and improve the accuracy of the agent's responses.

Designing the ReAct prompt

The ReAct prompt is central to enabling the agent to follow the **Thought–Action–Observation** loop in a controlled and repeatable way. It typically includes several key elements:

- **Task description**: A clear statement of the user's goal, ensuring the agent understands the scope and constraints of the task.
- **Available tools**: A description of the tools the agent can use, along with their usage formats, so the agent knows exactly how to invoke them.
- **Output structure**: A specific format for the agent's responses, often something like:

```
Thought: [Reasoning about the next step]
Action: [Tool name and parameters]
Observation: [Tool output]
```

- **Looping instruction**: Guidance on when to repeat the cycle and when to stop.

The most important feature is the structured output, which makes it possible to implement the agentic workflow programmatically. By parsing the output into distinct fields, the orchestration layer can execute actions, feed observations back into the reasoning process, and maintain control over the workflow.

Care must be taken to phrase the prompt unambiguously, avoid excessive verbosity in intermediate thoughts, and ensure that the agent does not hallucinate tool names or formats. A well-crafted prompt directly impacts the stability and effectiveness of the agent's behavior.

Example of a ReAct prompt

The ReAct prompt can be illustrated using the example of a travel booking agent. Here is a sample:

```
You are a travel booking assistant.
Your task is to help the user plan and book a trip based on their preferences
and constraints.
You have access to the following tools:
1. FlightSearch[origin, destination, date] - Searches for flights between two
cities on a specific date.
```

```
2. HotelSearch[city, checkin_date, checkout_date] - Finds hotels in a city for the specified dates.
3. CurrencyConvert[amount, from_currency, to_currency] - Converts currency values.
4. WeatherCheck[city, date] - Provides weather forecast for a specific date in a city.
5. PaymentGateway[amount, currency] - Processes a payment.

You also have access to the following memory:
- User's preferences (e.g., budget, preferred airlines, hotel ratings)
- Past search results
- Any constraints given by the user

You must work in the following loop until the task is completed:
Thought: Reason about the next step based on the goal, memory, and current observations.
Action: Select the most appropriate tool and provide its parameters in the given format.
Observation: Record the result returned by the tool.

When all subtasks are completed, output a final answer summarizing the itinerary and costs.
```

This prompt defines the role of the agent, enumerates the **tools** it can use, and describes the **memory** available for decision-making. The **Thought–Action–Observation** loop is clearly specified, enabling the orchestration layer to parse and control the workflow. Explicit tool formats ensure predictable outputs, while memory access instructions help maintain context and avoid redundant work. Finally, the **stop condition**—producing a final itinerary—ensures the agent concludes its operation once the user's goal is met.

Since this is an example, the tools are assumed to be built and available. When the prompt runs, it will take several iterations to complete its task. Here is a sample output:

```
User Goal: "Book me a trip from New York to Paris from 15th to 20th September, budget $1500."
Step 1
Thought: The user wants a trip from New York to Paris within a budget of $1500. First, I need to find available flights for the given dates.
Action: FlightSearch[New York, Paris, 2025-09-15]
Observation: Found 3 flights; cheapest is $650 (round trip).
Step 2
Thought: With $650 spent on flights, $850 remains for hotels and other costs.
```

```
Next, I should find a suitable hotel in Paris.
Action: HotelSearch[Paris, 2025-09-15, 2025-09-20]
Observation: Found hotels ranging from $100 to $250 per night; a 4-star hotel
is available for $150/night.
Step 3
Thought: The selected hotel will cost $750 for 5 nights. Total so far is $650
+ $750 = $1400, which is within budget. I should check the weather to confirm
suitable travel conditions.
Action: WeatherCheck[Paris, 2025-09-15]
Observation: Forecast shows mild and sunny weather for the entire trip.
Step 4
Thought: All constraints satisfied—good flight, suitable hotel, within budget, and
favorable weather. I can now present the final itinerary to the user.
Action: None (final output)
Observation: None
Final Answer:
"Your trip from New York to Paris from 15-20 September is booked with AirFrance
(round trip $650) and Le Grand Paris Hotel (5 nights at $150/night, total $750).
Total cost is $1400. Expected weather: sunny and mild."
```

Real-world implementations and applications

The ReAct framework has been successfully applied in multiple domains, showcasing its ability to combine reasoning and tool usage in iterative workflows. Key application areas include:

- **Research and knowledge work**
    - o Building intelligent research assistants that break down complex queries.
    - o Searching academic databases, summarizing findings, and synthesizing conclusions.
- **Customer service**
    - o Developing agents that diagnose technical issues through clarifying questions.
    - o Querying internal systems and suggesting targeted, actionable solutions.
- **Data analysis**
    - o Creating conversational agents that query databases, perform calculations, and generate visualizations.
    - o Making advanced analytics accessible to non-technical users.

- **Travel and logistics**
    - o Implementing agents that search flights, check weather, calculate budgets, and confirm bookings.
    - o Adapting dynamically to user preferences and constraints.

Frameworks and platforms that support ReAct-style implementations include:

- **LangChain**: Offers native patterns for Thought–Action–Observation loops.
- **LlamaIndex**: Integrates retrieval capabilities into ReAct orchestration.
- **Haystack**: Designed for RAG but adaptable for ReAct style reasoning.
- **OpenAI function calling**: Enables structured execution of actions in ReAct loops.

These examples highlight that ReAct is not only a conceptual framework but also a practical, production-ready methodology for developing autonomous agents that integrate seamlessly with diverse tools and memory systems.

Reflexion framework

The Reflexion framework is a conceptual approach for developing AI agents that integrates self-reflection into their operation. Unlike the ReAct framework, which focuses on step-by-step reasoning and action execution, Reflexion introduces an additional stage where the agent evaluates its own reasoning, detects potential errors, and generates improved responses. This self-assessment loop allows the agent to refine its outputs before presenting them to the user, increasing both accuracy and reliability.

Reflexion is particularly valuable for complex, ambiguous, or high-stakes tasks where a single pass of reasoning might not yield optimal results. By reviewing its earlier reasoning and results, the agent can identify gaps, inconsistencies, or alternative solutions, and then incorporate these insights into a revised plan of action. This makes the framework useful across domains such as problem-solving, research, planning, and creative tasks, where thoughtful iteration can significantly enhance performance.

Basics of Reflexion framework

The Reflexion framework focuses on enhancing the orchestration layer by adding a meta-reasoning capability. While traditional orchestration executes a sequence of planned steps, Reflexion adds an iterative process where the agent pauses to assess its own outputs before deciding whether to proceed or revise its approach.

The framework typically follows a three-phase loop that continues until the task is completed or a stopping condition is met:

1. **Reasoning phase**: The agent generates an initial solution or response using its standard reasoning and tools. This is similar to the output from a ReAct-style orchestration.
2. **Reflection phase**: The agent critically evaluates its own reasoning and output. This may involve identifying logical errors, missing information, irrelevant steps, or opportunities for improvement. The reflection can be guided by prompts that encourage error detection and solution refinement.
3. **Refinement phase**: Based on the insights from reflection, the agent updates its plan or modifies its solution, potentially re-running certain steps or exploring alternative strategies.

Reflexion can be implemented using prompt engineering with large language models, where each phase is explicitly defined and guided. Memory plays a key role in preserving both the original reasoning and the reflections, ensuring that improvements are cumulative rather than repetitive. Tools are invoked during both reasoning and refinement phases to gather additional data, verify facts, or test new hypotheses.

In the context of a travel booking agent, Reflexion could be used to re-check proposed itineraries for better prices, improved scheduling, or overlooked user preferences before finalizing the booking.

Example of a Reflexion prompt

To demonstrate the approach, the same travel booking agent example is implemented using a prompt designed according to Reflection principles. The sample prompt is as follows:

```
You are an AI travel booking agent. Your task is to plan and book a trip for the user based on their requirements.
You have access to the following tools:
- Flight Search Tool
- Hotel Search Tool
- Weather Information Tool
- Currency Conversion Tool
- Payment Gateway

Follow this process:

1. Reasoning:
   - Think step-by-step about the travel request.
    - Break it into subtasks (e.g., find flights, check hotels, review weather, calculate total cost).
   - Decide the best sequence for completing the subtasks.
```

```
2. Reflection:
   - Critically evaluate your reasoning and results.
   - Check for:
      a) Flight and hotel mismatches in dates or locations
      b) Costs exceeding budget
      c) Missing or unclear user preferences
      d) Opportunities for better deals or options
   - Suggest improvements.

3. Refinement:
   - Adjust the plan based on the reflection.
   - Re-run any necessary searches or calculations.
   - Output the improved travel itinerary.

Format your output as:
Thought: [reasoning for the current step]
Action: [tool call or step taken]
Observation: [result of action]
Reflection: [critical evaluation]
Refined Thought: [improved reasoning or plan]
Final Answer: [final improved travel plan for the user]

Important:
- Always preserve the user's budget, preferred dates, and destinations across steps.
- Use the reflection phase to actively improve the travel plan, not just restate it.
```

The following sample output represents a dummy run:

```
User Request:
"I want to travel from New York to Paris from September 15-22, with a budget of $2,500, including flights and hotel. I prefer a 4-star or better hotel and would like to avoid overnight flights."
Step 1 - Thought:
The trip requires finding a round-trip flight from New York to Paris within the given dates, avoiding overnight departures, and finding a 4-star hotel for 7 nights. I need to keep the total cost under $2,500.
```

```
Step 2 - Action:
Call Flight Search Tool for flights from New York to Paris, departing Sept 15,
returning Sept 22, avoiding overnight flights.
Step 3 - Observation:
Found a direct flight on Air France: Depart 10:00 AM Sept 15, Return 1:00 PM Sept
22. Price: $1,200 round trip.
Step 4 - Action:
Call Hotel Search Tool for Paris, Sept 15-22, 4-star or better.
Step 5 - Observation:
Hotel Le Parisien (4-star) available for $1,050 total for 7 nights.
Step 6 - Thought:
Flight + Hotel = $2,250. This is within budget.
Step 7 - Reflection:
Dates match - Yes
Location correct - Yes
No weather check performed—could impact trip enjoyment
Budget within limit - Yes
Opportunity: Check if slightly cheaper flight/hotel could allow for extra
activities.
Step 8 - Refinement:
Search alternative hotel for $950, saving $100 for activities. Also check Paris
weather forecast.
Step 9 - Observation:
Alternative hotel found: Hôtel Jardin (4-star) for $950. Weather forecast:
Mostly sunny, 20-24°C.
Step 10 - Final Answer:
Flight: Air France, direct, $1,20
Hotel: Hôtel Jardin, $950
Total: $2,150 (leaves $350 for activities)
Weather: Mostly sunny, 20-24°C
```

Real world implementation and applications

While Reflexion is a conceptual framework, its ideas can be implemented using a variety of programming tools and agent development platforms. These frameworks provide the infrastructure to integrate the core elements of Reflexion, i.e., reasoning, reflection, and improved action selection, into practical systems.

Commonly used options include:

- **LangChain**: Offers memory management, tool integration, and customizable agent workflows. Reflexion can be implemented using chains that include both reasoning and reflection steps before producing a final output.
- **LlamaIndex**: Useful for data-rich applications, enabling the agent to reflect on retrieved knowledge before responding.
- **Auto-GPT and BabyAGI**: Autonomous agent frameworks that can be adapted to include reflection cycles, ensuring more accurate and context-aware task execution.
- **Haystack**: Particularly suited for search-heavy tasks, where reflection can be applied to improve retrieval accuracy and reasoning over large knowledge bases.

By selecting the right platform and combining it with thoughtful prompt design, developers can operationalize Reflexion for a wide range of applications, from research assistants to complex planning agents.

Applications of agents

AI agents are increasingly being adopted across industries and business functions due to their ability to operate autonomously, integrate multiple data sources, and adapt to complex workflows. By combining tools, orchestration, and memory, agents can perform tasks ranging from routine automation to sophisticated decision-making. Their flexibility allows them to be tailored for specific domains or functions, improving efficiency, reducing costs, and enabling new capabilities that were previously impractical. This section explores two key perspectives: how agents are applied across various industries, and how they support different functions within a company, regardless of the industry.

Applications in various industries

AI agents are reshaping operations across a wide range of industries by automating complex processes, improving decision-making, and enabling highly personalized services. Their versatility allows them to tackle sector-specific challenges while utilizing shared capabilities such as data analysis, predictive modeling, and workflow orchestration. The following sub-sections examine key industries where AI agents are driving significant impact and innovation.

Healthcare

AI agents are increasingly being deployed in the healthcare industry to enhance efficiency, accuracy, and patient outcomes. Key applications include:

- **Clinical decision support**: By analyzing patient data, medical histories, and relevant medical literature, AI agents assist healthcare professionals in identifying potential diagnoses and recommending suitable treatment options. This enables faster, evidence-based decision-making while reducing the chances of oversight.

- **Virtual health assistants**: AI agents provide patients with round-the-clock access to health information, reminders for medication, and post-treatment guidance. This continuous support improves adherence to treatment and reduces the need for frequent consultations.
- **Administrative automation**: Tasks such as appointment scheduling, insurance verification, and medical coding can be efficiently handled by AI agents. Automating these processes allows healthcare staff to devote more time to direct patient care.

Financial services

AI agents are playing a significant role in transforming banking and financial services by improving security, personalization, and operational efficiency. Notable applications include:

- **Fraud detection and risk management**: AI agents continuously monitor transaction patterns to detect anomalies that may indicate fraudulent activity. They can flag suspicious transactions in real-time, enabling rapid investigation and prevention of financial losses.
- **Personalized financial advisory**: By analyzing a customer's financial history, spending habits, and investment goals, AI agents can offer tailored advice on budgeting, saving, and investing. This personalized approach enhances customer engagement and helps individuals make more informed financial decisions.
- **Process automation**: Agents handle routine tasks such as loan application processing, compliance checks, and account management. This automation speeds up service delivery while reducing human error and operational costs.

Retail

AI agents are reshaping the retail industry by enabling personalized shopping experiences, optimizing operations, and improving customer service. Key applications include:

- **Personalized product recommendations**: By analyzing customer browsing history, purchase patterns, and preferences, AI agents suggest relevant products in real-time. This personalization boosts customer satisfaction and increases sales conversions.
- **Inventory and supply chain optimization**: Agents monitor stock levels, predict demand trends, and coordinate with suppliers to prevent overstocking or stockouts. These capabilities help retailers maintain efficiency and reduce operational costs.
- **Customer service chatbots**: AI-powered agents provide instant responses to customer inquiries, assist with order tracking, and process returns. This 24/7 support enhances the shopping experience while reducing the workload on human staff.

Travel and hospitality

AI agents are transforming the travel and hospitality industry by enhancing trip planning, streamlining operations, and delivering personalized guest experiences. Key applications are:

- **Personalized travel planning**: Agents recommend destinations, itineraries, and activities based on user preferences, budget, and travel history. This customization makes trip planning more efficient and enjoyable for travelers.
- **Dynamic pricing:** AI agents analyze market trends, competitor prices, and booking patterns to adjust prices in real-time. This helps airlines, hotels, and tour operators maximize revenue while remaining competitive.
- **Guest experience enhancement**: Virtual concierge agents assist guests with room service requests, local recommendations, and itinerary changes. These services improve convenience and overall satisfaction during the stay.

Applications to business functions

AI agents are increasingly being embedded into core business functions, enabling organizations to operate more efficiently, make better decisions, and deliver enhanced value to customers and employees alike. By automating routine tasks, providing data-driven insights, and enabling personalized interactions, these agents help businesses achieve greater speed, accuracy, and scalability. Their applications span diverse areas such as marketing, customer service, human resources, and supply chain management, where they optimize workflows, improve engagement, and support strategic decision-making. The following sub-sections explore how AI agents are transforming each of these functions, reshaping the way organizations work and compete in a fast-changing business environment.

Marketing

Marketing is one of the most dynamic areas where AI agents are making a strong impact. Their ability to process vast amounts of customer and market data in real-time allows marketers to make faster, more informed decisions. AI agents not only automate repetitive tasks but also enhance creativity and precision in targeting audiences. Applications include:

- **Personalized campaign optimization**: AI agents analyze customer behavior, preferences, and interaction history in real-time to design and adjust marketing campaigns for specific audience segments. This ensures higher engagement rates and improved return on marketing investment.
- **Lead qualification and nurturing**: Agents automatically evaluate incoming leads based on data from multiple sources, assigning scores and triggering relevant follow-up actions. They also maintain ongoing communication with prospects until they are ready for direct sales engagement.

- **Content creation and curation**: AI agents generate marketing copy, social media posts, or ad creatives tailored to different customer personas. They also curate relevant content from external sources to keep audiences engaged.
- **Market trend analysis**: By continuously monitoring competitor activities, consumer sentiment, and emerging market signals, AI agents provide marketers with timely insights to adjust strategies ahead of changing market conditions.

Customer service

Customer service has rapidly evolved with the introduction of AI agents, enabling organizations to provide faster, more consistent, and more personalized support. These agents handle a wide range of interactions across channels, reducing the need for human intervention in routine cases and allowing service teams to focus on complex issues. The result is improved customer satisfaction and lower operational costs. Some use cases in customer service are:

- **24/7 multichannel support**: AI agents can manage customer inquiries through chat, email, voice, and social media at any time, ensuring instant responses and consistent quality of service.
- **Intelligent case routing**: By analyzing the content and urgency of incoming queries, AI agents direct cases to the most suitable human agent or department, minimizing resolution time.
- **Proactive issue resolution**: Agents monitor product usage patterns, detect potential problems, and reach out to customers with solutions before they encounter an issue.
- **Knowledge base management**: AI agents continuously update and optimize internal and public knowledge bases by identifying gaps and improving content, making self-service more effective.

Human resources

HR functions benefit greatly from AI agents that can automate administrative tasks, enhance recruitment efficiency, and improve employee engagement. These agents act as digital HR Assistants, streamlining processes while ensuring data-driven decision-making. This allows HR teams to focus more on strategic workforce initiatives and less on repetitive operations. Applications of agents in HR include:

- **Automated candidate screening**: AI agents evaluate resumes, match qualifications with job requirements, and shortlist suitable candidates, reducing manual effort and bias.
- **Interview scheduling and coordination**: By integrating with calendars and communication tools, AI agents manage interview logistics seamlessly for both recruiters and candidates.

- **Employee onboarding assistance**: Agents guide new hires through paperwork, policy familiarization, and training schedules, ensuring a smooth transition into the organization.
- **Employee query handling**: AI agents serve as the first point of contact for HR-related inquiries, instantly providing accurate answers about leave policies, benefits, and procedures.

Supply chain management

Supply chain operations involve complex coordination across procurement, production, logistics, and distribution. AI agents can enhance visibility, optimize decision-making, and respond quickly to disruptions. By analyzing large volumes of real-time data, these agents help maintain efficiency, reduce costs, and improve service levels across the supply chain network. Some applications are as follows:

- **Demand forecasting support**: AI agents process market trends, sales history, and external factors to provide accurate demand predictions, enabling better inventory planning.
- **Supplier performance monitoring**: Agents continuously track supplier reliability, delivery times, and quality metrics to identify potential risks early.
- **Route and delivery optimization**: By evaluating traffic, weather, and delivery constraints, AI agents recommend the most efficient transportation routes.
- **Inventory replenishment automation**: AI agents monitor stock levels and automatically trigger purchase orders when thresholds are reached, preventing shortages and overstocking.

Practical issues of debugging and optimization

Developing AI agent systems presents unique challenges that differ significantly from building traditional software. These systems are designed to operate with a high degree of autonomy, making decisions and taking actions without step-by-step human oversight. While this autonomy enables powerful and adaptive behavior, it also creates practical problems for developers. Troubleshooting becomes difficult because the internal reasoning and decision-making of agents are often opaque. Furthermore, developers cannot fully control the execution path, leading to unpredictable or suboptimal workflows. Understanding these challenges is essential to improving reliability, efficiency, and performance in agentic system development.

Debugging AI agents

The workflow of an AI agent is largely determined by its orchestration module. This module acts as the decision-making layer that interprets the agent's goals, evaluates the current context, and selects the next action or tool to invoke. Unlike traditional programs, where execution follows a predefined sequence of instructions, the orchestration module dynamically constructs the workflow in real-time. It does so by analyzing the agent's observations, reasoning over multiple options, and then determining the most appropriate next step. This flexibility allows the agent to adapt to changing situations but also introduces significant complexity when developers attempt to trace or debug its behavior.

For instance, consider a travel booking agent tasked with arranging a customer's trip. Initially, the orchestration module might decide to start with searching for available flights. After retrieving the flight options, it observes that the prices are unusually high. Based on this observation, the module may decide to switch strategies, perhaps by checking alternative travel dates or nearby airports instead of proceeding directly to hotel bookings. This change in course happens dynamically, without explicit instructions from the developer. While this adaptability is valuable for achieving better outcomes, it also means that the agent's execution path can vary widely from one run to another.

Debugging AI agents poses unique challenges because many traditional software debugging techniques are difficult to apply directly. Here are some conventional debugging techniques that cannot be used for agents:

- **Breakpoints**: In traditional code, breakpoints can halt execution at a specific line, but in AI agents, much of the decision-making happens inside opaque model inference, where pausing and inspecting are not straightforward.
- **Step-by-step execution**: Stepping through instructions works in deterministic programs, but AI agents often follow non-deterministic paths influenced by probabilistic outputs.
- **Variable inspection**: While standard debugging allows easy inspection of variable values, AI agents rely heavily on hidden states and embeddings that are not human-readable.
- **Logging**: Logging is still useful, but logs from AI agents may be massive, unstructured, and hard to interpret due to the complexity of the model's internal reasoning.
- **Unit testing**: Testing isolated functions is challenging because AI agent behavior often depends on context and prior interactions, making it hard to isolate components.
- **Integration testing**: While possible, the agent's adaptive behavior can cause different outcomes even when the same test conditions are applied.

Due to these limitations, debugging AI agents often shifts from inspecting fixed code paths to understanding dynamic, adaptive behavior. This is where the **orchestration module** plays a critical role. Instead of relying on static execution, the orchestration layer observes the agent's interactions, decisions, and outcomes in real-time. It can then adjust the workflow, reroute steps, or insert additional checks based on what is actually happening rather than what was expected in the initial plan. This dynamic oversight helps maintain reliability even when the agent's underlying reasoning remains a *black box*.

Optimization

While AI agents excel at adapting to changing circumstances, their **autonomous workflows** can sometimes drift into sub-optimal patterns of operation. Since these agents decide their own sequence of actions—often without human intervention—small inefficiencies can accumulate unnoticed. For example, the agent may repeatedly choose longer paths to a goal, call expensive external APIs more often than necessary, or retrieve redundant information. Over time, such patterns can increase cost, slow down execution, and even reduce the quality of outcomes.

The underlying reason is that, unlike a fixed software pipeline where each step is predetermined and refined by developers, an agent's path can vary from run to run depending on inputs, context, and observations. Without active monitoring and tuning, this flexibility can come at the expense of efficiency.

To ensure AI agents operate efficiently, developers can employ several strategies:

- **Action cost analysis**: Monitor and measure the resource usage (time, API calls, compute cost) for each action the agent takes, and redesign high-cost steps.
- **Caching and reuse of results**: Store frequently accessed or previously computed results so the agent does not repeat expensive operations.
- **Pruning unnecessary steps**: Introduce logic that detects and removes redundant actions in the agent's plan.
- **Dynamic goal refinement**: Periodically reassess the agent's target and approach to ensure it is still aligned with the overall objective.
- **Adaptive action selection**: Use performance feedback to bias the agent towards historically more efficient actions for similar situations.
- **Simulation-based testing**: Run the agent in simulated environments to identify common inefficiencies before deployment.
- **Parameter tuning**: Adjust internal thresholds (e.g., confidence scores, retrieval depth) to balance speed, cost, and accuracy.

These optimization steps are not a one-time exercise; in agentic workflows, performance tuning needs to be an ongoing process because the agent's behavior can change as its environment or available tools evolve.

As an example, consider an AI travel booking assistant tasked with planning a business trip. It autonomously searches for flights, hotels, and local transport. Without optimization, the agent might:

- Search multiple airline websites sequentially, even if earlier results already meet the requirements.
- Repeatedly query the same hotel database in different parts of the workflow.

- Recommend routes that look optimal from a cost perspective but involve impractical layovers.

By applying optimization methods:

- **Action cost analysis** can reveal that querying certain APIs is expensive and slow, leading the agent to prioritize faster, cheaper sources.
- **Caching** can prevent re-fetching hotel availability data that was retrieved minutes ago.
- **Pruning unnecessary steps** ensures that once a suitable flight is found, the agent stops searching for alternatives unless the criteria change.
- **Adaptive action selection** lets the agent favor travel providers that historically give better matches for the user's preferences.

Introduction to LlamaIndex

LlamaIndex is an open-source framework designed to help developers connect LLMs with external data sources and tools in a structured, efficient manner. At its core, it provides data connectors, indexing methods, query interfaces, and orchestration capabilities that allow LLMs to retrieve, process, and act on information beyond their built-in knowledge. This makes it a versatile foundation for applications that require complex reasoning and multi-step workflows.

One reason LlamaIndex has become popular for building AI agents is its strong focus on modularity and extensibility. It offers ready-to-use components for tool integration, memory management, and query planning, while allowing developers to easily customize workflows. Its orchestration features enable agents to reason over data, select actions dynamically, and combine multiple capabilities in a single cohesive pipeline, making it a preferred choice for agentic AI development. In this section, the aspects of LlamaIndex useful for building agentic workflows will be explored.

Core concepts for agents in LlamaIndex

In the earlier section on *Components of agents*, three key elements, **tools**, **orchestration**, and **memory**, were introduced as the backbone of agent functionality. LlamaIndex builds on these elements and provides a set of well-defined concepts that make it easier to assemble them into working agent systems:

- **Data connectors**: Similar in role to tools, these components link agents to external data sources such as databases, APIs, files, or enterprise platforms, ensuring timely and relevant information access.
- **Indexes**: Specialized data structures that organize retrieved information for efficient querying. LlamaIndex supports vector indexes, keyword indexes, and hybrid approaches to balance accuracy and performance.

- **Query engines**: Interfaces that process user input, execute searches across the indexes, and deliver refined, relevant results to the agent.
- **Tool interfaces**: Wrappers that allow the agent to perform actions via external services or APIs, extending its capabilities beyond retrieval and text generation.
- **Memory management**: Mechanisms for storing and recalling context over multiple interactions, supporting coherent reasoning across steps or sessions.
- **Query planning and orchestration**: The agent's decision-making layer, determining which indexes, tools, or reasoning steps to use in a given situation.

Together, these components form a structured foundation for building agents that can combine data retrieval, contextual reasoning, and actionable output to operate effectively in complex, real-world tasks.

Implementing agents in LlamaIndex

In the earlier sections on ReAct and Reflexion, the discussion focused on implementing orchestration, primarily through a prompt that could leverage tools and memory in a step-by-step manner. Therefore, a framework for building agents must be able to:

- Support prompt engineering
- Create tools
- Provide access to those tools through prompts
- Incorporate memory through prompts

LlamaIndex fulfills all these requirements. The example below shows how to create a simple agent in LlamaIndex that builds and uses a tool for web search. Other capabilities, such as orchestration and memory usage, will be covered in the next section, *Development of IT Ops Agent*.

First, import the necessary classes:

```
from llama_index.core.tools import FunctionTool
from llama_index.core.agent.workflow import FunctionAgent
import requests
import asyncio
```

Then follow these steps:

1. **Define the tool function**: A tool is simply a function with a clear purpose. In this case, the **`web_search_tool`** function accepts a query, calls DuckDuckGo's API, and returns a short answer:

```
def web_search_tool(query: str) -> str:
    url = f"https://api.duckduckgo.com/?q={query}&format=json&no_
redirect=1&no_html=1"
    response = requests.get(url)
    data = response.json()
    if data.get("AbstractText"):
        return data["AbstractText"]
    elif data.get("RelatedTopics"):
        return data["RelatedTopics"][0].get("Text", "No relevant
information found.")
    return "No search results found."
```

2. **Wrap the function as a tool**: The **`FunctionTool.from_defaults()`** helper converts the function into a usable tool with a name and description:

```
web_search = FunctionTool.from_defaults(
    fn=web_search_tool,
    name="web_search",
    description="Searches the web for up-to-date information on a given
query."
)
```

3. **Step 3: Create an agent and run a query**: A **`FunctionAgent`** is then created with the tool and given a query. The agent decides when to use the tool and returns the result:

```
agent = FunctionAgent(tools=[web_search])
async def main():
    response = await agent.run("Find the latest news on Mars
exploration.")
    print("Agent response:", response)
asyncio.run(main())
```

When executed, the agent interprets the prompt, uses the **`web_search`** tool, and fetches live results from the web. It should be noted that the calling of the agent has to be done in an asynchronous mode, as the web search activity can take time.

Development of IT Ops Agent

IT operations form the backbone of an organization's technology infrastructure, ensuring that systems, applications, and networks function reliably and securely. They directly impact employee productivity, business continuity, and the organization's ability to deliver products and services without disruption. Well-managed IT operations reduce downtime, prevent costly outages, and maintain the trust of both internal stakeholders and customers.

In a rapidly evolving digital environment, IT teams face increasing pressure to manage complex systems, address incidents quickly, and implement changes with minimal disruption. Proactive and streamlined IT operations are essential to keeping systems secure, stable, and aligned with business needs. Conversely, poorly managed IT operations can lead to frequent outages, security breaches, delayed projects, and reputational damage.

IT operations also serve as a source of valuable insights, identifying patterns in system performance, predicting potential failures, and revealing opportunities for process improvement. In competitive markets, operational excellence can become a critical differentiator, enabling faster innovation and greater resilience.

This section introduces the **IT Ops Agent** (**ITOA**), a GenAI-powered application that uses agentic workflows to automate both routine and complex IT operations. By incorporating autonomous monitoring, predictive capabilities, and intelligent task orchestration, the IT Ops Agent enhances operational efficiency, strengthens system security, and enables faster, more reliable service delivery.

Features of the ITOA

The IT team faces several challenges that directly affect system performance, service availability, and overall business continuity. Common issues include:

- **Incident response delays**: Large volumes of alerts and service requests overwhelm the team, slowing resolution and increasing downtime.
- **Complex system maintenance**: Managing diverse infrastructure across on-premises and cloud environments is time-consuming and prone to human error.
- **Reactive problem management**: Issues are often addressed only after they impact users, leading to service disruptions and productivity loss.

These challenges not only increase operational risk but also strain team resources and limit the ability to focus on strategic improvements.

The IT Ops Agent addresses these issues by acting as an intelligent assistant that automates both routine and complex tasks. Leveraging agentic workflows and autonomous monitoring, it delivers timely, contextual insights, streamlines operations, and enables a shift from reactive to proactive IT management.

The main features of the ITOA are covered in the following sub-sections.

Automated incident triage and resolution

IT teams often face the challenge of handling incidents quickly and accurately. Common incidents in IT infrastructure include server crashes, high CPU or memory usage, application errors, network connectivity issues, and security alerts. Delays in identifying the root cause or determining the right response can lead to prolonged downtime and user dissatisfaction.

The ITOA addresses this challenge by automatically classifying incoming incidents, identifying probable causes, and triggering predefined resolution workflows. This reduces manual effort, speeds up recovery, and ensures consistent handling of recurring issues, ultimately improving system availability and user experience.

Unified system monitoring

In complex IT environments, monitoring is often spread across multiple tools—one for servers, another for networks, and others for applications and security. This patchwork approach leaves blind spots, making it difficult to detect emerging issues or connect related events. Typical monitoring requirements include observing CPU and memory usage, tracking network anomalies, checking application uptime, and spotting security threats.

The ITOA addresses this by aggregating data from all these sources into a single, continuously updated view. This integrated perspective not only speeds up detection but also improves decision-making, allowing teams to act before minor irregularities escalate.

Proactive issue detection

IT systems often experience problems that build up silently before causing major disruptions—such as gradual memory leaks, increasing disk usage, slow database queries, or abnormal network traffic patterns. These issues frequently go unnoticed until they trigger downtime or degrade performance. The ITOA mitigates this risk by continuously analyzing system metrics, logs, and event patterns to spot early warning signs. Using predictive analytics, it identifies anomalies and trends that indicate potential failures. By alerting the team in advance, ITOA enables preventive action, reducing outages, minimizing performance drops, and ensuring smoother IT operations.

Solution overview

The ITOA is designed as an **agentic workflow** system that operates continuously in the background, monitoring infrastructure health, identifying issues, and taking appropriate actions without constant human intervention. Its autonomous nature allows it to process large volumes of system data in real-time, enabling faster response to operational challenges.

The system is paired with a user-facing front end that provides clear visibility into the agent's findings and actions. Through this interface, IT team members can review incident reports, monitor system status, and intervene when necessary by providing additional input or approving automated actions. This ensures that while the agent can act independently, human oversight remains an integral part of the workflow.

The ITOA offers three core capabilities:

- Automated Incident Triage and Resolution
- Unified System Monitoring
- Proactive Issue Detection

Together, these functionalities streamline IT operations, reduce downtime, and improve service reliability.

In this chapter, the focus will be on building and demonstrating the Automated Incident Triage and Resolution feature. This implementation will showcase how the ITOA can classify incidents, suggest resolution steps, and even execute automated fixes for common infrastructure problems—illustrating the potential of intelligent agents to transform IT operations management.

Architecture

The architecture for **Automated Incident Triage and Resolution** in the ITOA system is designed as an intelligent, agentic workflow that operates autonomously while allowing human oversight when needed. It focuses on streamlining the journey from incident detection to resolution with minimal manual effort. The system contains the following modules:

- **Data ingestion and monitoring module**: This module gathers logs, alerts, and performance metrics from servers, applications, and network devices. It includes connectors for existing monitoring systems, APIs for real-time data streaming, and a normalization layer to unify various data formats.
- **Incident detection and classification module**: Implemented as part of the agentic workflow in **LlamaIndex**, this module uses the **OpenAI GPT-4o** model to classify incidents, assess severity, and enrich context. Its components include:
    - **Pattern Recognition Engine** for matching incidents to known issue signatures.
    - **Severity Assessment Unit** to assign priority based on potential business impact.
    - **Contextual Enrichment Layer** for gathering related historical data.
- **Automation module**: Also built in **LlamaIndex** and powered by **GPT-4o**, this module suggests or executes resolutions by referring to a knowledge base of SOPs and past incident resolutions. It contains:
    - **Recommendation Engine** to generate step-by-step solutions.
    - **Automation Executor** to run scripts, API calls, or system commands.
    - **Feedback Capture Unit** to record results for iterative improvement.
- **UI module**: The user interface is developed in **Streamlit**, allowing operators to view incident details, approve or modify resolutions, and provide additional instructions. It features real-time dashboards and historical reports for operational insights.

By combining an LLM-powered agentic workflow with a simple, interactive UI, the system ensures that triage and resolution tasks are both efficient and transparent, while remaining scalable for future functionality.

Development

The ITOA development involves creating both the agent and the user interface. The agent will be built using the ReAct framework, while the UI will follow a design approach similar to that used for previous systems.

Development of the agent

The agent's development approach differs from the GenAI systems discussed earlier in this book. Conventional systems such as prompt engineering or RAG typically follow a predefined workflow, where a main function sequentially calls other functions. In contrast, the agent architecture relies on a set of tools that the orchestration module can dynamically select and use to achieve its goal, in this case, issue detection and resolution.

The agent will therefore consist of:

- **Orchestration module**
- **Tools**: The choice of tools depends on the external functionality required by the agent, as outlined earlier in the *Architecture* subsection. Based on those requirements, the following tools will be included for each function:
- **Data ingestion tool**
    - o Reads system logs.
    - o Converts to LlamaIndex documents.
- **Incident detection and classification tool**
    - o GPT-4o via LlamaIndex for log interpretation.
    - o Anomaly detection models for metric-based alerts (not implemented in this example, but can be added to enhance the system).
- **Resolution recommendation tool**
    - o GPT-4o for solution generation.
    - o LlamaIndex **retrieval-augmented generation** (**RAG**) pipeline (optional; not implemented in this example).

The development of the various tools is discussed first, beginning with the **data_ingestion** tool:

```
from pathlib import Path
import re
import pandas as pd
from llama_index.core import Document
```

The first step is to read the given log file.

```
def read_log_file(file_path: str) -> list:

    # Reads a log file and returns a list of lines.

    path = Path(file_path)
    if not path.exists():
        raise FileNotFoundError(f"Log file not found: {file_path}")

    with open(path, "r", encoding="utf-8") as f:
        lines = [line.strip() for line in f if line.strip()]

    return lines
```

Next, the **pandas** library is used to parse the log file and return a **dataframe**:

```
def parse_logs_to_dataframe(log_data: list):
    # Apache common log format regex with username field
    log_pattern = re.compile(
        r'(?P<ip>\S+) '                        # IP address
        r'\S+ '                                # RFC 1413 identity (ignored)
        r'(?P<user>\S+) '                      # Authenticated user or '-'
        r'\[(?P<time>.*?)\] '                  # Timestamp
        r'"(?P<method>\S+) '                   # HTTP method
        r'(?P<url>\S+) '                       # URL
        r'(?P<protocol>HTTP/\d\.\d)" '         # Protocol
        r'(?P<status>\d{3}) '                  # Status code
        r'(?P<size>\d+)'                       # Response size
    )

    records = []
    for line in log_data:
        match = log_pattern.match(line)
        if match:
            records.append(match.groupdict())

    df = pd.DataFrame(records)
    df['time'] = pd.to_datetime(df['time'], format='%d/%b/%Y:%H:%M:%S %z')
```

```
    df['status'] = df['status'].astype(int)
    df['size'] = df['size'].astype(int)
    return df
```

The data loader function creates the LlamaIndex documents from the **`dataframe`**:

```
def dataframe_to_llama_documents(df: pd.DataFrame) -> list:
   # Converts a DataFrame of logs into LlamaIndex Document objects.
   #Each row becomes one document.

    documents = []
    for _, row in df.iterrows():

        text = f"[{row['time']}] Status: {row['status']}, Size: {row['size']},
URL: {row['url']}"
        documents.append(Document(text=text, metadata={
            "time": row['time'],
            "status": row['status'],
            "size": row['size'],
             "URL": row["url"]
        }))
    return documents
```

The **`data_ingestion_tool`** function reads the log file from the given location (in an actual system, an ingestion pipeline such as Apache Kafka will be used for the purpose). The function then calls the other three functions to complete the job. The documents created are persisted in a vector store, which works as the **memory** for the agent:

```
def Data_ingestion_tool():
    #Reads, parses Apache logs and stores into LlamaIndex documents
    # Example log file path
    file_path = "sample_data/Sample Log.log"
    storage_path = "sample_data"

    raw_lines =  read_log_file(file_path)
    parsed_df = parse_logs_to_dataframe(raw_lines)
    docs = dataframe_to_llama_documents(parsed_df)

    index = VectorStoreIndex.from_documents(docs)

    # Persist the index
    index.storage_context.persist(persist_dir=storage_path)
```

The next development is for the **Detect_issue** tool that uses the memory created by the earlier tool. This function utilizes prompt engineering to identify the issue from logs:

- `from llama_index.core import StorageContext, load_index_from_storage`
- `from llama_index.core.query_engine import RetrieverQueryEngine`
- `from llama_index.llms.openai import OpenAI`

Refer to the following code:

```
def Detect_issue_tool(storage_path="log_index", query="Identify any system
issues in the logs."):

    #Detect issues from previously ingested logs stored in a vector index.
    # Load the index from storage
    storage_context = StorageContext.from_defaults(persist_dir=storage_path)
    index = load_index_from_storage(storage_context)

    # Create a retriever and query engine
    retriever = index.as_retriever(similarity_top_k=5)
    query_engine = RetrieverQueryEngine(retriever=retriever)

    # Construct a targeted prompt for issue detection
    prompt = f"""
    You are an expert system log analyst. Your task is to analyze the given
logs and identify any errors, failures, or anomalies that may indicate system
issues. Summarize the main issue in 2-3 concise sentences.

    Logs:
    {query}
    """

    # Use the query engine to get relevant log snippets
    response = query_engine.query(prompt)

    return str(response)
```

Using a vector index and running a query using LlamaIndex is quite simple, as can be seen in the code.

The final tool is the **Recommend_resolution** tool. It uses the issue analysis created by the **Detect_issue** tool, along with the logs to suggest a solution:

```
def Recommend_solution_tool(issue_description, storage_path):

    #Recommend a solution for the detected issue using logs and LLM reasoning.

    # Load the index from storage
    storage_context = StorageContext.from_defaults(persist_dir=storage_path)
    index = load_index_from_storage(storage_context)

    # Create a retriever and query engine
    retriever = index.as_retriever(similarity_top_k=5)
    query_engine = RetrieverQueryEngine(retriever=retriever)

    # Construct the solution prompt
    prompt = f"""
    You are an expert IT operations engineer.
    You have access to system logs and an identified issue description.
    Using the retrieved logs and your domain expertise, recommend a clear,
    actionable solution to fix the problem. The solution should include:
    1. Root cause explanation
    2. Recommended fix steps
    3. Any preventive measures to avoid recurrence.

    Issue:
    {issue_description}
    """

    # Query the vector store with the prompt
    response = query_engine.query(prompt)

    return str(response)
```

This completes the development of the tools. The remaining part is to write the LlamaIndex ReAct agent. The ReAct agent is similar to the **FunctionAgent** built in the earlier section, *Introduction to LlamaIndex*. The first part of the code wraps the tool function in the LlamaIndex **FunctionTool** objects:

```
from llama_index.core.agent import ReActAgent
from llama_index.core.tools import FunctionTool
from llama_index.llms.openai import OpenAI
```

```
# Create FunctionTool objects
ingest_logs_ft = FunctionTool.from_defaults(
    fn=Data_ingestion_tool,
    name="DataIngestionTool",
    description="Ingests system log file, parses it, and stores it into the log index."
)

detect_issue_ft = FunctionTool.from_defaults(
    fn=Detect_issue_tool,
    name="DetectIssueTool",
    description="Detects and summarizes issues in logs."
)

recommend_solution_ft = FunctionTool.from_defaults(
    fn=Recommend_solution_tool,
    name="RecommendSolutionTool",
    description="Recommends solution based on detected issue and stored logs."
)
```

The remaining part is to create the agent:

```
llm = OpenAI(model="gpt-4o", temperature=0)

agent = ReActAgent(
    tools=[ingest_logs_ft, detect_issue_ft, recommend_solution_ft],
    llm=llm,
    verbose=True,
    max_iterations=5
)
```

The agent can be used by using the following code:

```
response = await agent.run(
    "We have a log file at 'sample_data'. "
    "Please ingest it, detect any issues, and recommend a solution."
)
```

Development of the UI module

The UI module will be built using **`streamlit`**. The interface will have two main elements:

- The **Run ITOA** button. This button will invoke the agent.
- A text area displaying the issue and the suggested resolution returned by the agent.

Implementation of this UI should be straightforward for the reader.

Conclusion

This chapter explored the concept of agentic workflows and how they enhance the capabilities of language models through reasoning, planning, and tool integration. It began with the fundamentals of agents, covering their definition and the three key components: tools, memory, and orchestration. Two prominent frameworks for building agents, ReAct and Reflexion, were examined, along with practical examples of how AI agents are applied in industry.

To demonstrate real-world implementation, the chapter presented ITOA, an AI agent built using the LlamaIndex framework, designed to analyze logs, detect issues, and recommend solutions for IT system incidents. This example illustrated how agents can function as intelligent collaborators, working seamlessly alongside industrial teams.

With this, the discussion on GenAI application development concludes. The next chapter will shift focus to deploying GenAI applications in production environments and the critical considerations involved in that process.

Chapter 9
Deploying GenAI Systems

Introduction

The preceding chapters have introduced a range of techniques for constructing **generative AI** (**GenAI**) systems, including prompt engineering, fine-tuning, retrieval-augmented generation, and agentic workflows. These techniques enable effective utilization of GenAI models to develop business applications that provide tangible benefits to industrial teams.

For such applications to be adopted by business teams, they must be deployed and made readily accessible to end users. If the deployment does not meet the necessary requirements, the business cannot effectively leverage the capabilities of GenAI, even when the solution has been designed and developed appropriately. Consequently, deployment becomes a critical element in delivering GenAI solutions to enterprises.

To achieve practical utility, a deployed solution must demonstrate availability, optimization, and the ability to meet user expectations. This creates a set of challenges for GenAI engineers, who are tasked with ensuring that the solution delivers measurable value to the organization. Establishing the appropriate infrastructure and configuring the system correctly represent foundational steps in this process. Additional challenges include managing computational costs, ensuring security and regulatory compliance, optimizing performance, and maintaining reliability under dynamic workloads.

This chapter explores the various dimensions of deploying GenAI solutions. It provides developers with an understanding of deployment requirements and outlines methods to align systems with these needs. Technologies central to deployment, such as cloud platforms, model servers, and containerization, are discussed in detail, along with the challenges they present and the strategies available for their mitigation.

Structure

This chapter covers the following topics:

- Critical aspects of deploying GenAI systems
- Cloud deployment and scaling
- Model server deployment
- Model selection

- Cost implications
- Optimization
- Evaluation

Objectives

By the end of this chapter, you will have a clear understanding of how GenAI systems are deployed in real-world environments. You will learn the key requirements for production systems and the architectural components that enable deployment, including infrastructure, compute, networking, and licensing. Cloud-based deployment will be explored with examples such as **Amazon Web Services** (**AWS**), along with approaches for model deployment and continuous model selection. A significant emphasis will be placed on GenAI model deployment, including server-based and cloud-hosted approaches, as well as the process of selecting and updating models for production use. You will also examine cost and **returns-on-investment** (**ROI**) considerations and understand how optimization and evaluation ensure long-term efficiency and reliability of GenAI systems in practice.

Critical aspects of deploying GenAI systems

Deployment plays a decisive role in transforming a GenAI system from a developed solution into a practical tool that delivers value to enterprises. Its effectiveness depends on several interconnected aspects that ensure the system remains reliable, efficient, and aligned with organizational objectives. These include understanding deployment requirements, defining the overall architecture, designing the deployment strategy, and evaluating infrastructure considerations. This section explores these aspects in detail to provide a comprehensive view of the factors that underpin successful deployment.

Understanding deployment requirements

Understanding the requirements of deployment is a fundamental step in planning the implementation of a GenAI solution within an organization. These requirements influence not only the choice of infrastructure but also decisions regarding model selection, scalability, cost management, security, compliance, and integration with existing systems. Careful consideration of these factors ensures that the deployed solution aligns with organizational goals and operates effectively in practice. The following sections examine these requirements in detail.

Users

The central consideration in deploying a GenAI solution within an organization is the profile of its users. Understanding who will access the system and under what conditions is essential for determining infrastructure needs and ensuring reliable performance. Key parameters include:

- **Number of users**: The scale of infrastructure must correspond to the expected user base, as higher numbers of users require greater computational resources and robust load management.
- **Time of usage**: If users are geographically distributed, the system may need to operate continuously, whereas limited time windows of usage may allow for more efficient resource allocation.
- **Location**: The deployment strategy must account for whether users operate primarily within office environments or in the field, as this influences connectivity requirements and the reliability of internet access.

Data

Data is a fundamental consideration in the deployment of a GenAI solution, as it determines both the functionality of the application and the infrastructure required to support it. The nature, sources, and volume of data must be carefully evaluated to ensure seamless integration and efficient operation. Key parameters include:

- **Organizational data**: Existing internal data must be integrated into the system, along with mechanisms to track updates, new entries, and modifications over time.
- **External subscriptions**: Many organizations rely on third-party or subscribed data sources that need to be incorporated into the application.
- **Open internet sources**: Publicly available data from websites, social media, and other online platforms may also form part of the information ecosystem.
- **Volume of data**: The scale of data directly impacts storage requirements and influences decisions regarding database systems, data pipelines, and associated infrastructure.

Application

The nature of the application is a key factor in planning the deployment of a GenAI solution. Different types of applications place distinct demands on infrastructure, availability, and optimization strategies. Important considerations include:

- **Mode of operation**: Online applications, such as customer service chatbots or virtual assistants, require minimal latency and very high availability to ensure a seamless user experience. In contrast, batch-processing applications, such as automated document summarization or large-scale report generation, can be scheduled in a more resource-efficient manner, allowing for greater flexibility in deployment.
- **Business criticality**: The role of the application within the organization must be evaluated. Solutions that support core business functions, such as financial risk analysis or compliance monitoring, require more stringent deployment measures to guarantee stability, security, and continuity of service.

Confidentiality

Data confidentiality is a crucial aspect in the deployment of GenAI solutions. Certain applications rely on highly sensitive information, such as financial records, legal documents, or internal business data, which require stringent protection measures and controlled access. In such cases, deployment strategies must prioritize secure environments, compliance with regulatory standards, and robust mechanisms for data governance. Other applications, by contrast, may rely on less sensitive or publicly available data, such as patents, government notifications, or general web content. The confidentiality level of the data, therefore, directly influences the choice of infrastructure, deployment model, and security practices.

Architecture of GenAI systems

The architecture of a GenAI system is a central determinant of how the solution is deployed and operated. Along with user, data, and application requirements, architectural choices define the structure of the system, the flow of information, and the mechanisms that enable scalability, reliability, and performance.

In the earlier chapters of this book, several GenAI applications were developed using techniques such as prompt engineering, retrieval-augmented generation, and agentic workflows. While each system followed a distinct architectural design tailored to its purpose, certain foundational elements were consistently present across them. The following subsections discuss these common architectural components in detail.

GenAI model

The GenAI model forms the central component of any system, defining its core capabilities and performance. As discussed in *Chapter 2, The SOTA GenAI Models*, a variety of models are available, each offering distinct strengths for different applications. These models may be self-hosted on the organization's servers, providing greater control and data security, or accessed through APIs offered by model providers, which allow rapid integration and scalability without the need for extensive infrastructure.

User interface

The user interface provides the point of interaction between the GenAI system and its users. It determines how effectively the system can be accessed and utilized in practice. Interfaces may take the form of chat-based applications, web dashboards, or integrations within existing enterprise tools. The design of the interface must prioritize ease of use, responsiveness, and accessibility, ensuring that users can efficiently communicate with the model and derive value from its capabilities.

Application services

Application services provide the functional layer that connects the GenAI model to business use cases. They handle tasks such as pre-processing inputs, post-processing outputs, integrating with organizational systems, and enforcing business logic. These services ensure that model outputs are contextually relevant and aligned with the user requirements. By acting as the bridge between raw model capabilities and practical applications, this layer enables the deployment of reliable, task-oriented solutions.

Storage and database

Storage and database systems form a critical backbone of GenAI deployments, supporting both the application and its data requirements. They store user inputs, model outputs, retrieved documents, and metadata necessary for system operation. Depending on the use case, this may involve structured databases, vector databases for semantic search, or large-scale storage for unstructured data. The design of storage solutions directly impacts scalability, retrieval speed, and reliability.

Configuration

Configuration defines how a GenAI system is tailored to specific organizational and user needs. It includes parameters such as model selection, prompt templates, access controls, integration settings, and resource allocation. Proper configuration ensures that the system operates securely, efficiently, and in alignment with business requirements. Since different applications demand varying levels of precision, latency, and scalability, configuration provides the flexibility to adjust the deployment without altering the underlying architecture.

User management and security

User management and security components ensure that the GenAI system is accessed safely and only by authorized individuals. User management defines roles and privileges, determining the level of interaction each user can have with the system. Security mechanisms, such as authentication, authorization, and encryption, protect data both in transit and at rest. Firewalls and intrusion detection further strengthen the environment against external threats. Together, these components form the architectural layer that safeguards system integrity and confidentiality.

Monitoring and logging

Monitoring and logging components provide visibility into the performance and operation of the system. Monitoring tools track metrics such as latency, throughput, resource utilization, and system health, enabling proactive detection of issues. Logging records user interactions, errors, and system events, creating an audit trail for analysis and compliance. Together, these components support reliability, performance optimization, and accountability, ensuring that the deployed system continues to meet organizational requirements.

The following figure illustrates the various components of the architecture of a typical GenAI system:

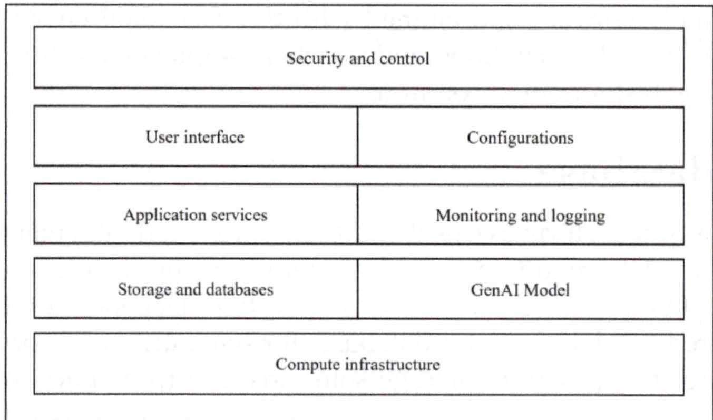

***Figure 9.1**: Architecture of a GenAI system*

Deployment design

The design of deployment plays a decisive role in determining the reliability, efficiency, and security of a GenAI solution. It involves decisions about infrastructure, computing resources, networking, licensing, and system security, each of which directly affects the system's performance and sustainability. The following subsections examine these considerations in detail.

Deciding the infrastructure

A fundamental decision in deployment design is the choice between cloud-based and on-premises infrastructure. Cloud deployments provide scalability, elasticity, and access to advanced managed services, making them suitable for dynamic workloads. However, they introduce challenges in areas such as data security, compliance, and cost management. On-premises deployments, while less flexible, may offer greater control over sensitive data and system security. These trade-offs are discussed further in the section *Cloud deployment and scaling*.

Finalizing the compute requirements

Each component of a GenAI system, including the model, application services, user interface, database, and storage, requires dedicated compute resources. These must be mapped to specific compute elements, such as physical servers or cloud instances, with appropriate specifications. The selection of processors, memory, and accelerators should reflect both the expected workload and latency requirements of the application. Proper planning ensures that resources are neither underutilized nor insufficient, striking a balance between cost efficiency and system performance. The following table shows the compute design for a hypothetical deployment:

Component	Compute name	Type	Specifications
GenAI model	AI-Model-Node-1	Cloud GPU	4 × A100 GPUs, 256 GB RAM, 5 TB SSD storage
Application services	App-Service-VM	On-prem server	16 vCPUs, 64 GB RAM, 2 TB SSD storage
User interface	UI-Web-Instance	On-prem server	8 vCPUs, 32 GB RAM, 500 GB SSD
Database	Org-DB-Server	On-prem Server	24 vCPUs, 128 GB RAM, 10 TB high-speed disk
Storage	Cloud-Storage-S1	On-prem server	SSD, 100 TB capacity

***Table 9.1**: Sample compute design for a GenAI deployment*

Designing the networking

Networking connects all components of the GenAI system, enabling smooth interaction across the architecture. Internal or external networks must be designed depending on whether the components are deployed within the organization or distributed across external services. When models or services reside outside organizational boundaries, secure communication channels are essential. End users accessing the user interface must also be provided with encrypted and authenticated connections to safeguard sensitive data and maintain trust in the system.

Ensuring proper licensing

All software used in deployment, including system software, middleware, and security tools, must be appropriately licensed. Proprietary software requires valid licensing agreements, while open-source tools demand careful review of licensing terms to ensure compliance with organizational policies and legal requirements. Selecting the correct license type for open-source software is particularly important, as certain licenses impose restrictions on modification or commercial use. Proper licensing not only ensures legality but also protects the organization from potential operational and financial risks.

Designing the security

Security is a critical element of deployment design, ensuring that access to the system is controlled and protected against unauthorized use. For system users, access must be granted according to defined privileges, limiting their ability to modify or influence components beyond their roles. Non-users must be prevented from gaining any form of entry into the system. Security measures should be continuously validated and strengthened through methods such as **Vulnerability Assessment and Penetration Testing** (**VAPT**), ensuring the system remains resilient to threats.

Cloud deployment and scaling

In recent years, cloud deployment has become more common than on-premises deployment for GenAI systems. The flexibility, scalability, and pay-as-you-go model of cloud infrastructure make it a preferred choice for many organizations. It allows teams to build and test applications without the need for significant investment in physical hardware.

The major cloud providers, i.e., AWS, Microsoft Azure, and **Google Cloud Platform** (**GCP**), offer services that support GenAI deployment. These include managed model APIs, scalable compute instances, storage solutions, networking, and security features. Together, they reduce the complexity of running GenAI applications. This section will discuss the advantages and limitations of cloud deployment and examine deployment options on two of the major providers: AWS and Azure.

Pros and cons of cloud deployment

Cloud deployment is increasingly chosen for GenAI systems due to its flexibility and the range of managed services it provides. However, it brings both advantages and challenges that must be carefully considered.

The advantages are as follows:

- **Scalability**: Resources can be scaled up or down to match varying workloads.
- **Cost efficiency**: The pay-as-you-go model minimizes upfront capital expenditure.
- **Managed services**: Providers offer tools for deployment, monitoring, and maintenance.
- **Global reach**: Distributed infrastructure ensures availability and resilience worldwide.

Cloud deployment has the following limitations:

- **Security and privacy risks**: Sensitive data may be exposed outside organizational boundaries.
- **Vendor lock-in**: Migration between cloud providers can be complex and costly.
- **Operational costs**: Expenses can rise significantly for large-scale or continuous workloads.
- **Latency and connectivity**: Dependence on network stability can affect performance.

Deploying GenAI applications on Azure

Microsoft Azure provides a broad ecosystem of services that support the deployment of GenAI applications. From model hosting to application services and data management, Azure offers integrated solutions to handle every component of the architecture. Its cloud-native tools simplify scaling, monitoring, and maintaining AI-driven applications.

Model deployment

GenAI models can be deployed on Azure using Azure Machine Learning or accessed through Azure AI Foundry. Azure AI Foundry provides access to a variety of foundation models, including those from OpenAI (such as GPT series), as well as open-source models integrated through Hugging Face. These models can be fine tuned, deployed as managed endpoints, and scaled as APIs for application use. Azure also supports GPU-backed compute clusters for hosting custom-trained models, ensuring low latency and high availability.

Application services

For applications built in Python, developers can use Azure App Service or **Azure Kubernetes Service** (**AKS**) to host services. Azure Functions offers a serverless option for lightweight workloads or event-driven tasks. Code repositories can be integrated with Azure DevOps or GitHub for **continuous integration and continuous deployment** (**CI/CD**). Containerization using Azure Container Instances or AKS provides flexibility and scalability, ensuring Python-based services can run reliably in production environments.

User interface

User interfaces developed in modern frameworks such as React or Node.js can be deployed using Azure Static Web Apps or Azure App Service for web applications. Static Web Apps integrates well with GitHub Actions or Azure DevOps pipelines, streamlining deployment. For interactive and dynamic applications, scaling and routing can be managed through **Azure Front Door** and **Azure Content Delivery Network** (**CDN**), ensuring global reach and low-latency performance for end users.

Data storage and databases

Azure offers a wide range of storage and database options. Azure Blob Storage supports unstructured data such as documents and media files. For relational data, Azure SQL Database or Azure Database for PostgreSQL/MySQL can be used. Vector search workloads can be implemented using Azure Cognitive Search with vector indexing, or Azure Cosmos DB with integrated vector support. For graph data, Azure Cosmos DB Gremlin API provides graph database capabilities, suitable for relationship-driven queries in GenAI solutions.

The following summary table maps GenAI architecture components to relevant Azure services:

GenAI component	Azure services
Model deployment	Azure Machine Learning, Azure AI Foundry, GPU-backed Compute Clusters, Managed Endpoints.
Application services	Azure App Service, **Azure Kubernetes Service** (**AKS**), Azure Functions, Azure Container Instances, Azure DevOps
User interface	Azure Static Web Apps, Azure App Service, Azure Front Door, Azure CDN
Data storage and databases	Azure Blob Storage (files), Azure SQL Database, Azure Database for PostgreSQL / MySQL (RDBMS), Azure Cognitive Search (vector database), Azure Cosmos DB (vector and Gremlin API for graph)

Table 9.2: *Mapping GenAI application components on Azure services*

Deploying GenAI applications on AWS

AWS provides a wide range of services that support the deployment of GenAI applications. These services allow organizations to host models, run application services, deploy user interfaces, and manage data storage with scalability and security. The following subsections describe how different components of a GenAI architecture can be implemented using AWS.

Model deployment

AWS offers multiple options for hosting and serving GenAI models. Amazon SageMaker is the primary service for building, training, and deploying ML models, including custom LLMs. Pretrained models can also be accessed via Amazon Bedrock, which provides API-based access to foundation models from various providers without requiring infrastructure management. For compute-intensive workloads, EC2 GPU instances such as P4d or G5 can be used. This flexibility enables organizations to choose between managed model endpoints, custom deployments, or third-party models integrated via APIs.

Application services

Python-based application services can be deployed on AWS using several managed and container-based solutions. AWS Elastic Beanstalk provides an easy way to run Python applications with minimal infrastructure management. For more control, **Amazon Elastic Kubernetes Service** (**EKS**) or **Amazon Elastic Container Service** (**ECS**) allows containerized deployments at scale. AWS Lambda offers a serverless option for running Python functions triggered by events. These services integrate with IAM for secure access control and **CloudWatch** for monitoring, ensuring scalability and reliability for GenAI backends.

User interface

Front-end applications developed using React, Node.js, or other frameworks can be deployed using AWS Amplify, which provides an end-to-end platform for building and hosting web applications. Alternatively, Amazon S3 can be used for static file hosting, often paired with Amazon CloudFront for content delivery and global caching. For more complex needs, Elastic Beanstalk or container services like ECS or EKS can host full-stack web apps. These services provide secure endpoints and integrate with AWS Certificate Manager to enable HTTPS for user-facing applications.

Data storage and databases

AWS provides a broad range of data storage and database services suitable for GenAI applications. Amazon S3 serves as a scalable storage solution for files and unstructured data. Relational databases can be managed through Amazon RDS, which supports MySQL, PostgreSQL, and SQL Server. For vector search, Amazon OpenSearch Service now supports KNN-based vector similarity search. Graph data can be managed using Amazon Neptune, which supports Gremlin and SPARQL queries. Together, these services provide robust options for structured, unstructured, and semantic data storage.

The following table summarizes GenAI components and AWS services that can be used for deployment:

GenAI component	AWS services
Model deployment	Amazon SageMaker, Amazon Bedrock, EC2 GPU Instances (P4d, G5)
Application services	AWS Elastic Beanstalk, Amazon ECS, Amazon EKS, AWS Lambda
User interface	AWS Amplify, Amazon S3 (Static Hosting), Amazon CloudFront, Elastic Beanstalk
Data storage and databases	Amazon S3 (File Storage), Amazon RDS (Relational DB), Amazon OpenSearch (Vector Search), Amazon Neptune (Graph Database)

Table 9.3: Mapping of GenAI components and AWS services

Model server deployment

Model deployment is the most critical aspect of running GenAI applications in production. While using an external API, such as OpenAI, provides a convenient way to access advanced models without managing infrastructure, there are many scenarios where private model deployment is necessary. This section will examine the various aspects of deploying models locally, which we will refer to as **model server deployment**.

Need for model deployment

While many organizations rely on external APIs to access generative AI models, there are situations where deploying models in-house becomes necessary. Running a private model server provides greater flexibility, control, and assurance in how AI is used in production. The following are the key reasons why organizations choose to deploy their own models:

- **Security and privacy**: Sensitive data, especially in regulated industries such as healthcare, finance, or government, cannot always be shared with third-party APIs. Deploying models locally ensures that all data remains within the organization's control, reducing the risk of data leaks and ensuring compliance with internal security standards.
- **Cost optimization**: For applications with heavy or continuous usage, relying on API calls can become prohibitively expensive over time. By deploying their own models, organizations can control infrastructure costs and achieve better cost predictability, especially when usage is high.
- **Customization and fine-tuning**: Off-the-shelf models may not always deliver the performance required for specific domains. Deploying models in-house allows organizations to fine-tune them on domain-specific data, improving accuracy and relevance for tasks such as legal analysis, customer support, or medical research.
- **Scalability and performance**: APIs often come with rate limits and latency constraints. Private deployments allow organizations to scale their infrastructure based on workload demands, ensuring low-latency responses and higher throughput without being restricted by external providers.
- **Availability of models**: Not all models are available as APIs from major providers. Open-source or specialized models may need to be hosted privately to meet unique requirements. In some cases, organizations may also want to experiment with multiple models and compare their performance in-house.
- **Control and independence**: Dependence on a single external provider creates risks such as pricing changes, service outages, or discontinuation of services. Hosting models privately gives organizations more independence and control over their AI roadmap.
- **Regulatory and compliance requirements**: In certain jurisdictions, data residency laws may require that data and models remain within specific geographical boundaries. Deploying models locally or in a private cloud ensures compliance with such legal mandates.

Challenges of model deployment

While private model deployment offers many advantages, it also introduces significant complexities. Hosting and maintaining large-scale generative models require careful planning, specialized skills, and ongoing resource investment. The following points highlight the common challenges organizations face when deploying models in-house:

- **High infrastructure costs**: Large generative models demand powerful GPUs or specialized hardware such as TPUs. Procuring and maintaining such infrastructure can be expensive, particularly when scaling to production-level workloads.
- **Operational complexity**: Unlike using APIs, running models internally requires setting up servers, managing dependencies, and ensuring continuous uptime. This adds layers of operational burden that many organizations may not be prepared for.
- **Resource management**: Efficiently allocating compute, memory, and storage resources is critical for performance. Without proper monitoring and optimization, resource bottlenecks can lead to degraded model performance or system failures.
- **Scalability challenges**: Scaling model servers to handle thousands of requests per second is non-trivial. Organizations must design for load balancing, autoscaling, and fault tolerance to ensure reliable service at scale.
- **Model updates and maintenance**: AI models evolve rapidly. Keeping deployed models up-to-date with the latest research or security patches requires ongoing effort. Without proper versioning and update strategies, organizations risk falling behind.
- **Specialized expertise**: Deploying models effectively requires skills in MLOps, distributed systems, and deep learning infrastructure. A shortage of such expertise can slow down implementation or lead to fragile deployments.
- **Energy consumption and sustainability**: Running large models continuously consumes significant energy. This raises concerns not only about cost but also about sustainability and the environmental impact of large-scale AI systems.
- **Compliance and governance**: Organizations must ensure that deployed models meet regulatory requirements, such as auditability, explainability, and data governance. Implementing these safeguards adds to the overall complexity.

Deploying local models with Ollama

As an example of model server deployment, this section illustrates the use of **Ollama**. Ollama is a lightweight framework designed to make it simple to run and serve LLMs locally. It provides a unified runtime that allows developers to download, configure, and interact with open-source models through a command-line interface or a built-in API. With its ease of installation and pre-packaged model support, Ollama offers a practical way to experiment with local LLM deployment, build prototypes, and integrate models into applications without relying on external cloud services.

Installation and setup

Ollama is designed for ease of use and can be installed with a single command. Once installed, it sets up a local runtime environment that allows models to be pulled and executed without additional dependencies. Installation packages are available for macOS, Windows, and Linux, ensuring compatibility across major platforms. The simplicity of setup makes it an attractive choice for developers who want to quickly experiment with local model deployment.

Model availability

Ollama supports a wide range of open-source models such as LLama 2, Mistral, Gemma, Phi, and others. These models can be pulled directly from the Ollama library using simple commands, eliminating the need to manage model weights and configurations manually. Users can also import custom fine-tuned models in supported formats, which broadens applicability for specialized use cases.

Running models locally

Once a model is downloaded, it can be executed locally using a straightforward command-line interface. Ollama provides interactive prompts for testing and supports chat-like workflows. It manages memory allocation and hardware optimization automatically, enabling efficient use of system resources. This capability allows developers to run sophisticated LLMs even on standard hardware, though higher-performance machines are recommended for large models.

API integration

Ollama includes a local API endpoint, which makes it easy to connect deployed models with external applications. Developers can send queries and retrieve responses programmatically via HTTP requests. This enables seamless integration with applications built in languages like Python, Node.js, or Java, making Ollama suitable not only for experimentation but also for embedding models into production-ready workflows.

Resource management and performance

Ollama optimizes resource usage by dynamically handling GPU and CPU allocations depending on the hardware available. It supports quantized model formats, which reduce memory requirements while maintaining acceptable accuracy. This makes it possible to run models on less powerful hardware without significant performance loss. However, scaling beyond a single machine requires additional orchestration outside of Ollama's native capabilities.

Customization and extensions

Beyond pre-built models, Ollama allows users to load custom models or fine-tuned variants. Configurations such as system prompts, context window size, and quantization levels can be adjusted to match specific application needs. This flexibility ensures that Ollama is not limited to generic use cases but can be tailored to specialized domains.

Role of Ollama in GenAI deployment

To summarize, Ollama plays an important role as a lightweight model server for running large language models locally. The important points to consider while designing are:

- **Useful for small-scale scenarios**: Ollama is well-suited for individual developers, research projects, or teams needing local inference without cloud reliance.
- **Limitations in large-scale serving**: Not designed for distributed or enterprise-level workloads, where more robust orchestration tools are required.
- **Best as a bridge solution**: Serves as a practical middle ground between using public cloud APIs and building fully customized enterprise deployments.

Deploying models on cloud

Deploying models on cloud instances is often the preferred choice for organizations that need to handle high or unpredictable workloads. Cloud platforms offer scalability, reliability, and managed infrastructure, which significantly reduce the operational overhead of maintaining large-scale model servers. This makes them particularly suitable for production environments where availability and performance are critical.

Advantages of cloud model deployment

Some advantages of using cloud for model deployment are as follows:

- **Scalability for large workloads**: Cloud instances allow horizontal and vertical scaling, making it possible to serve thousands or even millions of requests without compromising performance.
- **Global availability**: Services can be deployed across multiple regions to ensure low latency and redundancy.
- **Cost optimization options**: Pay-as-you-go pricing and auto-scaling features ensure that organizations only pay for what they use.
- **Integration with ecosystem services**: Direct support for data pipelines, monitoring, and security tools makes it easier to manage end-to-end deployment.

Model deployment on AWS example

Consider an enterprise deploying a large language model to serve 500,000 API calls per day. On AWS, this setup might include:

- **Amazon EC2 GPU instances** (e.g., p4d or g5 series) to host the model for inference. A framework suitable for high workloads, such as TensorRT or vLLM, can be used for the deployment.
- **Amazon Elastic Load Balancer (ELB)** to distribute traffic across multiple instances.
- **Amazon Auto Scaling** to adjust the number of running instances based on traffic spikes.
- **Amazon CloudWatch** for monitoring usage, latency, and errors.
- **Amazon S3** for storing model weights and related data.
- **AWS API Gateway** to provide a managed interface for client applications to send requests.

With this setup, the model can efficiently handle the workload while maintaining performance and reliability. Scaling policies ensure that during peak usage (e.g., a surge to 1 million requests), additional instances are automatically provisioned.

The following figure shows the schematic representation of the deployment of model on AWS:

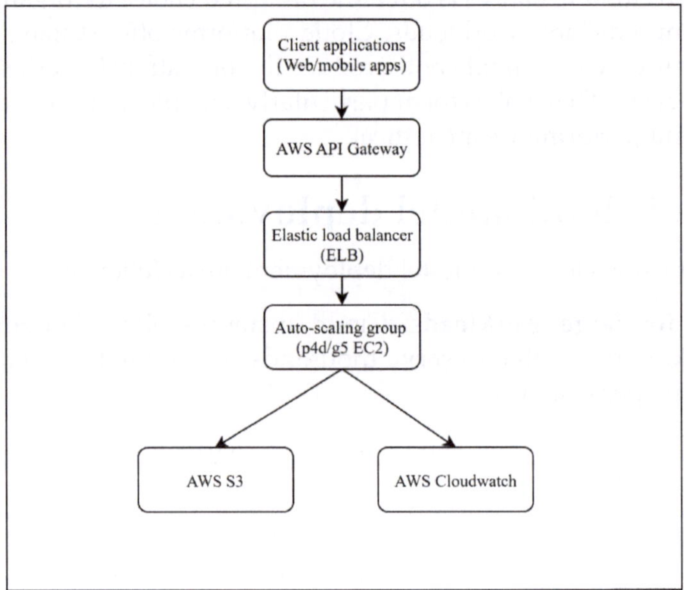

Figure 9.2: Model deployment on AWS

Model selection

Selecting the right model is a critical step in building and deploying GenAI applications. While the application domain, such as text, image, or audio, determines the broad category of models to be used, the exact choice is often finalized during deployment. Model selection is not a one-time task but an ongoing process, as new variants are introduced and older versions are deprecated by providers. A systematic approach to selecting and periodically revisiting the model ensures that the application continues to meet performance, cost, and reliability requirements. The following subsections discuss various aspects of model selection important for GenAI deployment.

Lifecycle of model selection

Model selection is not limited to the initial stages of development. It is an ongoing activity that occurs at multiple points in the lifecycle of a GenAI application. The three key stages are outlined as follows:

1. **During development**: At the prototyping stage, teams often rely on readily available APIs to accelerate development and validate ideas quickly. This approach allows rapid iteration and proof-of-concept creation, but it may not always reflect long-term needs. The trade-off here lies between the speed of development and the suitability of the chosen model for production environments.

2. **During deployment**: The actual deployment phase demands careful evaluation of model options, as the choices made here directly affect cost, security, and scalability. Often, enterprises shift from API-based prototypes to local or private model deployments to meet organizational requirements. Deployment-time selection is critical to ensure alignment with enterprise infrastructure and performance expectations.

3. **Continuous re-evaluation**: Model selection does not end with deployment. Continuous monitoring of new model releases, provider updates, and performance in production is necessary. Providers may discontinue older versions or introduce new ones, prompting re-evaluation. The decision to switch models must balance potential improvements in capability or efficiency against risks such as retraining costs or operational disruptions.

Factors influencing model selection

Selecting the right model involves balancing multiple considerations. These factors ensure that the chosen model not only meets the functional requirements of the application but also performs efficiently within the available infrastructure. The major influencing factors are outlined as follows:

- **Application requirements**: The starting point of model selection is the type of application being developed. Different use cases may require language, vision, audio, or multimodal models. Beyond the type, the specific capabilities, such as reasoning, summarization, content generation, or classification, determine the suitability of a model. Understanding the end-user expectations and application goals is essential in narrowing down the right family of models.

- **Performance requirements**: A model's performance has a direct impact on user experience and system reliability. Key considerations include response time (latency), accuracy, and overall throughput measured in requests per second. Applications requiring real-time interaction must prioritize low latency, while others may emphasize high accuracy or reliability. Balancing these factors ensures that the model can consistently deliver the desired outcomes under expected workloads.
- **Infrastructure considerations**: The final factor is the infrastructure available to support the model. Deployment environments can vary from local servers to cloud platforms or hybrid setups, each with different implications. Compute resources, whether GPU, TPU, or CPU, define what model sizes can be feasibly hosted. Cost is also a critical element, as running large models on high-performance hardware may strain budgets, making optimization and resource alignment necessary.

Parameters for model selection

Choosing a model involves examining multiple parameters beyond the general requirements. These parameters define how well the model aligns with application needs, infrastructure constraints, and performance expectations. The main parameters to consider are outlined as follows:

- **Model family**: The first choice is selecting the appropriate family of models such as GPT, LLaMA, Falcon, or Mistral. Each family has different strengths in terms of capabilities, availability, and ecosystem support. A key trade-off exists between open-source models, which provide flexibility and customization, and closed-source models, which often deliver stronger performance but with higher costs and limited control.
- **Model variant and size**: Within a model family, multiple variants and sizes are available, such as GPT-3.5 vs. GPT-4-mini, or LLaMA-2 with 7B, 13B, or 70B parameters. Larger models typically offer better reasoning and accuracy, but they demand significantly more compute and memory resources. The right balance must be struck between capability and resource consumption, ensuring the model delivers adequate results without overwhelming infrastructure limits.
- **Quantization level**: Quantization techniques allow models to run more efficiently by reducing precision from FP32 to FP16, INT8, or even 4-bit representations. Lower precision improves inference speed and reduces hardware requirements, making deployment more cost-effective. However, this often comes at the expense of some accuracy. The decision depends on whether the application prioritizes maximum accuracy or operational efficiency.

Evolving model choices

Model selection is not just a one-time decision but an evolving process shaped by practical realities. The following scenarios illustrate how organizations typically navigate model choices in real-world contexts:

- **Prototype vs. production model choice**: During the prototype stage, teams often use easily accessible APIs such as OpenAI's GPT-4 or Anthropic's Claude to accelerate development. This helps validate the application concept quickly without investing in infrastructure. However, for production, the team may switch to an open-source alternative like LLaMA-2-13B or Mistral deployed on enterprise GPUs, ensuring better cost control and data ownership while still maintaining the required performance.
- **Switching from API-based to local deployment**: An organization developing a contract analysis tool might begin with GPT-4 API calls for accuracy and speed of integration. As usage grows, API costs escalate and sensitive legal data raises security concerns. To address this, the company transitions to a locally hosted model such as Falcon-40B, optimized with TensorRT on EC2 instances. This reduces recurring costs and provides greater control over sensitive data handling.
- **Re-evaluating with new versions**: A customer support system may initially deploy GPT-3.5 for handling FAQs and summarizing queries. When GPT-4-mini becomes available with lower latency and improved reasoning at a comparable cost, the enterprise re-evaluates and switches models. This change reduces response times, improves customer satisfaction, and keeps the system aligned with the latest technology advances.

Cost implications

When moving from experimentation to production, costs become one of the most critical considerations in GenAI deployment. Unlike the prototype phase, where quick results are prioritized, running an application in production demands sustainable financial planning. Organizations must account for the full range of expenses associated with keeping a system reliable, scalable, and secure.

These costs generally fall into two categories: capital costs and operational costs. Capital costs represent one-time investments, such as infrastructure setup or model licensing, while operational costs reflect recurring expenses, such as compute usage, storage, and staffing. A clear understanding and estimation of both categories is essential before seeking project approval and long-term sustainability.

Capital costs

Capital costs represent the upfront investments required to set up a GenAI application for production. These are typically one-time expenses that establish the foundation for long-term operations and cannot be avoided if the deployment is to be robust and sustainable. The following subsections discuss some of the capital costs involved.

Infrastructure setup

Capital costs become significant when an enterprise decides to host GenAI infrastructure on-premises. Unlike cloud services, where resources are consumed on demand, on-premises infrastructure requires building a strong foundation of hardware and supporting systems. These typically include:

- **High-performance servers**: Equipped with GPUs or TPUs to handle intensive training and inference workloads. Required only when models are hosted locally.
- **Application servers**: To host the application services and databases
- **Networking equipment**: Firewalls, switches, and related hardware to ensure connectivity, security, and scalability.
- **Secure storage systems**: Large-capacity and resilient storage solutions to manage datasets, model weights, and logs.

Software licensing

Software licensing is another important component of capital costs in GenAI deployment, particularly when the infrastructure is hosted on-premises. This includes system software such as operating systems, frameworks for model development, and optimization or deployment tools. While many libraries and frameworks are free for experimentation or non-commercial use, production deployments often require commercial licenses.

Enterprises may also choose enterprise licensing options, which not only grant access to advanced features but also provide technical support, security patches, and service-level agreements. These costs, while upfront, ensure reliability and compliance in large-scale production environments.

Model acquisition

Model acquisition represents another form of capital cost that may arise in GenAI deployment. While many models are open source and freely available, certain situations require investment to access or develop specialized models. The acquisition costs include:

- **Specialized paid models**: Some AI companies provide proprietary models that can be purchased for specific use cases. For example, Cohere's Command R+ or Anthropic's Claude Enterprise versions may require licensing fees for enterprise deployment.
- **Fine-tuning expenses**: Preparing high-quality datasets and allocating compute resources for fine-tuning can represent significant costs.
- **Additional costs**: This may include licensing pretrained checkpoints, domain-specific datasets, or consultancy support for custom model development.

Development and integration

Development and integration form a major part of capital expenditure in GenAI projects. Costs include building essential components such as application services, user interfaces, and supporting databases. These tasks may be handled by internal engineering teams or outsourced to specialized development partners, both contributing to the overall budget.

Another significant aspect is integration with existing enterprise systems. Connecting GenAI applications to platforms like CRM, ERP, or data warehouses often requires custom connectors, middleware, and rigorous testing. These efforts ensure smooth workflows but can substantially increase upfront costs in the deployment process.

Operational costs

Operational costs represent the ongoing expenses of running a GenAI application once it has been deployed. Unlike capital costs, which are one-time investments, these costs recur as part of day-to-day functioning. They include infrastructure usage, cloud services, model inference charges, maintenance, and human oversight. Careful estimation of operational costs is critical for long-term sustainability and scalability. The following subsections discuss some of the operational costs involved in production.

Cloud compute

When GenAI applications are deployed on the cloud, compute-related charges form a significant part of operational costs. These expenses vary depending on the services consumed and the scale of usage. A broad view of such costs includes:

- **Compute instances**: Charges for CPU, GPU, or TPU-based instances used to host models and applications.
- **Storage services**: Costs of storing structured, unstructured, and model-related data in secure cloud storage.
- **Networking components**: Expenditure on load balancers, firewalls, and data transfer across regions.
- **Managed databases**: Charges for specialized services like vector databases or graph databases.

API and external services

Third-party APIs are often integrated into GenAI applications to extend functionality and reduce development effort. Many large language models, such as OpenAI GPT-4, Anthropic Claude, or Cohere Command, are consumed directly as APIs. These services typically charge based on consumption, with model APIs often priced according to the number of tokens processed for prompts and responses.

Beyond models, external APIs provide domain-specific data and utilities that enhance applications. Examples include web search APIs for knowledge retrieval, weather APIs for contextual decision-making, payment gateway APIs for transactions, and translation APIs for multilingual support. These costs scale with usage, making monitoring and optimization essential for controlling operational expenses.

System monitoring

Monitoring the system is a critical operational expense in GenAI deployments. Services such as AWS CloudWatch, logging tools, and custom dashboards track application performance, resource utilization, and anomalies. In addition, model health monitoring ensures accuracy, response times, and drift detection are managed continuously, safeguarding reliability and user trust while incurring recurring costs.

Human resource and maintenance contract

Resource and maintenance costs form another significant operational component. Skilled engineers, data scientists, and support staff are required for smooth running and troubleshooting of the system. Additionally, **annual maintenance contracts** (**AMCs**) with vendors or cloud providers ensure timely upgrades, patches, and technical support, helping sustain system reliability.

Returns on investment

The deployment of GenAI systems requires significant financial commitment, but the potential returns often justify these costs. Measuring ROI helps organizations evaluate whether the benefits outweigh the expenses and provides a basis for scaling further adoption. The returns from GenAI deployment can be seen across multiple dimensions:

- **Productivity gains**: Automation of repetitive tasks, faster information retrieval, and improved workflows reduce manual effort.
- **Enhanced customer experience**: Personalized interactions, faster response times, and intelligent support improve satisfaction and retention.
- **New revenue opportunities**: Innovative products, services, or business models can emerge from leveraging GenAI capabilities.
- **Improved decision-making**: Better insights from unstructured data and predictive analytics support strategic planning.
- **Competitive advantage**: Early adoption helps organizations differentiate and stay ahead in rapidly evolving markets.

The ROI of GenAI systems is not only financial but also strategic, driving both efficiency and innovation. By balancing upfront investments with operational costs, organizations can create long-term value. Proper planning, monitoring, and scaling ensure that GenAI initiatives deliver measurable benefits and position businesses for sustained success.

Optimization

Optimization in the context of GenAI systems refers to the process of refining models, infrastructure, and workflows to achieve the best possible balance between performance, cost, and user experience. As these systems can be resource-intensive, optimization ensures they run efficiently without compromising quality. It is necessary because unoptimized deployments often lead to higher costs, slower response times, and poor scalability. By applying optimization techniques, organizations can reduce expenses, improve speed and accuracy, and deliver a smoother experience for end users. Ultimately, optimization transforms GenAI deployments into sustainable, reliable, and value-driven solutions. This section discusses various aspects of optimization of GenAI deployments.

Reasons of unoptimized deployment

Unoptimized GenAI deployments often result from oversight, resource limitations, or a lack of systematic planning. These factors can reduce efficiency, inflate costs, and negatively impact user experience. Key reasons include:

- **Overprovisioning of resources**: Allocating excessive compute, storage, or network capacity without assessing actual workload needs.
- **Lack of monitoring and feedback**: Absence of tools or processes to track performance, usage, and cost metrics in real-time.
- **Inefficient model selection**: Using larger or more complex models than required for the task, leading to unnecessary computation.
- **Poor integration practices**: Incomplete or rushed integration with existing systems causing redundancies or bottlenecks.
- **Limited expertise**: Teams lacking specialized knowledge in AI deployment and optimization strategies.

Adverse effects of unoptimized systems

Unoptimized GenAI systems can create inefficiencies that not only increase costs but also degrade overall system value. These adverse effects can be significant and long-lasting if not addressed promptly. Common issues include:

- **Higher operational costs**: Excessive spending on compute, storage, and third-party services without proportional benefits.
- **Slower response times**: Inefficient resource use or oversized models leading to latency and poor user experience.

- **Scalability challenges**: Difficulty handling growing workloads due to a lack of streamlined resource management.
- **System instability**: Increased chances of downtime or performance degradation under varying loads.
- **Lower return on investment**: Reduced business value as resources are consumed inefficiently without delivering expected outcomes.

Optimizing system components

Optimization can be applied to different parts of a GenAI system to improve efficiency, reduce costs, and enhance performance. Each component, whether infrastructure, software, or models, offers opportunities for fine-tuning. The following subsections explore how individual components can be optimized for better overall results.

Model optimization

Improving the performance of GenAI models is one of the most effective ways to optimize a system. Models can be fine-tuned or adjusted to balance accuracy, speed, and cost, depending on the application. Key approaches to model optimization include:

- **Model compression and quantization**: Reducing the size and precision of models to lower compute and memory requirements while maintaining acceptable accuracy.
- **Fine-tuning with domain-specific data**: Training models on targeted datasets to improve relevance and efficiency for specific use cases.
- **Distillation techniques**: Creating smaller, faster models by transferring knowledge from larger, more complex models.

Infrastructure optimization

Optimizing the underlying infrastructure ensures that GenAI systems run efficiently without unnecessary overhead. This involves selecting the right mix of compute, storage, and networking resources that balance performance with cost. Key approaches to infrastructure optimization include:

- **Right-sizing resources**: Using appropriately scaled instances (CPU, GPU, TPU) and storage based on workload demands to avoid over-provisioning.
- **Autoscaling and load balancing**: Dynamically adjusting resources based on usage patterns while distributing requests evenly to ensure smooth performance.
- **Hybrid or multi-cloud strategies**: Combining on-premises and cloud infrastructure, or using multiple providers, to reduce costs and improve flexibility.

Third-party API optimization

Third-party APIs often add significant value to GenAI systems, but their costs and performance can quickly become challenging if not managed well. Optimizing API usage ensures both efficiency and cost-effectiveness. Key strategies include:

- **Selective usage**: Calling APIs only when necessary and caching frequent responses to reduce repeated requests.
- **Cost monitoring**: Tracking usage patterns, especially for token-based model APIs, to avoid unexpected bills.
- **Fallback mechanisms**: Using alternative APIs or in-house models when external services are slow, costly, or unavailable.

Security and compliance optimization

Security and compliance are critical for GenAI systems, especially when handling sensitive or regulated data. Optimizing these aspects ensures the system remains both safe and compliant without introducing unnecessary overhead. Key strategies include:

- **Data handling practices**: Encrypting data in transit and at rest while minimizing storage of sensitive information.
- **Access control**: Implementing role-based access and strict authentication to prevent unauthorized use.
- **Regulatory alignment**: Regular audits and adherence to standards such as GDPR, HIPAA, or ISO ensure compliance while keeping processes efficient.

User interface optimization

The **user interface** (**UI**) plays a key role in how effectively people interact with a GenAI system. An optimized UI not only improves usability but also enhances the overall user experience and adoption of the system. Key strategies include:

- **Simplified design**: Keeping layouts clean and intuitive so users can navigate easily.
- **Personalization**: Offering adaptive interfaces that adjust to user preferences and roles.
- **Feedback and responsiveness**: Providing quick responses, clear error messages, and interactive guidance to ensure smooth interactions.

Evaluation

Evaluating a GenAI system is the process of assessing how well it performs in real-world use. It ensures that the system is not only functional but also effective, safe, and reliable for its users. Without proper evaluation, even a technically sound deployment can fail to meet its objectives. The following subsections discuss the various aspects of the evaluation of GenAI systems in production.

Importance of system evaluation

Evaluating a GenAI system is essential to confirm that it meets its intended goals and provides value to its users. Proper evaluation helps identify gaps, weaknesses, or risks early, reducing the chances of costly failures after deployment. It also builds trust among stakeholders by ensuring that the system is accurate, fair, and dependable. Key benefits of systematic evaluation include:

- **Reliability assurance**: Ensures the system consistently delivers expected outcomes.
- **Risk management**: Identifies issues such as bias, security risks, or compliance gaps.
- **User confidence**: Strengthens acceptance by validating usability and accuracy.
- **Sustained performance**: Supports continuous improvement as the system evolves.

Lifecycle of system evaluations

The evaluation of a GenAI system follows a structured lifecycle to ensure quality at every stage of development and use. Each phase serves a specific purpose and contributes to the system's long-term success:

- **Design and preparation**: Define evaluation goals, select metrics, and plan for both AI and engineering assessments.
- **Pre-production evaluation**: Test the system in controlled environments to assess accuracy, bias, latency, and user experience before release.
- **Continuous or periodic evaluation**: Monitor performance after deployment, using metrics and feedback to refine the system regularly.

This lifecycle ensures that evaluation is not a one-time activity but an ongoing process that maintains system effectiveness and trustworthiness.

Two aspects of evaluation

The evaluation of GenAI systems can be broadly divided into two categories, each addressing different but equally important dimensions of performance:

- **Engineering aspects**: These focus on the system's technical performance, including speed, scalability, uptime, reliability, and overall user experience. Strong engineering evaluation ensures that the system runs smoothly under real-world conditions.

- **AI aspects**: These focus on the model's intelligence and behavior. Parameters such as accuracy, fairness, transparency, explainability, and absence of bias are assessed to ensure the system delivers trustworthy and acceptable results.

By combining both engineering and AI evaluations, organizations can achieve a balanced view of system quality, covering both functionality and responsible AI performance. In this section, focus is on the evaluation of AI parameters.

Evaluation of AI parameters

Evaluating AI-specific parameters is critical to ensure that a GenAI system is not only functional but also reliable, ethical, and aligned with user expectations. The following dimensions are central to such evaluations:

- **Accuracy and relevance**: The system should produce outputs that are correct, meaningful, and contextually aligned with user inputs.
- **Consistency and robustness**: Responses should remain stable across varied queries and not degrade under slightly modified inputs.
- **Fairness and lack of bias**: Models must be tested to minimize harmful stereotypes, biases, or discriminatory behavior in outputs.
- **Safety and ethical compliance**: Evaluations must ensure that the system avoids generating unsafe, offensive, or harmful content.
- **User acceptability**: The outputs should meet the expectations of end users, considering both utility and comfort in interacting with the system.

Accuracy constitutes the most significant parameter in the evaluation process. Its assessment is examined in detail in the subsequent section.

Evaluation of accuracy

Accuracy is a central parameter in the evaluation of GenAI systems. Unlike traditional machine learning systems where accuracy can often be measured by straightforward comparisons between predicted and actual labels, GenAI systems produce open-ended outputs such as text, images, or audio. This makes the evaluation of accuracy more nuanced, requiring domain-specific methods, advanced metrics, and a balance between objective and subjective assessments.

Methods of evaluation

The evaluation of accuracy in GenAI systems requires diverse approaches, each suited to the type of output and application context. Key methods include:

- **Human evaluation**: Relies on experts or end-users to assess the correctness, factual alignment, coherence, and absence of hallucinations in generated outputs.
- **Reference-based evaluation**: Compares generated outputs against a set of verified references. For example, in text summarization, overlap with human-written summaries is measured using automated metrics.
- **Task-oriented evaluation**: Examines accuracy within the context of intended use. This includes checking whether a generated contract clause adheres to legal standards or verifying that a generated SQL query executes as expected.

Metrics for measuring accuracy

Accuracy in text-based systems is assessed using both traditional and advanced metrics, with a focus on factual reliability, semantic depth, and minimization of hallucinations.

- **Factual consistency metrics**: Measure whether generated content aligns with verified source data, using approaches such as *FactCC* or *QAGS*.
- **Semantic similarity metrics**: Capture meaning beyond surface overlap; BERTScore is widely used to assess semantic closeness between generated and reference texts.
- **Hallucination detection**: Identifies fabricated, unverifiable, or misleading content introduced by the model.
- **Traditional metrics:** Metrics such as *BLEU*, *ROUGE*, *METEOR*, and *Exact Match* are still used, though they often fall short of capturing deeper semantic and contextual accuracy.

Accuracy in multimodal systems

Evaluating accuracy in multimodal systems requires specialized methods tailored to the type of output, whether visual or auditory, with both automated metrics and human judgment playing a role. It involves:

- **Image generation accuracy**: Assessed using metrics such as **Fréchet Inception Distance** (**FID**) and **Inception Score** (**IS**) to evaluate realism and distributional alignment. Human evaluation complements these by checking fidelity to prompts (e.g., confirming that *a cat on a skateboard* contains both specified elements).
- **Audio generation accuracy**: Measured through intelligibility (e.g., word error rate for speech outputs), naturalness (using Mean Opinion Score), and adherence to prompts, including correct pronunciation in text-to-speech or preservation of intended emotion.

Additional considerations

Beyond general evaluation, several nuanced aspects of accuracy are critical to ensuring trustworthy GenAI performance:

- **Domain-specific accuracy**: In sensitive areas such as healthcare, law, or finance, even minor factual errors can lead to severe consequences, making strict accuracy checks indispensable.
- **Contextual accuracy**: Accuracy extends beyond factual correctness to include contextual relevance and appropriateness, ensuring that responses align with the specific needs and intent of the user.
- **Continuous evaluation**: Accuracy must be monitored and reassessed regularly, as models can experience performance drift or degradation when exposed to new, evolving, or adversarial data.

Example

A GenAI model is used to generate radiology reports from medical images. Accuracy is evaluated by comparing the generated reports with expert-written ones using semantic similarity measures. Radiologists also review a sample set for factual consistency, checking for missing or hallucinated findings. In parallel, the model's ability to generate clinically relevant images (e.g., simulated X-rays for training) is tested using FID scores and domain-expert evaluation. This multi-faceted approach ensures that both textual and visual outputs meet the required accuracy standards.

Conclusion

The deployment of GenAI systems is critical for translating cutting-edge models into practical, value-generating applications. Without effective deployment, even the most advanced models remain theoretical assets rather than operational solutions.

In this chapter, the discussion centered on the real-world deployment of GenAI systems. The requirements for production-grade systems were examined, followed by an overview of the typical architectural components that enable them. Key aspects of deployment design, such as infrastructure, compute resources, networking, and licensing, were highlighted, with particular attention to the growing role of cloud environments. An illustrative example of deployment on AWS was presented to ground these concepts. At the heart of every system lies the GenAI model, whose deployment strategy received detailed treatment. Beyond this, practical considerations such as model selection, cost management, and ROI determination were emphasized as central to long-term success. Finally, the chapter explored optimization and evaluation, both of which ensure that deployed systems remain efficient, accurate, and relevant in real-world contexts.

Looking forward, one of the most important aspects of GenAI systems is governance. The next chapter addresses governance in detail.

CHAPTER 10
AI Governance and Ethics

Introduction

Generative AI has demonstrated significant potential in enterprises, enabling innovations in customer engagement, process optimization, product development, and decision-making. Earlier chapters have highlighted these opportunities and shown how organizations can successfully adopt and implement AI solutions. Yet, with this promise comes a set of challenges that cannot be overlooked. If inadequately managed, the risks associated with AI can jeopardize implementations, disrupt operations, and expose enterprises to reputational, financial, and even legal consequences.

In addition to these operational risks, GenAI raises profound ethical concerns. Questions of fairness, transparency, accountability, and privacy must be addressed to ensure that AI serves not only enterprise objectives but also the broader interests of society. Responsible AI has emerged as a discipline aimed at providing principles and practices to guide the ethical development and use of AI systems in business environments.

At the same time, governments and regulators across the world are responding to the rapid evolution of AI technologies. Initiatives such as the European Union's AI Act, emerging guidelines in the United States, and policy frameworks in countries like India and Singapore illustrate a growing recognition of the need for oversight. These regulatory efforts are shaping the way enterprises must design, deploy, and govern AI solutions.

Finally, the impact of AI extends beyond technology and ethics into the social sphere, particularly in relation to jobs and workforce transformation. Enterprises must anticipate and address these shifts to ensure sustainable adoption.

This chapter examines these dimensions, risks, ethics, responsible AI, regulations, and workforce impact within the enterprise context.

Structure

This chapter covers the following topics:

- Risks of GenAI
- Ethical issues
- Responsible AI toolbox

- AI regulations
- Impact on jobs

Objectives

By the end of this chapter, you will understand the key governance and ethical considerations essential for the responsible deployment of GAI. You will learn about major risks, such as bias, privacy breaches, misinformation, and over-reliance, and how they can affect enterprises and society. The chapter explains practical mitigation strategies, including governance frameworks, technical safeguards, and human oversight.

You will also explore the global regulatory landscape, covering policies in the European Union, the United States, China, and India, and identify common regulatory themes. Ethical dimensions such as fairness, transparency, privacy, autonomy, and environmental responsibility are examined, along with methods to embed these principles into organizational culture and operations.

Risks of GenAI

While generative AI offers significant opportunities for enterprises, it also introduces a set of risks that cannot be overlooked. These risks span technical, operational, ethical, and reputational dimensions, each with the potential to disrupt business outcomes if not managed carefully. Understanding these challenges is the first step toward building safe, reliable, and sustainable AI systems for enterprise use. The following subsections discuss the major risks in detail, along with their implications and possible mitigations.

Hallucination and accuracy risks

Generative AI models are known to produce content that appears convincing but may be factually incorrect, incomplete, or entirely fabricated. This phenomenon, commonly called hallucination, arises because models generate responses based on patterns in training data rather than true verification of facts. In enterprise settings where precision and reliability are critical, such inaccuracies can have serious consequences. The problem is further compounded by the authoritative tone of AI outputs, which makes errors harder to detect. Unlike traditional software, these systems cannot guarantee consistency across repeated queries, adding unpredictability to enterprise use.

Impact on enterprise

Hallucinations can erode the reliability of AI systems and create serious risks for decision-making and compliance. Some of the risks are:

- **Decision errors**: Wrong outputs may mislead business leaders into flawed strategic or operational decisions.

- **Compliance breach**: In regulated industries, inaccurate information can result in non-compliance with legal or policy requirements.
- **Financial loss**: Misleading insights can cause revenue loss, wasted resources, or penalties.
- **Erosion of trust**: Stakeholders may lose confidence in enterprise AI systems if inaccuracies are frequent.

Example in litigation

In the legal sector, a law firm experimenting with AI-generated case briefs faced embarrassment when the system cited court rulings that did not exist. Such hallucinations could misinform legal strategy, delay case preparation, and damage the firm's reputation.

Mitigation

Enterprises should establish controls to detect and limit the impact of hallucinated outputs. Examples are:

- **Human-in-the-loop**: Require expert review before using AI outputs in critical workflows.
- **Source verification**: Cross-check AI-generated content against trusted databases or systems.
- **Domain-specific fine-tuning**: Adapt models with curated enterprise data to improve factual accuracy.
- **Usage boundaries**: Restrict generative AI applications to low-risk domains unless robust safeguards exist.

Bias and fairness

Generative AI models learn from vast datasets collected from the internet and other sources, which often contain cultural, social, or historical biases. These biases can become embedded in model behavior, leading to outputs that systematically favor or disadvantage certain groups. In an enterprise environment, where AI-driven decisions affect customers, employees, or partners, biased outputs can create significant ethical and operational challenges. Ensuring fairness is not only a moral obligation but also a practical necessity for sustaining trust and compliance.

Impact on enterprise

Bias in AI systems can undermine inclusivity and expose organizations to reputational and legal risks. Some of the risks are:

- **Discrimination risk**: AI outputs may unfairly disadvantage individuals based on gender, race, or background.
- **Reputation damage**: Perceived bias in enterprise AI can harm brand image and stakeholder confidence.
- **Legal liability**: Biased outcomes in hiring, lending, or insurance decisions may expose enterprises to lawsuits.
- **Customer attrition**: Unfair treatment can alienate customers, resulting in reduced loyalty and lost business.

Example in recruitment

In recruitment, AI-driven résumé screening tools have shown bias by favoring male candidates for technical roles due to patterns in historical data. Such unfair outcomes can undermine diversity goals and expose organizations to discrimination claims.

Mitigation

Reducing bias requires both technical interventions and governance mechanisms, such as:

- **Bias testing**: Regularly audit AI systems for biased outputs across different user groups.
- **Diverse training data**: Use datasets that represent varied demographics and contexts.
- **Fairness constraints**: Apply algorithms that limit discriminatory patterns in outputs.
- **Oversight committees**: Establish review boards to monitor fairness in AI deployments.

Data privacy and security

Generative AI systems rely on large volumes of data to generate meaningful outputs. When enterprises feed sensitive information into these systems, there is a risk of data leakage, unauthorized access, or unintended retention. In addition, if external AI services are used without proper safeguards, proprietary business data may end up outside organizational control. Privacy concerns are further heightened when AI models inadvertently reproduce fragments of their training data, potentially exposing confidential or personal information.

Impact on enterprise

Some of the risks are:

- **Data breach**: Sensitive information may be exposed to external parties, intentionally or accidentally.

- **Regulatory non-compliance**: Mishandling personal or proprietary data can violate laws such as GDPR or HIPAA.
- **Loss of competitive edge**: Leakage of intellectual property or trade secrets may erode strategic advantage.
- **Trust deficit**: Customers and employees may lose confidence in enterprise systems if data misuse occurs.

Example in financial services

A financial services company using an external AI assistant to draft client communications faced a risk of exposing customer account details, as employee inputs could be stored or accessed outside the enterprise firewall.

Mitigation

Enterprises can reduce privacy and security risks by combining preventive measures with robust governance. Some of the measures are:

- **Data anonymization**: Remove or mask personal identifiers before feeding data into AI systems.
- **Access controls**: Restrict who can use AI tools and what data can be shared.
- **Private AI deployment**: Use on-premise or enterprise-grade cloud AI solutions to keep data within organizational boundaries.
- **Regular audits**: Monitor AI usage and conduct compliance reviews to detect potential leakage or misuse.

Intellectual property-related risks

Generative AI models are trained on vast amounts of online content, some of which may include copyrighted, trademarked, or patented material. As a result, the outputs generated by these systems can inadvertently resemble protected works or use proprietary information without authorization. For enterprises, this raises the risk of intellectual property disputes, especially when AI-generated content is used externally in marketing, product design, or customer communication.

Impact on enterprise

Enterprises face both legal and reputational consequences when AI-generated outputs infringe on intellectual property rights. Some of the risks are:

- **Legal disputes**: Unauthorized use of copyrighted material can result in lawsuits or settlements.

- **Financial penalties**: Infringement claims may lead to fines, compensation costs, or licensing fees.
- **Reputational harm**: Perceived misuse of others' content can damage brand credibility.
- **Operational delays**: Disputes over IP can stall product launches or marketing campaigns.

Example in marketing

A consumer goods company used a generative AI tool to create product advertisements, only to later discover that the imagery closely resembled stock photos owned by another firm, exposing the company to copyright infringement claims.

Mitigation

To minimize IP risks, enterprises must combine policy, process, and technical safeguards, as follows:

- **Content review**: Implement human-in-the-loop checks before publishing AI-generated content.
- **Clear usage policies**: Define acceptable use of generative AI outputs within the organization.
- **Licensed training data**: Prefer AI systems trained on properly licensed or enterprise-owned datasets.
- **Legal consultation**: Engage legal teams to evaluate ownership rights of AI-generated assets.

Regulatory and compliance risks

The regulatory landscape for AI is evolving rapidly as governments and international bodies attempt to keep pace with technological advances. Enterprises deploying generative AI must navigate requirements related to transparency, accountability, data protection, and auditability. Non-compliance can result not only from ignorance of new rules but also from insufficient governance practices within organizations. Since regulations vary across regions, multinational enterprises face additional complexity in aligning AI implementations with diverse legal frameworks. A more detailed discussion of global AI regulations will be provided later in this chapter.

Impact on enterprise

Regulatory and compliance risks can disrupt business continuity and expose enterprises to legal and financial consequences. Risks include:

- **Legal penalties**: Violations of AI-related regulations may lead to fines or sanctions.
- **Operational constraints**: Enterprises may need to pause or redesign AI systems to meet compliance standards.
- **Cross-border complexity**: Differing laws across regions complicate global deployments of enterprise AI.
- **Reputation damage**: Non-compliance signals irresponsibility, eroding trust with regulators and stakeholders.

Example in healthcare

A hospital group adopting AI-powered diagnostic tools had to suspend deployment after regulators questioned whether the system complied with medical device certification requirements. This led to delays in implementation and additional compliance costs.

Mitigation

Enterprises should embed compliance into the AI lifecycle through proactive monitoring and governance. Some example measures are:

- **Regulatory tracking**: Continuously monitor evolving AI regulations across relevant jurisdictions.
- **Compliance frameworks**: Align AI development with standards such as ISO, NIST, or EU AI Act provisions.
- **Audit trails**: Maintain documentation of data sources, model decisions, and testing results for regulatory review.
- **Cross-functional governance**: Involve legal, compliance, and risk management teams in AI projects.

Security and adversarial risks

Generative AI systems are vulnerable to manipulation through malicious inputs or deliberate attacks. Adversaries can exploit weaknesses in models by injecting harmful prompts, altering training data, or crafting adversarial examples that cause incorrect or unsafe outputs. In enterprise environments, these risks extend beyond the AI system itself, as compromised outputs can be used for phishing, misinformation, or other forms of cyberattacks. The openness and flexibility of generative models make them particularly attractive targets for exploitation.

Impact on enterprise

Security vulnerabilities in AI can expose enterprises to operational disruption and malicious exploitation. Examples are:

- **Prompt injection attacks**: Attackers can manipulate instructions to override intended behavior.
- **Data poisoning**: Malicious inputs during training or fine-tuning can corrupt system reliability.
- **Phishing and fraud**: AI-generated content can be weaponized to deceive customers or employees.
- **System downtime**: Exploited vulnerabilities may force suspension of AI services, affecting business continuity.

Example in banking

A bank piloting an AI-powered customer support chatbot discovered that adversarial prompts could make the system reveal internal process details, creating potential security exposure.

Mitigation

Enterprises can strengthen resilience against adversarial risks by combining technical safeguards such as:

- **Robust prompt filtering**: Detect and block malicious or suspicious inputs in real-time.
- **Secure fine-tuning**: Use controlled and verified datasets to prevent data poisoning.
- **Continuous monitoring**: Track AI behavior to identify anomalies and unauthorized use.
- **Red-team testing**: Simulate attacks to proactively uncover and patch vulnerabilities.

Operational and integration risks

Generative AI solutions do not operate in isolation; they must fit seamlessly into existing enterprise workflows, IT systems, and governance structures. Poor integration can lead to inefficiencies, inconsistent user experience, or even process breakdowns. Additionally, over-reliance on experimental AI systems without proper monitoring or fallback mechanisms can cause operational disruptions. These risks often stem from the complexity of aligning AI outputs with enterprise standards, data pipelines, and business objectives.

Impact on enterprise

Operational challenges can reduce the effectiveness of AI solutions and create downstream issues. Example issues include:

- **Workflow disruption**: Misaligned AI outputs can break established business processes.
- **System incompatibility**: Integration with legacy IT systems may be difficult or costly.

- **Over-reliance on AI**: Lack of human oversight can magnify errors in critical decisions.
- **Scalability issues**: Pilots may work well, but full-scale deployments face technical or cost hurdles.

Example in healthcare

A hospital attempted to integrate a generative AI tool for summarizing patient records. However, mismatches with its **electronic health record** (**EHR**) system created delays and data inconsistencies, ultimately reducing clinician trust in the system.

Mitigation

Enterprises can minimize operational risks by adopting structured deployment strategies such as:

- **Pilot before scaling**: Test AI solutions in controlled settings before full rollout.
- **Human-in-the-loop**: Maintain oversight to validate critical AI-driven decisions.
- **Standards-based integration**: Use APIs and interoperability protocols for smooth system alignment.
- **Monitoring and feedback**: Continuously track performance and incorporate user feedback.

Reputational and trust risks

Generative AI outputs directly shape how customers, employees, and stakeholders perceive an enterprise. If the system produces biased, offensive, or inaccurate content, the organization's reputation can be quickly damaged. Trust, once lost, is difficult to rebuild, and in highly competitive markets, reputational harm can lead to loss of customers, partnerships, and employee confidence. In regulated industries, public missteps can also invite scrutiny from authorities and media.

Impact on enterprise

Reputational harm can undermine both short-term and long-term business value. Some of the issues faced can be:

- **Customer trust erosion**: Inaccurate or offensive AI responses can alienate users.
- **Brand damage**: Negative publicity from AI failures can tarnish the enterprise's image.
- **Stakeholder concerns**: Investors and partners may lose confidence in governance practices.

- **Employee morale**: Internal trust in enterprise technology can weaken, reducing adoption.

Example in retail

A large e-commerce platform faced backlash when its AI-driven product description tool generated culturally insensitive content. The incident went viral, forcing the company to issue public apologies and tighten review processes.

Mitigation

Reputation risks can be managed through proactive governance and transparency. Some measures employed are:

- **Content review policies**: Ensure AI-generated outputs undergo quality checks.
- **Bias audits**: Regularly assess models for fairness and inclusivity.
- **Clear communication**: Inform customers about AI use to set realistic expectations.
- **Crisis management plans**: Prepare strategies to respond quickly to reputational incidents.

Over-reliance and skill degradation

Generative AI can become so efficient at automating cognitive tasks that enterprises risk over-relying on it at the expense of human expertise. Employees may gradually lose critical thinking, problem-solving, or domain-specific skills if they depend too heavily on AI for routine or complex decision-making. This phenomenon can reduce organizational resilience, as the enterprise becomes less capable of functioning effectively when AI tools fail, are unavailable, or produce errors.

Impact on enterprise

Excessive dependence on AI may weaken human expertise and adaptability. Some of the adverse effects can be:

- **Skill atrophy**: Employees may lose proficiency in essential analytical or creative tasks.
- **Decision quality risks**: Lack of independent judgment increases the impact of AI errors.
- **Compliance gaps**: Over-reliance may neglect the human oversight required by regulations.
- **Reduced resilience**: Organizations may struggle to adapt during AI outages or failures.

Example in consulting

A consulting firm introduced an AI tool to automate business proposal writing. While efficiency improved, junior consultants relied solely on the system, leading to weaker skill development in persuasive writing and strategic thinking.

Mitigation

Balanced adoption ensures that AI supports rather than replaces human expertise. Some examples practices are:

- **Human-AI collaboration**: Use AI as an assistant, not a substitute, in decision-making.
- **Training programs**: Continuously upskill employees to maintain core competencies.
- **Oversight protocols**: Define areas where human review is mandatory.
- **Rotation of tasks**: Encourage employees to practice skills AI often automates.

Ethical issues

When discussing ethical issues in generative AI, the focus shifts from the enterprise to society at large. These issues concern the ways in which AI systems affect people, employees, consumers, and other groups, sometimes even when there is no direct organizational impact. They include questions of fairness, privacy, autonomy, and broader social responsibility.

In this section, the discussion will center on the major ethical concerns enterprises must consider when deploying GenAI solutions. Later in the chapter, the *AI regulations* section will explore how governments are framing laws to address these concerns, and the *Responsible AI toolbox* section will present mechanisms and practices to mitigate them. Together, these perspectives help build a holistic understanding of ethics in enterprise AI.

Fairness and bias

GenAI does not operate in a neutral space; it reflects the data it was trained on. When these systems generate text, images, or recommendations, they may unintentionally privilege some groups while creating disadvantage for others. The problem arises because historical imbalances, stereotypes, or exclusions encoded in data are reproduced in AI outputs. In enterprise use, this can mean that important decisions or customer interactions are shaped by unfair assumptions rather than objective criteria.

Impacted groups

Bias in GenAI can affect multiple stakeholders who interact with enterprise systems. Some examples are:

- **Job applicants**: Recruitment tools that favor certain demographic groups may reduce opportunities for equally qualified candidates from underrepresented communities.
- **Customers**: AI-powered credit or insurance assessments can result in discriminatory decisions, excluding groups based on socioeconomic or ethnic characteristics.
- **Employees**: Workplace AI tools for performance evaluation or task allocation may disadvantage certain groups, affecting promotions and career progression.
- **Society at large**: Biased content in public-facing applications can reinforce harmful stereotypes, deepening social divisions over time.

Transparency and explainability

GenAI systems often function as *black boxes*, producing results without clear reasoning that humans can easily follow. While these outputs may appear accurate, the lack of transparency raises ethical concerns when people are affected by decisions they cannot understand or challenge. In enterprise settings, the inability to explain how AI reached an outcome undermines trust and accountability, especially in areas where fairness, safety, or compliance are critical.

Impacted groups

Limited transparency and explainability can negatively affect different stakeholders who rely on or are subject to enterprise AI systems. Some examples of stakeholders are:

- **Customers**: When denied a loan or given an unusual recommendation, customers may feel frustrated if no clear explanation is provided.
- **Employees**: Workers using AI tools for decision-making may lack confidence in outputs they cannot justify to managers or clients.
- **Regulators**: Oversight bodies may find it difficult to evaluate whether enterprise systems comply with legal or ethical standards.
- **General public**: Communities may lose trust in enterprises that use opaque AI systems, leading to resistance against adoption.

Privacy and surveillance

Generative AI systems often rely on vast amounts of personal or sensitive data for training and operation. If such data is mishandled, individuals' privacy can be compromised through unintended disclosure, re-identification, or misuse. In enterprise settings, AI can also be deployed in ways that increase surveillance of employees or customers, raising concerns about consent, autonomy, and proportionality. These practices not only pose ethical questions but also risk eroding trust in the organization.

Impacted groups

Privacy intrusions and surveillance practices can affect multiple groups touched by enterprise AI systems. Some examples of such groups are:

- **Customers**: Personal data used in training or for targeted services can be exposed, misused, or shared without proper consent.
- **Employees**: Monitoring tools that track productivity or communication can create a sense of constant surveillance, undermining workplace morale.
- **Vulnerable populations**: Groups such as children, patients, or marginalized communities face heightened risks if sensitive data about them is leaked or exploited.
- **Society at large**: Widespread use of surveillance-driven AI can normalize intrusive practices, reducing expectations of privacy for everyone.

Autonomy and manipulation

Generative AI has the capacity to influence human behavior by shaping opinions, emotions, or decisions through the content it produces. When used irresponsibly, it can blur the line between assistance and manipulation, raising ethical concerns about respect for human autonomy. In enterprise contexts, this may occur through persuasive marketing, nudging in financial advice, or subtle framing of choices, where users are guided toward actions they may not have otherwise taken.

Impacted groups

The erosion of autonomy through manipulative AI practices can touch various stakeholders, such as:

- **Consumers**: Targeted advertising or personalized recommendations may push individuals toward unnecessary purchases or harmful financial decisions.
- **Employees**: AI-driven performance nudges or workplace tools can pressure workers into behaviors that serve organizational goals but reduce their sense of agency.
- **Citizens**: Generative AI used in political campaigns or social messaging can manipulate public opinion, influencing democratic processes.
- **Vulnerable individuals**: People with limited digital literacy or higher susceptibility to influence may be disproportionately affected by manipulative AI outputs.

Misinformation

Generative AI makes it possible to create realistic text, images, audio, and video at scale. While this enables powerful enterprise applications, it also increases the risk of producing or spreading misinformation. Deepfakes, fabricated news, or misleading content can erode public trust, damage reputations, and destabilize social discourse. In enterprise use, even unintentional dissemination of false or misleading outputs raises serious ethical questions about authenticity and responsibility.

Impacted groups

The spread of AI-generated misinformation can harm different parts of society in distinct ways. Some examples are:

- **Consumers**: False product information or deceptive marketing content can mislead customers, leading to poor decisions or financial harm.
- **Public figures**: Deepfake content can damage the credibility of individuals, exposing them to reputational or personal harm.
- **Society at large**: Widespread misinformation can fuel polarization, weaken trust in institutions, and create confusion in democratic processes.

Environmental impact

Generative AI models, particularly large-scale ones, require vast computational resources for both training and deployment. This translates into significant energy consumption and a large carbon footprint, raising concerns about the sustainability of AI adoption at scale. For enterprises, while the direct impact may be less visible than operational risks, the ethical responsibility to consider environmental consequences is becoming increasingly important. Ignoring this dimension may not only harm the planet but also affect the organization's reputation among environmentally conscious stakeholders.

Impacted groups

The environmental costs of generative AI extend beyond the enterprise to wider communities and ecosystems. Examples of such communities can be:

- **Communities near data centers**: High energy consumption and water usage for cooling can strain local resources, directly affecting residents.
- **Global society**: The overall carbon footprint of AI adds to climate change challenges, which impact health, agriculture, and biodiversity worldwide.
- **Future generations**: Unsustainable energy use contributes to climate change, creating long-term risks for younger populations and those yet to come.

Responsible AI toolbox

Enterprises adopting generative AI face a range of ethical challenges, from fairness and transparency to privacy, manipulation, and even environmental impact. These issues extend beyond business outcomes, influencing how employees, customers, and society experience the technology. As discussed earlier, the ethical risks are complex and multifaceted, requiring more than ad hoc fixes; they demand structured responses that build trust and accountability.

Over the past decade, the idea of responsible AI has emerged as a guiding framework to address these concerns. Initially shaped by academic debates and policy discussions, it has now evolved into practical guidelines, regulatory expectations, and enterprise practices. Large organizations, governments, and international bodies have put forward principles and toolkits aimed at making AI safer, fairer, and more reliable. For enterprises, this shift means that ethical considerations are no longer optional but central to long-term success.

The following discussion examines specific responsible AI principles and the measures available to put them into practice. Each principle corresponds to the concerns discussed in the ethics section, offering both conceptual clarity and practical techniques for mitigation.

Governance and accountability

Strong governance structures are the foundation of responsible AI in enterprises. Governance ensures that the development and deployment of generative AI systems follow established policies, standards, and ethical principles. Accountability mechanisms clarify who is responsible for decisions made by AI, preventing ambiguity when outcomes cause harm or violate norms. Without such structures, even the most advanced technical safeguards risk being inconsistently applied or ignored. Key practices include:

- **AI ethics boards and committees**: organizations often create cross-functional bodies that review projects, assess risks, and provide guidance on ethical dilemmas.
- **Policy frameworks and guidelines**: clearly documented principles and procedures define acceptable uses of AI and set boundaries for sensitive applications.
- **Defined roles and responsibilities**: assigning accountability at executive, managerial, and technical levels ensures that decision-making is traceable.
- **Audit trails and reporting**: documenting model development, data sources, and decision logic enables internal oversight and external compliance checks.

Governance and accountability not only protect enterprises from reputational or legal damage but also demonstrate commitment to building AI systems that stakeholders can trust.

Technical methods and tools

While governance sets the rules, technical methods and tools bring responsible AI principles into practice. These approaches enable enterprises to design, test, and monitor generative AI systems in ways that actively reduce risks and improve reliability. Given the complexity of AI models and their reliance on massive datasets, technical safeguards are essential to ensure fairness, transparency, privacy, and robustness at scale. Some important techniques are:

- **Bias detection and mitigation**: Tools can analyze training data and model outputs to identify imbalances or unfair patterns, followed by techniques such as reweighting data, synthetic data generation, or post-processing corrections. Open-source libraries like IBM AI Fairness 360 and Fairlearn provide ready-to-use methods for these tasks.
- **Explainability techniques**: Methods like **Local Interpretable Model-Agnostic Explanations** (**LIME**), **Shapley Additive Explanations** (**SHAP**), and attention visualization provide insights into why models produce certain results, making outputs more understandable to developers, auditors, and users. Toolkits such as InterpretML support explainability in enterprise contexts.
- **Robustness and adversarial testing**: Stress-testing models against adversarial prompts, edge cases, or distribution shifts helps identify vulnerabilities before deployment. Platforms like **Adversarial Robustness Toolbox** (**ART**) offer specialized techniques for this purpose.
- **Privacy-preserving methods**: Approaches such as differential privacy, homomorphic encryption, and federated learning allow enterprises to protect sensitive information while still training powerful models. Google's TensorFlow Privacy and PySyft are common implementations.
- **Monitoring and drift detection**: Continuous surveillance of deployed systems detects when models begin to diverge from expected behavior, either due to data drift, changing contexts, or adversarial misuse. Commercial MLOps platforms often embed these features.
- **Content moderation and filtering**: For generative systems, automated filters and human-in-the-loop mechanisms can prevent the generation of harmful or inappropriate outputs.

Enterprises often integrate these methods into standardized documentation frameworks like model cards and datasheets for datasets, or use comprehensive platforms such as the Microsoft responsible AI toolbox. By embedding these technical practices across the AI lifecycle, organizations move beyond policy aspirations and ensure that Responsible AI principles are consistently operationalized.

Organizational culture and training

Responsible AI cannot be achieved through policies and tools alone; it requires an organizational culture that values ethics, accountability, and long-term trust. Enterprises that embed these values into their workforce practices create conditions where responsible AI becomes a shared responsibility rather than the job of a single team. Training employees to recognize risks and empowering them to act ethically are critical steps in bridging the gap between principle and practice. Some key practices:

- **Awareness programs**: Regular workshops, internal campaigns, and training modules help employees understand the ethical risks of AI and their role in mitigating them. Large organizations such as Google and Microsoft have created internal AI ethics curricula for this purpose.
- **Role-specific training**: Developers, data scientists, business managers, and legal teams each need tailored training that matches their responsibilities in the AI lifecycle. For example, technical staff may learn bias detection methods, while managers focus on governance frameworks.
- **Ethics champions**: Some enterprises designate individuals or teams as *ethics champions* who serve as points of contact for Responsible AI concerns and guide project teams in ethical decision-making.
- **Incentives and accountability structures**: Linking performance metrics and recognition systems to responsible behavior encourages employees to align with ethical AI practices.
- **Cross-disciplinary collaboration**: Encouraging dialogue between technical experts, domain specialists, and social scientists enriches the enterprise perspective on AI's human impact.

A strong culture and workforce training ensure that responsible AI is not confined to compliance documents or specialized toolkits but becomes part of daily decision-making across the organization.

Human autonomy and oversight

A core principle of responsible AI is ensuring that humans remain in control of critical decisions. Generative AI can create persuasive outputs, but enterprises must prevent over-reliance on automated systems that could manipulate behavior or bypass human judgment. Human oversight provides a safeguard, balancing efficiency with accountability. Key practices include:

- **Human-in-the-loop systems**: Embedding checkpoints where humans review and approve AI-driven recommendations before action is taken.
- **Clear boundaries of automation**: Defining which decisions AI may handle autonomously and which require human authority, particularly in high-stakes areas like finance or healthcare.
- **Escalation mechanisms**: Ensuring there are clear processes to flag and correct problematic outputs or unintended consequences.

- **Training for critical review**: Equipping staff to question AI outputs rather than accept them at face value.

By maintaining human oversight, enterprises protect both organizational integrity and societal trust.

Environment and sustainability

The environmental impact of generative AI is becoming a central concern in responsible AI discussions. Training and deploying large-scale models require significant computational resources, leading to high energy consumption and carbon emissions. For enterprises, this raises not only ethical questions about sustainability but also practical challenges around cost and resource efficiency. Some measures are:

- **Energy-efficient model design**: Using smaller, optimized models or fine-tuning existing ones rather than training from scratch.
- **Green data centers**: Leveraging cloud providers or facilities powered by renewable energy sources to reduce carbon footprints.
- **Resource monitoring**: Tracking energy use and emissions during model training and deployment to align with enterprise sustainability goals.
- **Lifecycle optimization**: Retiring or compressing underused models and encouraging reuse of components to minimize waste.

By incorporating sustainability into AI practices, enterprises can align technological innovation with broader environmental and corporate responsibility goals.

AI regulations

The earlier sections of this book examined the potential downsides of enterprise AI. Risks highlighted how generative AI can harm organizations if left unchecked. The discussion on ethics shifted the focus outward, exploring the broader effects on employees, customers, and society. The responsible AI section then outlined practical steps, governance frameworks, human oversight, and technical safeguards that organizations can adopt to address these challenges internally. Together, these sections have shown that while enterprises can act proactively, the scale and complexity of AI demand collective action that goes beyond individual companies.

AI regulations represent this collective response. Around the world, governments and international bodies are drafting laws to ensure that AI systems are developed and deployed in ways that protect human rights, preserve fairness, and reduce harm. Regulation can appear as binding legislation or as non-binding guidelines and standards, but enterprises should treat both with equal seriousness. Guidelines often set the direction for future laws and are frequently adopted by industry partners, regulators, and customers as de facto requirements.

This section examines the emerging landscape of AI regulation. It will review key laws and frameworks from different regions, highlight themes such as data protection and algorithmic transparency, and discuss how enterprises can navigate this evolving legal environment. The following subsections will explore major global regulations, sector-specific requirements, and practical considerations for compliance.

Global landscape of AI regulation

AI regulation is taking shape across the world, with each major region adopting its own mix of legal requirements and policy frameworks. These approaches reflect different social priorities, levels of technological maturity, and political contexts, but all aim to balance innovation with safeguards for individuals and society. For enterprises operating internationally, understanding these differences is essential. Compliance strategies must account for the strict data and safety standards in some jurisdictions as well as the more flexible, innovation-driven policies in others.

The following discussion provides a brief overview of key regulatory environments that are shaping the global AI landscape. They highlight the European Union's comprehensive AI Act, the United States' sector-based and state-level initiatives, China's centrally directed but rapidly evolving rules, and India's emerging policy framework.

Regulation in the European Union

The European Union has taken a leading role in establishing a comprehensive and binding legal framework for artificial intelligence. The cornerstone of this effort is the **EU AI Act**, which introduces a risk-based approach to governing AI systems and is expected to influence global standards much like the GDPR did for data privacy. Enterprises planning to deploy generative AI in Europe must be aware of these obligations even if they are headquartered elsewhere, as the rules apply to any organization offering AI products or services within the EU.

Key features of the EU regulatory approach include:

- **Risk classification**: AI systems are categorized as unacceptable, high, limited, or minimal risk, with requirements increasing sharply for high-risk applications.
- **Transparency obligations**: Providers must disclose when users are interacting with AI, especially for generative models.
- **Governance and oversight**: Mandatory documentation, human oversight mechanisms, and post-market monitoring are required for high-risk systems.
- **Enforcement and penalties**: Non-compliance can attract significant fines, modeled after GDPR enforcement levels.

Regulation in the United States

The United States does not yet have a single, comprehensive federal AI law. Instead, regulation is evolving through a mix of executive actions, sector-specific rules, and state-level initiatives. For enterprises operating in or with the U.S., this patchwork landscape means careful attention to both national guidance and local legislation.

Key elements shaping the U.S. regulatory environment include:

- **Executive Order on AI (2023)**: Directs federal agencies to set safety, security, and privacy standards, and requires developers of powerful AI models to share safety test results with the government.
- **Sector-specific rules**: Agencies such as the **Federal Trade Commission** (**FTC**), **Food and Drug Administration** (FDA), and **Securities and Exchange Commission** (**SEC**) apply existing consumer protection, healthcare, and financial regulations to AI-driven products and services.
- **State-level initiatives**: States like *California*, *Colorado*, and *New York* are advancing privacy and AI-specific bills, creating varying compliance requirements.
- **Voluntary frameworks**: The NIST AI risk management framework offers best practices for responsible AI design and deployment, encouraging enterprises to adopt self-regulation even before federal mandates emerge.

Regulation in China

China has adopted a proactive and centralized approach to AI regulation, aiming to maintain state oversight while promoting innovation. Its rules are among the most detailed globally, placing strong emphasis on content control, security, and accountability. Enterprises operating in or with China must navigate a tightly governed environment where compliance is critical.

Key regulations in China include:

- **Generative AI measures (2023)**: Require providers of generative AI services to ensure content aligns with socialist values, prevent discrimination, and conduct security assessments before public release.
- **Algorithmic recommendation rules (2022)**: Mandate transparency in recommendation systems, including disclosure of algorithms and the ability for users to opt out of personalized feeds.
- **Cybersecurity and data laws**: The **Personal Information Protection Law** (**PIPL**) and the Data Security Law set strict requirements for handling and transferring personal data, with significant penalties for violations.

- **Licensing and registration**: AI service providers must register with regulators and maintain detailed records of data sources and training processes to demonstrate compliance.

Regulation in India

India's approach to AI regulation is evolving, with a focus on encouraging innovation while safeguarding citizens' rights and national interests. Unlike the European Union's prescriptive framework, India currently relies on sectoral guidelines and broad digital governance laws, but concrete AI-specific regulations are steadily emerging. Enterprises working in or with India must stay alert to these fast-changing requirements.

Some existing and emerging frameworks are:

- **Digital Personal Data Protection Act (DPDPA) 2023**: Establishes a framework for collecting, processing, and storing personal data, emphasizing user consent and accountability for data breaches.
- **Sectoral guidelines**: Financial, healthcare, and telecom regulators have issued directives on responsible AI use, covering areas such as algorithmic decision-making and bias reduction.
- **National AI strategy (NITI Aayog)**: Outlines principles for ethical AI development, including fairness, transparency, and inclusivity, offering a policy foundation for future regulations.
- **Upcoming AI-specific framework**: The government has signaled its intent to draft AI regulations focused on risk-based oversight, expected to address generative AI, deepfakes, and critical infrastructure applications.

Common regulatory themes

While each country's AI regulation reflects its own political priorities and legal traditions, several principles consistently appear across jurisdictions. These shared themes provide enterprises with a useful guide for building AI systems that meet global expectations, even when operating in different markets. They also align closely with the ethical concerns and responsible AI practices discussed in earlier sections, reinforcing the need for consistent governance and oversight.

Some common regulatory themes are given as follows:

- **Transparency and explainability**: Laws worldwide require that AI systems provide clear information about how they function, including data sources, decision logic, and limitations, so that users and regulators can understand outcomes.
- **Accountability and governance**: Organizations are expected to assign clear responsibility for AI outputs, maintain documentation, and implement oversight structures to ensure compliance and traceability.

- **Data protection and privacy**: Regulations emphasize lawful data collection, explicit consent, and safeguards against misuse, reflecting the growing importance of individual rights in the digital economy.
- **Fairness and non-discrimination**: Rules call for proactive steps to detect and mitigate bias, ensuring that AI systems treat all groups equitably.
- **Risk management and security**: Enterprises must assess and mitigate potential harms, from adversarial attacks to operational failures, and establish processes for monitoring and incident response.

Recognizing these recurring principles helps enterprises design AI solutions that remain compliant across borders and adaptable to future regulatory changes.

Impact on jobs

Generative AI is transforming how work is performed and how value is created inside organizations. Beyond automating routine tasks, it reshapes roles, decision-making, and the skills employees need to thrive. For enterprises, understanding these shifts is critical, not only to remain competitive but also to ensure that their workforce adapts successfully to a rapidly changing environment.

The impact extends in two directions. Within an organization, existing job profiles evolve as AI tools handle content creation, data analysis, and customer interactions, while new roles emerge to design, monitor, and govern AI systems. At the same time, the wider job market experiences both disruption and opportunity, as entire industries reconfigure their demand for human talent.

This section examines these changes from an enterprise perspective. The following subsections explore how generative AI transforms internal job profiles and skill requirements, and how it influences employment patterns and economic dynamics across society.

Impact on internal workforce

Generative AI is reshaping the nature of work within enterprises, influencing roles, responsibilities, and the skills employees need to succeed. Automating repetitive tasks and enhancing creative and analytical processes creates opportunities for greater productivity and innovation. However, these benefits come with challenges that require careful planning to ensure employees remain engaged and valued.

Impact of GenAI

GenAI tools automate content generation, report writing, customer service interactions, and even parts of software development, reducing the need for routine manual work. Knowledge workers can focus more on strategic decision-making, complex problem-solving, and creative oversight, using AI as a collaborative partner. New roles are emerging, such as AI trainers, prompt engineers, and AI ethics specialists, to design, monitor, and govern AI systems. At the same time, some traditional positions may shrink or shift, particularly those centered on repetitive information processing.

Measures to ensure smooth transitions

Enterprises must prepare employees to adapt and thrive in an AI-augmented workplace. Example actions are:

- **Reskilling and upskilling**: Provide continuous learning programs in AI literacy, data analysis, and human–AI collaboration to help employees move into higher-value roles.
- **Change management**: Communicate openly about AI adoption plans, addressing fears of displacement and involving staff in planning and pilot projects.
- **Career mobility pathways**: Create clear opportunities for employees to transition into emerging roles, such as AI operations or governance.
- **Supportive culture**: Foster an environment where experimentation and innovation are encouraged, and where employees view AI as a tool to enhance their contribution rather than replace it.

By combining technological investment with proactive workforce development, enterprises can capture the advantages of generative AI while maintaining employee trust, morale, and long-term organizational resilience.

Impact on the wider job market

Generative AI is reshaping employment across the global economy, creating both disruption and new opportunities. Its influence varies widely between industries and professions, requiring workers and job-seekers to adapt. The following themes illustrate how these changes unfold and how individuals can prepare.

Sectoral effects

The degree of disruption differs sharply by sector. Some examples include:

- **High exposure**: Content creation, customer service, legal research, and parts of software development face significant automation of routine tasks.
- **Moderate exposure**: Healthcare, education, and engineering experience augmentation rather than replacement, as human expertise remains essential.
- **Low exposure**: Jobs requiring manual dexterity or on-site presence—construction, hospitality, skilled trades are less affected and may even gain from AI-driven productivity tools.

New opportunities

Generative AI is also a powerful job creator, opening career paths that did not exist a few years ago. Here are some of the new opportunities:

- **Specialist roles**: AI trainers, data curators, ethics officers, and AI operations or security specialists.
- **Adjacent industries**: Growth in AI-enhanced design, personalized education platforms, and remote digital services that scale across borders.
- **Entrepreneurial ventures**: Start-ups built around custom AI applications for niche markets such as healthcare analytics or localized content generation.

Thriving in the new environment

Workers and job-seekers can remain competitive by building skills that complement AI. Recommended actions:

- **AI literacy**: Understanding how AI systems function, their limitations, and how to collaborate with them.
- **Creative and strategic abilities**: Strengthening problem-solving, innovation, and critical thinking skills, which are difficult to automate.
- **Lifelong learning mindset**: Pursuing continuous education, certifications, and cross-disciplinary expertise to pivot as new opportunities arise.

By anticipating these trends and developing adaptable skills, professionals can navigate the changing landscape and seize the benefits of an AI-driven economy.

Conclusion

GenAI has emerged as a transformative force, offering unprecedented opportunities alongside significant risks. Its rapid adoption makes governance and ethics essential for every enterprise, not as an afterthought but as a guiding principle. Without careful oversight, issues such as bias, privacy breaches, intellectual property disputes, and misinformation can undermine trust and damage both business and society.

This chapter highlighted why responsible AI practices must be integral to any deployment strategy. Clear governance frameworks, robust technical safeguards, and strong human oversight help organizations balance innovation with accountability. Evolving global regulations further reinforce the need for proactive compliance, while ethical considerations ensure that progress benefits people as much as it drives productivity.

Generative AI will continue to reshape roles within companies and influence the wider job market, creating both disruption and opportunity. By anticipating change and investing in skills, organizations and professionals can adapt and thrive.

GenAI is evolving rapidly. The readers will benefit enormously by keeping an eye on the future developments and how they will impact the enterprise. The next chapter discusses some of these upcoming trends.

CHAPTER 11
Future of Generative AI

Introduction

The preceding chapters have examined generative **artificial intelligence** (**AI**) from multiple angles, beginning with the construction of large models, moving through the development of applications built upon them, and addressing the practical concerns of deployment and governance. Together, these topics have offered a comprehensive view of how generative AI solutions are conceived, engineered, and managed in contemporary practice. They provide the essential context for understanding how the coming advances will build upon the foundations already established.

Yet generative AI remains a field in rapid motion. New research results appear almost daily, and technical milestones are achieved at a pace that renders any static account provisional. No single volume can encompass every facet of this domain, and any description of its present is quickly overtaken by new discoveries. Anticipating its future is therefore challenging, but patterns in current work provide enough evidence to outline plausible directions. This very uncertainty underscores the importance of examining trends that can guide research, policy, and investment despite the shifting landscape.

This chapter turns toward those emerging directions. It surveys trends in architectural innovation and in the scaling and refinement of models, highlighting areas where fundamental advances are already visible. The discussion then considers the evolving concept of artificial general intelligence and the growing role of autonomous AI agents, which many view as a potential pathway toward more general capabilities. Finally, the chapter closes the book with an exploration of the broader social and economic consequences of generative AI, reflecting on how these technologies may reshape work, creativity, and collective life in the years ahead. Through this progression, the chapter serves both as a conclusion to the book and as a vantage point from which to contemplate the unfolding trajectory of the field.

Structure

This chapter covers the following topics:

- Emerging architectures
- Model advancements
- Future of agents and AGI
- Impact on society

Objectives

By the end of this chapter, you will be able to describe emerging architectures in GenAI, including innovations beyond transformers and the growing role of model communication protocols in enabling complex multi-agent interactions. You will understand the key trends in model advancements, such as improvements in accuracy, efficiency, speed, size reduction, and multi-modality. The chapter will also equip you with a perspective on the evolving landscape of AI agents and the ongoing discussions around **artificial general intelligence** (**AGI**). Finally, you will be able to analyze the potential societal impact of GenAI, including its influence on education, healthcare, work, creativity, and daily life, while appreciating both the opportunities and the challenges posed by its adoption.

Emerging architectures

GenAI is entering a phase where the underlying structures of models and the ways they interact are rapidly evolving. New architectures are emerging to overcome the limitations of transformers, enabling greater scale, efficiency, and flexibility. Alongside these innovations, communication protocols now allow different models to coordinate and share information, laying the groundwork for complex, multi-model AI systems.

The following subsections explore these developments in detail, beginning with the advances in core model architectures and continuing with the rise of model communication protocols that enable collaborative and distributed intelligence.

Architectures beyond transformers

Transformer models have driven most of the breakthroughs in GenAI. Their self-attention mechanism made it possible to learn rich patterns in language, images, audio, and more. Yet, the search for better foundations continues. New ideas are emerging that aim to handle longer inputs, use computing resources more efficiently, and learn from fewer examples.

Limitations of transformers

Although highly successful, transformers show several structural weaknesses that motivate exploration of other designs:

- **High cost for long sequences**: Self-attention compares every token with every other token, causing memory and computation to grow rapidly as the input length increases.
- **Shallow memory**: Transformers rely on attention over a fixed context window, making it difficult to capture relationships that span very long distances.
- **Weak built-in structure**: They treat inputs as flat sequences, offering little help for tasks where natural order, hierarchy, or geometry are important.

- **Data and energy demands**: Training requires vast datasets and substantial computing power, limiting accessibility and slowing experimentation.

Survey of alternative architectures

Several research directions attempt to overcome these limits. Each takes a different path while keeping the goal of powerful sequence modeling. The following are some newer architectures that are under development:

- **State-space models**: State-space models view a sequence as a continuous signal moving through a hidden dynamic system. Instead of recalculating attention across all past tokens, they update a compact internal state that evolves with each new input. This makes the memory requirement grow only in proportion to sequence length, allowing efficient handling of inputs that extend to millions of steps. Their strength lies in capturing long-range dependencies with stable, mathematically grounded dynamics. They are especially suited for streaming data such as audio, sensor signals, or long documents. However, designing and tuning the underlying differential equations can be complex, and these models may be less flexible than transformers when the data is highly irregular or multimodal. Researchers continue to explore hybrid forms that combine state-space efficiency with the adaptability of attention.

- **Linear and kernel attention**: Linear-attention approaches keep the essence of self-attention but change the computation so that the cost scales linearly with input length. They achieve this by rewriting the attention operation using kernel functions or low-rank approximations, allowing interactions to be summarized efficiently without comparing every token to every other token. This reduction enables much longer context windows on the same hardware and can be applied to both text and audio streams. The trade-off is that approximations may lose some of the fine-grained relationships captured by full attention, occasionally reducing accuracy on tasks that rely on subtle global patterns. These methods are therefore attractive when very long inputs or limited computing budgets dominate, but less so when absolute precision in token interactions is essential.

- **Perceiver and latent bottleneck designs**: Perceiver-style models introduce a fixed set of latent vectors that act as an information bottleneck. Inputs of any size, images, video frames, sound waves, or combined modalities, first map into this latent space. The heavy computation of attention then occurs within the smaller latent array, so the cost depends on the latent size rather than the raw input. This architecture is well-suited for problems where inputs are huge or heterogeneous. It naturally supports multimodal learning because different data types can share the same latent interface. A potential drawback is that the latent set must be carefully chosen; too small and information may be lost, too large and efficiency gains diminish. Training can also be more complex, as the model must learn to compress and retrieve key features effectively.

- **All-MLP and mixing networks**: All-MLP designs replace attention entirely with layers of multilayer perceptrons that mix information across positions. Spatial mixing or learned projections allow tokens or pixels to influence one another without explicit pairwise comparisons. These networks are simple, hardware-friendly, and often easier to scale and optimize than attention-based models. They have shown competitive results in vision and some language tasks, proving that self-attention is not the only path to strong performance. Yet their inductive biases differ from transformers: capturing very long-range relationships can require deeper networks, and they may need more data or careful regularization to match transformer accuracy on complex natural-language tasks. They fit scenarios where simplicity, speed, and deployment on limited hardware are important.
- **Mixture of experts**: Mixture of experts models divide a giant network into many specialized expert modules. For each input, a gating mechanism routes tokens to only a small subset of these experts. As a result, the overall parameter count can be enormous, but the active computation per token remains modest. This structure allows efficient scaling to trillions of parameters and enables experts to specialize in different languages, domains, or skills. It can also support incremental updates, training only selected experts when new data arrives. The main challenges are engineering: routing must stay balanced to prevent certain experts from being overused, and communication overhead across experts can become a bottleneck. These models are powerful for large-scale systems where capacity and flexibility are more important than architectural simplicity. While this architecture is already being used both in open-source and closed-source models, a lot more work is being done on it by the researchers.
- **Neuro-symbolic hybrids**: Neuro-symbolic models combine the pattern-recognition ability of neural networks with the explicit reasoning of symbolic systems such as logic engines or program interpreters. The neural part handles perception, recognizing objects, parsing language, or identifying features, while the symbolic component performs structured reasoning or exact computation. This blend can improve interpretability, enforce rules, and handle tasks that demand precise multi-step logic, such as mathematical proof or complex planning. It also offers a natural path to integrate prior knowledge and constraints. The downside is complexity: integrating two very different paradigms can make training and debugging difficult, and performance gains are often domain-specific. Nonetheless, neuro-symbolic approaches remain a promising route toward more reliable and explainable generative AI.
- **Large concept models**: Large concept models aim to represent abstract ideas and relationships that go beyond raw tokens or pixels. Instead of learning only from sequences of words or images, these systems are trained on diverse data that capture human concepts, text, diagrams, structured knowledge bases, and even real-world interactions. The objective is to build a model that understands high-level notions such as *justice, gravity,* or *market dynamics,* and can connect them across languages

and modalities. As they operate on concepts rather than surface patterns, such models promise stronger reasoning, better transfer to new domains, and more meaningful answers to complex questions. They could provide a bridge between symbolic reasoning and generative capabilities, supporting applications like scientific discovery or policy analysis. The challenges are significant. Concepts are fuzzy and culturally dependent, making reliable training data difficult to define. Balancing breadth with depth, avoiding bias, and ensuring interpretability are open research problems. Yet the pursuit of large models that truly grasp abstract meaning is an exciting frontier in GenAI.

Model communication

Model communication protocols are a recent and fast-growing development in the generative-AI landscape. They define structured formats and conventions by which independent models and autonomous agents exchange information, requests, and intermediate results. Instead of treating a generative model as an isolated oracle, these emerging standards describe how context, metadata, function calls, and control signals can flow between components in a heterogeneous system. They specify message schemas, authentication and provenance tags, error semantics, and negotiation rules so that specialized models, language, vision, reasoning, or planning modules can interoperate smoothly across networks and deployment boundaries.

The push for such protocols reflects a new phase in AI design. As capabilities diversify and scale, purely monolithic models are proving costly and brittle, while modular ensembles promise easier composition and evolution. Communication standards lower integration barriers, let domain-specific experts be reused, and support deployments that respect privacy or regulatory limits, for example, keeping sensitive models on-premises while coordinating through a shared protocol. For today's generative-AI systems, these emerging protocols signal a shift in priorities: they make multi-model orchestration feasible, improve fault isolation and scalability, and move attention from single-model benchmarks toward system-level reliability, trust, and provenance.

Survey of model communication protocols

Several experimental protocols have appeared in just the past year, each aiming to standardize how AI models and agents exchange information. These efforts differ in scope and maturity, but all share a goal of making multi-model collaboration practical and reliable. The features are as follows:

- **Model Context Protocol (MCP)**: MCP defines a lightweight, JSON-based messaging layer so models can share context, capabilities, and execution results in real-time. It supports role-based permissions, typed message formats, and provenance tags, making it easier to plug specialized models into larger systems without custom integration code.

- **Agent-to-Agent (A2A)**: A2A focuses on peer-to-peer communication between autonomous agents. It includes discovery mechanisms, negotiation of goals, and secure transport of instructions or partial outputs. Designed for dynamic networks, it allows agents to join or leave without disrupting the overall workflow.
- **Open Function Calling (OFC)**: OFC standardizes how models request external functions or APIs. Instead of bespoke plugins, it uses a shared schema for describing callable actions and their parameters. This makes it possible for different models to trigger the same tools or services consistently.
- **Multi-Agent Message Passing (MAMP)**: MAMP is an experimental framework that borrows ideas from distributed computing, such as asynchronous queues and fault-tolerant routing. It enables large teams of specialized models to cooperate on long-running tasks where ordering, retries, and error handling matter.

These protocols are still evolving, but they collectively point toward a future where interoperable AI systems can be assembled as easily as today's web services.

Future of model communication protocols

Model communication protocols are expected to become a core layer of next-generation AI infrastructure. As multi-model systems expand, protocols will likely standardize authentication, data privacy, and semantic alignment, enabling secure collaboration across organizational and geographic boundaries. Integration with real-time streaming, edge computing, and specialized hardware will reduce latency and improve reliability. Over time, these protocols may evolve into open ecosystems comparable to today's internet standards, allowing independently developed models and agents to form large, adaptive networks. Such developments could transform generative AI from isolated applications into seamlessly connected, cooperative intelligence platforms.

Model advancements

GenAI is advancing not only through new architectures but also through steady improvements in the core characteristics of the models themselves. Accuracy continues to rise as training methods become more refined, data quality improves, and evaluation benchmarks grow more rigorous. At the same time, researchers and industry teams are achieving these gains with lower training costs and shorter development cycles, aided by algorithmic innovations and specialized hardware. Inference speed is also accelerating, enabling real-time interaction and large-scale deployment across diverse applications. Alongside these trends, techniques for reducing model size, such as pruning, distillation, and efficient fine-tuning, are making high-performance systems more practical for mobile devices and edge computing. Together, these advancements are reshaping expectations of what generative models can deliver, emphasizing efficiency and accessibility as much as raw capability, and ensuring that progress is measured not only by scale but by practical impact across research, industry, and everyday use.

The following subsections examine four key aspects of this progress: gains in accuracy, reductions in training cost and time, faster generation, and model size optimization, each illustrating how innovation is making generative AI more powerful and more widely usable.

Improvement in accuracy

Accuracy remains a central measure of progress in GenAI. Early breakthroughs showed that scaling model size and training data could yield dramatic gains, but recent work demonstrates that careful refinement often matters as much as raw scale. Better-curated datasets, improved pre-processing, and training objectives aligned with human feedback now drive much of the improvement. Techniques such as instruction tuning and **reinforcement learning from human feedback** (**RLHF**) help models follow complex prompts more reliably and produce outputs closer to user intent.

A persistent challenge is hallucination, the confident generation of information that is factually incorrect or unsupported. While all large language models are susceptible, research is steadily reducing this problem. Approaches include retrieval-augmented generation, where models consult external knowledge bases during inference, and fine-grained preference optimization, which rewards factual consistency. Emerging evaluation benchmarks explicitly test truthfulness and reasoning, providing clearer signals for training and model selection.

Looking ahead, several experimental approaches aim to push accuracy further:

- **Neuro-symbolic integration**: combines neural networks with symbolic reasoning engines to enforce logical consistency and verifiable steps.
- **Self-verification and debate systems**: They deploy multiple model instances to critique or cross-examine each other, detecting and correcting errors before output.
- **Continual and lifelong learning**: enables models to incorporate new information incrementally without full retraining, reducing drift and outdated responses.

These research avenues indicate that future gains in accuracy will arise from fundamentally new mechanisms for reasoning, validation, and adaptive knowledge acquisition, beyond better data and tuning.

Reduction in training cost and time

Lowering the expense and duration of model training has become a key priority as generative AI continues to scale. Early success often depended on vast computational resources and months of training, but ongoing advances are making high-performance models more accessible to both industry and research groups.

Several techniques directly reduce the amount of computation required. Some of these techniques have already been discussed in previous chapters. Parameter-efficient fine-tuning allows new tasks to be learned by updating only a small subset of weights or by adding lightweight adapters, rather than retraining the entire network. Curriculum learning organizes data from simple to complex examples, guiding the model to converge faster and with fewer passes. Large-scale distributed training systems spread workloads across clusters of GPUs or specialized accelerators, maximizing hardware utilization and shortening training cycles. The introduction of AI-specific chips such as **tensor processing units** (TPUs) and custom accelerators further cuts both energy use and wall-clock time.

Algorithmic improvements complement these hardware gains. Mixed-precision training exploits lower-bit computations without sacrificing accuracy, while advanced optimizers such as *AdamW* and *Lion* stabilize learning and reduce the number of required iterations. Together, these methods trim both energy costs and the duration of massive training runs.

Emerging research promises further breakthroughs:

- Progressive modular training, where models are assembled from smaller, specialized components trained in parallel, reducing the need for end-to-end retraining.
- Neural architecture search with adaptive pruning, which automatically discovers and removes redundant parameters during training, shrinking models while they learn.
- Federated and on-device pretraining, distributing the training process across millions of edge devices to tap idle compute power and cut reliance on centralized supercomputers.

The combined effect is a dramatic widening of access. Academic labs, startups, and smaller enterprises can now attempt projects that were once limited to the largest technology firms. By lowering barriers to experimentation and deployment, these innovations are helping to democratize generative AI development and accelerate the pace of discovery across fields.

Faster generation

As GenAI moves into interactive and real-time applications, reducing inference time has become as important as improving training efficiency. Faster generation enables streaming outputs, conversational agents, and large-scale deployment in environments where latency is critical. Achieving high-speed inference requires both architectural innovations and algorithmic optimizations, carefully balanced to preserve output quality.

Several techniques have emerged to accelerate generation. Speculative decoding allows models to predict multiple tokens in parallel and then verify correctness, reducing the number of sequential steps. Quantization converts model weights and activations to lower-bit representations, which cuts memory bandwidth and computation without severely impacting performance. Caching intermediate representations or previously computed attention matrices avoids redundant calculations, significantly improving throughput for repeated or long-context queries. These methods collectively make real-time interactions more feasible while keeping resource requirements manageable.

Future directions promise even greater acceleration:

- Dynamic token skipping, where models identify and bypass less informative computations during generation, reducing wasted effort.
- Adaptive multi-resolution decoding, which generates coarse-grained outputs first and refines them selectively, speeding early stages of response generation.
- Hardware-aware compilation and routing, tailoring computations to specialized accelerators for maximal parallelism and minimal latency.

These advances, while improving speed, involve careful trade-offs. Aggressive quantization or token skipping can degrade output fidelity, requiring strategies that balance responsiveness with accuracy and creativity. Faster generation, when combined with robust architectural design, opens the door to highly interactive, scalable generative AI applications across domains.

Model size reduction

Reducing model size has become a crucial trend in GenAI, enabling deployment on edge devices, lowering energy consumption, and making models more accessible to a broader range of users and organizations. Smaller models also reduce inference latency and memory requirements, which is essential for mobile applications, IoT devices, and other resource-constrained environments.

Several techniques are widely used to achieve size reduction without significant loss of performance. Distillation transfers knowledge from a large *teacher* model to a smaller *student*, allowing the smaller model to retain much of the teacher's capability. Pruning removes redundant or less important parameters, streamlining computation. **Low Rank Adaptation** (**LoRA**) modifies only selected weight matrices, reducing the number of trainable parameters for new tasks. Modular systems divide networks into specialized components that can be loaded or executed on demand, reducing the effective model footprint while maintaining versatility.

Emerging approaches aim to push size reduction further:

- Dynamic model slimming, where the model adapts its size at inference based on task complexity or resource availability.
- Neural architecture morphing, which automatically restructures networks to retain expressiveness while reducing parameters.
- Sparse and conditional computation networks, activating only relevant subnetworks for a given input to minimize active parameters and energy usage.

Through these innovations, smaller models can achieve performance close to their larger counterparts while enabling energy-efficient, scalable, and practical deployment across a wide range of devices and environments.

Advancements in multi-modality

GenAI is increasingly moving beyond single-modality inputs, integrating text, images, audio, video, and structured data into unified models. Multi-modal models enable richer understanding, more flexible generation, and applications that can reason across different types of information. This trend is driven by both research and practical demand, as real-world tasks often involve multiple forms of data simultaneously.

Current approaches focus on aligning representations across modalities. Cross-attention mechanisms allow models to relate information from different streams, while shared latent spaces provide a common embedding that captures the relationships between text, images, or audio. Techniques like modality-specific encoders combined with fusion layers improve the model's ability to extract features unique to each data type while maintaining coherence in joint outputs. Large-scale pretraining on multi-modal datasets further enhances generalization across tasks.

Looking forward, several promising directions are emerging:

- Dynamic modality selection, where models choose which modalities to attend to based on context or task requirements.
- Temporal multi-modal reasoning, enabling integration of sequential data such as video and audio with textual instructions for real-time applications.
- Concept-level multi-modality, combining high-level semantic concepts across modalities for more abstract reasoning and creative generation.

Advancements in multi-modality are expected to make generative AI models more versatile, capable of understanding and producing content across domains, and more effective in applications like robotics, virtual assistants, content creation, and scientific discovery.

Future of agents and AGI

Artificial intelligence agents have already transitioned from experimental prototypes to powerful tools driving automation and decision-making in many industries. From virtual assistants that schedule meetings to customer service bots resolving queries in real-time, agents have proven their utility in handling tasks that demand responsiveness, adaptability, and a degree of autonomy. Yet, what we are witnessing today is only the beginning. The rapid evolution of large language models, reinforcement learning techniques, and multi-modal capabilities is redefining what agents can achieve.

As these technologies advance, the line between narrow, task-specific agents and general-purpose problem-solvers is beginning to blur. Modern agents are no longer confined to following rigid instructions. Instead, they exhibit reasoning abilities, collaborate with humans, and integrate with complex digital ecosystems. The momentum points toward a future where agents are not just tools but active participants in workflows, innovation, and decision-making.

This section explores the emerging trends in AI agent technology and the opportunities they open up. It also considers how the trajectory of these advancements could shape the larger pursuit of AGI, bringing agents closer to performing at a level comparable to human intelligence in a wide range of domains.

Emerging trends in AI agents

The development of AI agents has moved beyond simple task automation into more sophisticated, adaptive systems. These agents are becoming capable of reasoning, planning, and acting in complex, uncertain environments. Several technological and conceptual shifts are driving this transformation. The following subsections highlight key trends that are shaping the future of AI agent design and deployment.

Increased autonomy and reasoning capabilities

Early AI agents were primarily reactive, executing predefined scripts or responding to limited sets of inputs. The integration of LLMs and reinforcement learning has enabled a new class of agents that can reason about goals, generate alternative strategies, and adapt to changing contexts. This progression is evident in planning-oriented frameworks such as chain-of-thought prompting and hierarchical reasoning systems. Some noteworthy developments in this area are:

- Agents are moving from reactive execution to proactive decision-making.
- Context-aware reasoning allows better alignment with user intent.
- Agents can decompose complex tasks into sub-tasks, reducing error and improving efficiency.

This trend reflects a shift toward agents that not only follow commands but also demonstrate initiative in solving problems.

Collaboration between agents and humans

Another important development is the enhancement of collaborative capabilities. Modern agents are being designed to work alongside humans as partners rather than mere tools. These agents can coordinate tasks, explain their reasoning, and adjust their behavior based on human feedback. This interaction goes beyond natural language interfaces, extending into multimodal communication such as speech, gesture, and visual cues. Some examples are:

- Improved transparency and explainability in decision-making.
- Support for multi-turn, mixed-initiative dialogues.
- Alignment techniques that prioritize human oversight and ethical considerations.

Such collaboration increases trust, making agents suitable for domains like healthcare, education, and creative industries where human judgment remains essential.

Multi-agent systems and collective intelligence

While individual agents are powerful, many complex problems require collaboration among multiple agents. Advances in multi-agent systems are enabling groups of agents to coordinate, negotiate, and share knowledge. This collective intelligence approach mirrors natural systems, such as swarms or social groups, and opens pathways to solving large-scale challenges. Some aspects of the multi-agent systems are:

- Distributed problem-solving across different domains or organizations.
- Emergent behaviors that go beyond the capacity of a single agent.
- Robustness through redundancy and specialization of roles.

For example, in supply chain management, different agents representing logistics, procurement, and sales can interact to optimize operations in real-time.

Integration with real-world environments

Another noticeable trend is the deepening integration of agents into real-world systems. Agents are increasingly deployed not only in digital platforms but also in physical contexts such as robotics, smart infrastructure, and **Internet of Things** (**IoT**) ecosystems. This shift requires agents to perceive, interpret, and act upon real-time data streams. The agents are fast developing the relevant capabilities, such as:

- Seamless connection with sensors, devices, and enterprise systems.
- Ability to function in partially observable and uncertain environments.
- Bridging digital intelligence with physical execution.

This integration is crucial for applications such as autonomous vehicles, disaster response systems, and industrial automation, where timely and accurate actions are vital.

Together, these trends highlight a trajectory where AI agents are becoming more autonomous, collaborative, interconnected, and embedded in real-world systems. These advancements not only expand the scope of agent applications but also bring them closer to contributing to broader goals such as general-purpose intelligence.

Towards AGI

AGI is often described as the next frontier of artificial intelligence, distinguished from today's narrow AI systems by its breadth of capability. While narrow AI excels at specific tasks, such as language translation, image recognition, or playing a particular game, AGI refers to systems capable of learning, reasoning, and adapting across a wide range of domains, much like humans. The vision is of machines that can not only solve predefined problems but also discover new ones, transfer knowledge from one context to another, and operate effectively without constant human guidance.

The idea of AGI has long fascinated researchers, philosophers, and technologists. It embodies the aspiration of building machines that do not merely mimic fragments of intelligence but exhibit a form of general adaptability. Importantly, AGI does not necessarily imply consciousness or human-like emotions; rather, it denotes competence across diverse cognitive tasks. In this sense, AGI is as much a technical objective as it is a conceptual benchmark, representing the transition from specialized intelligence to generalized capability.

As the pace of AI development accelerates, discussions around AGI are no longer purely theoretical. Advances in large language models, multi-modal systems, and agent frameworks have created stepping stones that make AGI appear less distant and more tangible than ever before.

Historical context of AGI

The roots of AGI trace back to the earliest days of computer science and artificial intelligence research. In the 1950s, pioneers such as *Alan Turing* speculated about whether machines could *think*, while *John McCarthy*, *Marvin Minsky*, and others framed AI as the quest to replicate the full breadth of human intelligence. Early symbolic AI systems attempted to capture intelligence through logic, rules, and explicit representations, reflecting the belief that reasoning could be formalized and programmed directly.

During the following decades, optimism alternated with setbacks. The limitations of symbolic approaches, highlighted during the *AI winters*, revealed that general intelligence required more than rule-based reasoning. The rise of machine learning and statistical methods in the 1980s and 1990s shifted focus toward systems that could learn patterns from data. Even so, these remained largely narrow in scope.

The emergence of deep learning in the 2010s reignited interest in AGI by demonstrating unprecedented progress in perception, language understanding, and generative capabilities. Milestones such as large-scale neural networks, reinforcement learning breakthroughs, and foundation models positioned AGI once again at the center of both scientific inquiry and public imagination. Today, AGI is seen not as a distant dream but as a pressing challenge with profound implications.

Definitions and interpretations of AGI

AGI is often defined as the capability of a machine to perform any intellectual task that a human can, demonstrating flexibility, adaptability, and transfer of knowledge across domains. Unlike narrow AI systems, which excel at specialized tasks such as translation or image recognition, AGI would possess the capacity to learn, reason, and apply knowledge in unfamiliar contexts without task-specific training.

Interpretations of AGI vary across research communities. Some view it as a continuum, where increasing generality in today's models gradually leads to AGI. Others see it as a qualitative leap, requiring fundamentally new paradigms beyond current machine learning techniques. There are also philosophical perspectives that question whether AGI should replicate human cognition or merely achieve functional equivalence in terms of problem-solving ability.

This diversity of interpretations influences the direction of research. For example, cognitive science–inspired approaches emphasize replicating human-like memory, reasoning, and perception, while engineering-focused approaches target measurable benchmarks of adaptability and performance. Despite differing perspectives, there is a broad consensus that AGI represents a threshold beyond which AI systems can autonomously handle a wide spectrum of challenges, potentially reshaping human interaction with technology at every level.

Technical pathways toward AGI

The pursuit of AGI is driven by multiple technical approaches, each reflecting different assumptions about how intelligence can be replicated or approximated. Current progress in large-scale machine learning suggests one path, but alternative paradigms are also under active exploration.

One prominent pathway is the scaling hypothesis, which posits that increasingly large models trained on vast and diverse datasets will naturally evolve more general intelligence. Foundation models such as GPT or Gemini represent early steps in this direction, showing how scale enhances reasoning, multi-modality, and task transfer. Proponents argue that with continued scaling, combined with efficiency improvements, emergent generality may become more pronounced. Critics, however, question whether scaling alone can overcome fundamental limitations such as reasoning gaps or grounding in real-world understanding.

Another pathway emphasizes hybrid approaches that combine neural networks with symbolic reasoning or structured knowledge representations. By integrating pattern recognition with explicit rules or logic systems, these methods aim to achieve both flexibility and reliability. This line of research revives older traditions of symbolic AI but augments them with the adaptive power of modern learning systems.

A third pathway lies in embodied and interactive learning, where agents develop intelligence through action, feedback, and exploration of real or simulated environments. Inspired by developmental psychology, this approach views intelligence as inseparable from interaction with the physical and social world, rather than as an abstract optimization problem.

Finally, some researchers explore neuromorphic computing and brain-inspired architectures, seeking to mimic biological structures more closely. These efforts suggest that progress toward AGI may require not only new algorithms but also new hardware optimized for cognitive processes.

In practice, these pathways are not mutually exclusive. Many researchers envision a convergence of scaling, hybrid reasoning, embodiment, and biologically inspired design, with AGI emerging from the synergies among them rather than a single dominant approach.

Challenges and barriers to AGI

Despite rapid advances, the road to AGI is marked by profound technical, conceptual, and practical challenges. Current AI systems, even the most advanced, still suffer from hallucinations, brittleness, and poor generalization when confronted with novel or ambiguous situations. True general intelligence requires not only scaling but also breakthroughs in reasoning, grounding, and contextual understanding.

Another barrier lies in the alignment problem, ensuring that increasingly autonomous systems act in ways consistent with human values, safety, and ethical norms. While narrow AI can be fine-tuned to specific guidelines, AGI's open-ended adaptability makes alignment vastly more complex.

From a technical perspective, resource constraints present additional difficulties. Training models approaching AGI capabilities demands enormous computational power and energy, raising sustainability concerns. Moreover, evaluation remains an unsolved challenge: there is no universally accepted benchmark for measuring *general intelligence,* making it difficult to track progress reliably.

Finally, there are sociotechnical barriers, including public trust, governance frameworks, and the potential for misuse. Without clear regulatory and ethical guardrails, AGI development risks amplifying inequalities or enabling destabilizing applications.

Together, these barriers highlight that progress toward AGI will not depend on algorithms alone but also on solving deep scientific, ethical, and societal problems that remain largely open.

Impact on society

The influence of GenAI extends far beyond technical domains, reaching into the very fabric of society. As these systems grow more capable, they are beginning to reshape how people learn, heal, work, and live. Their potential to democratize access, accelerate innovation, and enrich human creativity is matched by risks of inequality, dependency, and ethical tension. Understanding this duality is essential to envisioning the role GenAI may play in shaping the future.

Education is already witnessing early signs of transformation, as personalized learning systems adapt content to individual learners. Healthcare stands on the cusp of breakthroughs in diagnosis, treatment, and patient empowerment, while employment landscapes are evolving under the pressures of automation and augmentation. Even everyday life, how people interact, create, and experience the world, is being redefined by these systems.

The impact of GenAI on society cannot be understood solely as technological change; it must be seen as cultural, economic, and existential in scope. Each domain brings unique opportunities and challenges, requiring thoughtful integration and careful governance. The following subsections explore how education, healthcare, jobs, and broader aspects of human life may evolve in the era of generative intelligence, highlighting both the promise and the disruption that lie ahead.

Future of education

GenAI is set to transform education by making learning more personalized, accessible, and adaptive to diverse needs. The role of teachers, curricula, and institutions may evolve significantly as AI augments traditional systems. At the same time, challenges such as equity, trust, and human oversight must be addressed to ensure responsible integration. The following themes highlight key directions in this transformation.

Personalized and adaptive learning

GenAI enables the design of learning pathways tailored to individual students. Intelligent tutoring systems can adjust difficulty levels, provide targeted explanations, and generate practice exercises aligned with each learner's progress. This level of personalization promises to engage students more effectively and reduce dropout rates.

Some examples of this shift include:

- Adaptive feedback loops that encourage mastery at one's own pace.
- Automated assessments that provide continuous insights into strengths and weaknesses.
- Content generation that offers new examples suited to varying contexts.

Bridging traditional and skill-based learning

Education is no longer confined to formal classrooms. GenAI supports skill learners, individuals pursuing knowledge for careers, hobbies, or personal growth, by offering modular, on-demand learning experiences. This flexibility helps bridge the gap between institutional education and lifelong skill development.

The following are some illustrations of this trend:

- AI-curated resources that create focused pathways for different goals.
- Contextual explanations that adapt concepts for vocational or academic use.
- Certification systems that validate learning outside traditional degrees.

Expanding access and equity

GenAI can reduce barriers to education by making high-quality resources widely available. Students in underserved regions can access lessons, explanations, and interactive exercises in their native languages. Accessibility tools powered by AI can also assist learners with disabilities, widening participation in formal and informal education.

Some of the possibilities include:

- Automatic translation that enables global reach of curricula.
- Text-to-speech and image descriptions that support diverse learning needs.
- Low-cost AI tutors that reduce reliance on scarce human resources.

Global collaboration and cultural exchange

GenAI can act as a bridge across geographies and cultures, creating opportunities for students worldwide to learn together. By translating content seamlessly, adapting learning material to different cultural contexts, and enabling shared projects, AI opens classrooms to the world. This fosters not only knowledge exchange but also empathy, diversity of thought, and global problem-solving.

Some examples:

- AI-powered platforms that allow students from different countries to co-create projects.
- Translation systems that make lectures accessible in multiple languages.
- Virtual cultural immersion experiences guided by AI tutors.

Risks and future outlook

The integration of AI into education carries risks, including over-reliance on automated systems, propagation of errors, and reduced emphasis on human mentorship. Safeguards such as human-in-the-loop oversight, robust content validation, and ethical use policies will be critical. Looking ahead, the most promising future is one where AI and human teachers complement one another, blending efficiency with empathy to create inclusive and effective learning ecosystems.

Future of healthcare

Healthcare stands to be one of the most deeply transformed sectors through GenAI. From diagnostics and treatment planning to patient engagement and medical research, AI promises faster, more accurate, and more personalized care. At the same time, it raises important questions about trust, ethics, and equitable access. The following themes highlight how healthcare could evolve in the coming years under the influence of GenAI.

Precision diagnostics

GenAI can analyze medical images, genomic data, and clinical records to support earlier and more accurate diagnoses. By reducing human error and identifying subtle patterns that even experts may miss, AI augments clinical decision-making.

Some examples include:

- Automated analysis of X-rays and MRIs.
- Genomic sequencing interpretation for cancer treatment.
- Predictive modeling to detect diseases such as Alzheimer's at pre-symptomatic stages.

Personalized treatment and drug discovery

One of the most promising areas lies in tailoring treatments to individual patients. GenAI models can simulate drug interactions, predict patient responses, and optimize care plans in ways that minimize side effects.

Illustrative cases are:

- AI-driven identification of drug candidates.
- Modeling protein structures to accelerate vaccine development.
- Adaptive treatment protocols designed around a patient's genetic profile.

Virtual health assistants

Conversational AI systems are emerging as companions for patients, offering guidance, reminders, and even mental health support. These systems can handle routine queries, free up medical staff for complex cases, and improve patient adherence.

For instance:

- AI chatbots providing post-surgery instructions.
- Voice-based assistants reminding patients to take medications.
- Mental health tools offering preliminary counseling or emotional support.

Remote and decentralized healthcare

GenAI enables healthcare delivery beyond traditional clinical settings, making it possible to monitor, diagnose, and treat patients remotely. Telemedicine platforms, wearable devices, and AI-driven monitoring tools allow continuous care and early intervention, reducing the need for in-person visits and expanding access to underserved areas.

Some illustrative examples:

- AI-powered virtual consultations that assess symptoms and provide guidance.
- Continuous monitoring of vital signs through wearable devices with AI alerts for anomalies.
- Remote management of chronic conditions using personalized AI-driven care plans.

Operational efficiency in healthcare systems

Hospitals and clinics face significant logistical challenges, and GenAI can streamline many of them. Generative tools support scheduling, resource allocation, and documentation, reducing administrative overhead while improving service delivery.

Consider examples like:

- Predictive patient flow modeling to reduce wait times.
- Automated report generation for physicians.
- AI-based optimization of operating room schedules.

Ethical and global implications

While the potential benefits are immense, GenAI in healthcare must be approached with caution. Issues around bias in training data, patient privacy, and equitable access remain unresolved. At the same time, GenAI could help bring advanced healthcare to underserved regions by lowering costs and enabling remote services.

Some important considerations are:

- Ensuring unbiased training datasets.
- Protecting sensitive medical records.
- Establishing clear accountability for AI-driven decisions.
- Using telemedicine platforms powered by generative AI to reach rural populations.

Future of jobs

GenAI is reshaping the world of work at an unprecedented pace. By automating routine tasks and augmenting human capabilities, these systems are enabling higher productivity and creating opportunities for new types of roles across industries. At the same time, the rapid adoption of AI presents challenges, including the displacement of existing jobs and the pressing need for reskilling and lifelong learning. Understanding these dynamics is essential for both workers and organizations. The following subsections explore how AI is transforming job roles, the emergence of new careers, evolving workplace dynamics, and the policies required to navigate this transition.

Job transformation and augmentation

GenAI is not limited to replacing human labor; it is increasingly enhancing productivity by automating routine tasks while enabling workers to focus on higher-level, creative, and strategic responsibilities. In many industries, humans and AI are beginning to collaborate closely, forming hybrid roles that combine human judgment with AI's computational speed and pattern recognition capabilities. This collaboration allows for faster decision-making, improved accuracy, and more innovative problem-solving, while reducing cognitive load on employees.

Some examples of how AI augments work include:

- Financial analysts use AI to generate predictive models while focusing on investment strategy.
- Content creators leveraging generative AI for drafting articles, videos, or marketing campaigns, refining output for style and context.
- Software engineers using AI assistants to suggest code, detect bugs, and optimize performance.
- Healthcare professionals employing AI to summarize patient records and highlight anomalies for faster diagnoses.

Emergence of new job categories

GenAI is creating entirely new roles that did not exist a decade ago. As organizations adopt GenAI systems, there is a growing need for professionals who can design, manage, and oversee these technologies. These roles often blend technical expertise with ethical, creative, or strategic responsibilities, reflecting the interdisciplinary nature of AI applications.

Some emerging job categories can be:

- **AI trainers and prompt engineers**: Professionals who design prompts, curate datasets, and fine-tune models for specific applications.
- **AI ethicists and compliance officers**: Experts ensuring AI systems are transparent, fair, and aligned with societal norms.
- **Creative collaborators**: Designers, writers, and media producers who use AI to co-create art, literature, and multimedia content.
- **AI-augmented scientists and analysts**: Researchers leveraging AI for simulations, predictions, and hypothesis generation across domains like genomics, climate science, and finance.

These roles highlight the evolving landscape where human skills and AI capabilities intersect, driving innovation and creating entirely new career paths.

Reskilling and lifelong learning

As GenAI transforms industries, continuous learning and reskilling are becoming essential for workers to remain relevant. Many routine and repetitive tasks are being automated, creating a pressing need for employees to acquire new skills that complement AI capabilities. Organizations, governments, and educational institutions must invest in flexible, lifelong learning frameworks to help individuals adapt to these shifts.

Here are some approaches and examples:

- **Micro-credentialing and online courses**: Short, targeted programs that equip workers with AI-related skills or domain-specific expertise.
- **AI-assisted personalized learning**: Platforms that assess individual skill gaps and recommend customized learning pathways.
- **On-the-job reskilling programs**: Integrating AI tools into daily workflows while providing mentorship and guided training.
- **Collaborative knowledge networks**: Communities where employees share insights, best practices, and lessons learned from AI-augmented projects.

These initiatives ensure that the workforce can adapt to rapidly changing roles while maximizing the benefits of AI augmentation.

Workplace dynamics and human-AI collaboration

The integration of GenAI into workplaces is reshaping organizational culture, workflows, and employee responsibilities. Rather than fully replacing human roles, GenAI augments them, enabling employees to focus on creativity, critical thinking, and complex decision-making. Teams are increasingly structured around human–AI collaboration, where AI handles repetitive, data-intensive tasks while humans provide judgment, context, and empathy.

Some examples of this transformation:

- **Collaborative content creation**: GenAI drafts reports, presentations, or marketing material, which employees refine and contextualize.
- **Decision support systems**: GenAI provides predictive insights and simulations to assist managers and analysts in strategic planning.
- **Enhanced communication workflows**: GenAI summarizes meetings, generates emails, and organizes project updates, reducing administrative burden.
- **Creative problem-solving labs**: Teams use GenAI to model scenarios, explore innovations, and iterate solutions rapidly.

This collaboration fosters a more productive, innovative, and adaptable workforce while emphasizing the complementary strengths of humans and GenAI.

Risks, inequalities, and policy responses

While GenAI brings transformative opportunities, it also introduces risks that could exacerbate inequalities in the workforce. Automation of routine tasks may displace workers in certain sectors, disproportionately affecting lower-skill roles. Unequal access to AI tools and training resources can widen the digital divide, leaving some populations behind. Effective policies are essential to ensure that the benefits of GenAI are broadly shared and potential harms are mitigated.

Some of the important measures are:

- **Workforce reskilling initiatives**: Government and corporate programs to train displaced workers in AI-augmented roles.
- **Inclusive access to GenAI tools**: Subsidized platforms or open-access AI resources for underserved communities.
- **Regulatory oversight**: Guidelines for ethical deployment, transparency, and accountability in AI-driven decision-making.
- **Social safety nets**: Measures such as a universal basic income or targeted support for sectors most affected by automation.

These interventions are critical to creating a balanced and equitable AI-augmented economy.

Future of life

Breakthrough technologies have always reshaped human existence in profound ways. Electricity transformed industries, cities, and daily routines; information technology revolutionized communication, knowledge access, and the pace of innovation. Generative AI promises to be another transformative force, touching nearly every aspect of life with unprecedented speed and depth. Unlike past innovations, GenAI directly amplifies human thought, creativity, and problem-solving, allowing people to reimagine what is possible in both personal and collective spheres.

In the coming decades, GenAI will influence the way individuals and societies organize themselves. Tasks that once required immense time and effort will be streamlined, freeing people to focus on higher-order thinking, creative endeavors, and meaningful human interaction. By providing insights into patterns of behavior, productivity, and decision-making, GenAI can help individuals correct mistakes, adopt better habits, and maintain healthier lifestyles. Cognitive augmentation through AI tools will allow humans to explore complex ideas, simulate scenarios, and experiment with solutions at scales previously unimaginable. Creative expression, from writing and music to design and research, will flourish as GenAI acts as a collaborator and co-pilot, expanding the horizons of imagination.

Equally important, GenAI will reshape how people solve societal and global problems. With AI-driven modeling, scenario planning, and predictive analysis, communities and organizations will make decisions grounded in richer data and deeper understanding. Coordination, resource allocation, and problem-solving at scale will be faster and more efficient. Relationships, both personal and professional, will benefit from AI-enhanced communication, empathy modeling, and support in managing complex interactions. Humans will be able to focus on the subtleties of collaboration, trust, and creativity while delegating repetitive or computationally heavy tasks to AI systems.

Yet alongside these opportunities, there will be challenges. Malicious actors will exploit GenAI to create sophisticated deceptions, manipulate information, and commit fraud. These threats will require a heightened level of awareness, discernment, and collective vigilance among people. Just as societies adapted to new risks introduced by previous technological revolutions, humanity will develop strategies, norms, and tools to identify, counter, and mitigate GenAI-based harms. Awareness, education, and ethical frameworks will become critical components of everyday life, ensuring that the benefits of AI are realized without succumbing to its potential misuse.

Despite these challenges, the trajectory remains optimistic. History demonstrates that humans have consistently risen to the occasion, integrating powerful technologies into society while addressing unintended consequences. The arrival of GenAI represents an extraordinary opportunity to enhance human potential, creativity, and well-being. It offers tools to amplify intelligence, solve pressing problems, and enrich daily life, while also inviting the cultivation of new skills and discernment to navigate emerging risks.

In essence, the future of life with GenAI is one of expanded possibilities. People will live more informed, productive, and creative lives, supported by AI that amplifies their capabilities. Societal structures, work, learning, and personal growth will all benefit from this technology, even as vigilance and ethical mindfulness guide its application. Like the previous waves of transformative innovations, GenAI is poised to become an integral part of human progress, offering unprecedented opportunities to thrive, create, and shape a more enriched world.

Conclusion

As this exploration of generative AI comes to a close, it becomes clear that the field is advancing on multiple fronts simultaneously, architectures are evolving, models are becoming more capable and efficient, agents are taking on increasingly sophisticated roles, and the vision of artificial general intelligence continues to inspire research and innovation. Beyond technical achievements, the societal implications are profound: education, healthcare, work, creativity, and daily life are all poised for transformation. While challenges such as ethical concerns, misuse, and inequities must be addressed, history shows that humanity has consistently harnessed powerful technologies to expand opportunity and well-being. The journey of GenAI is one of accelerating discovery, collaboration, and adaptation, offering a future in which human potential can be amplified, imagination can flourish, and society can be reshaped for the better, guided by insight, responsibility, and vision.

Index

A

B

C

D

E

F

G

H

I

K

L

M

N

O

P

Q

R

S

T

U

V

W